UAE...................UNITED ARAB EMIRATES
YAR.....................YEMEN ARAB REPUBLIC
YMD.................YEMEN DEM. REPUBLIC

OCEANIA

AUS...AUSTRALIA
FIJ...FIJI
NZL...................................NEW ZEALAND
PNG........................PAPUA-NEW GUINEA
SAM................................WESTERN SAMOA
SOL............................SOLOMON ISLANDS
TGA...TONGA

THE OLYMPIC CENTURY
THE OFFICIAL 1ST CENTURY HISTORY OF THE MODERN OLYMPIC MOVEMENT

VOLUME 21

THE
XXIII OLYMPIAD

LOS ANGELES 1984
CALGARY 1988

BY
ELLEN GALFORD

WORLD SPORT RESEARCH & PUBLICATIONS INC.
LOS ANGELES

1996 © United States Olympic Committee

Published by:
World Sport Research & Publications Inc.
1424 North Highland Avenue
Los Angeles, California 90028
(213) 461-2900

1st Century Project
The 1st Century Project is an undertaking by World
Sport Research & Publications Inc. to commemorate the
100-year history of the Modern Olympic Movement.
Charles Gary Allison (Chairman)

Publishers: C. Jay Halzle, Robert G. Rossi,
James A. Williamson

Senior Consultant: Dr. Dietrich Quanz (Germany)
Special Consultants: Walter Borges (Germany), Ian
Buchanan (United Kingdon), Dr. Carl Lennartz
(Germany), Wolf Lyberg (Sweden), Dr. Norbert Müller
(Germany), Dr. Nicholas Yalouris (Greece)

Editor: Laura Foreman
Executive Editor: Christian Kinney
Editorial Board: George Constable, George G. Daniels,
Ellen Galford, Ellen Phillips, Carl A. Posey

Art Director: Christopher M. Register
Production Manager: Nicholas Pitt
Picture Editor: Debra Lemmonds Hannah
Designers: Kimberley Davison, Diane Farenick
Staff Researchers: Mark Brewin (Canada), Diana
Fakiola (Greece), Brad Haynes (Australia), Alexandra
Hesse (Germany), Pauline Ploquin (Senegal and France)
Copy Editor: Barbara F. Quarmby
Proofing Editor: Harry Endrulat
Fact Verification: Carl and Liselott Diem Institute;
German Sport University; Cologne, Germany
Statistician: Bill Mallon
Memorabilia Consultants: Manfred Bergman, James D.
Greensfelder, John P. Kelly, Ingrid O'Neill
Staff Photographer: Theresa Halzle
Office Manager: Christopher Jason Waters
Office Staff: Chris C. Conlee, Brian M. Heath,
Edward J. Messler, Elsa Ramirez, Brian Rand

International Contributors: Jean Durry (France),
Dr. Antonio Lombardo (Italy), Dr. John A. MacAloon
(USA), Dr. Jujiro Narita (Japan), Dr. Roland Renson
(Belgium).

International Research and Assistance: John S. Baich
(New York), Matthieu Brocart (Paris), Alexander
Fakiolas (Athens), Bob Miyakawa (Tokyo), Rona Lester
(London), Dominic LoTempio (Columbia), George
Kostas Mazareas (Boston), Georgia McDonald
(Colorado Springs), Wendy Nolan (Princeton), Jon
Simon (Washington D.C.), Valéry Turco (Lausanne),
Laura Walden (Rome), Jorge Zocchi (Mexico City).

Map Compilation: Mapping Specialists Inc. Madison,
Wisconsin
Map Artwork: Dave Hader, Studio Conceptions,
Toronto
Film Production: Global Film Services, Toronto
Marketing Consultant: Robert George

Bookstore and Library Distribution:
Firefly Books Ltd.
3680 Victoria Park Avenue
Willowdale, ON M2H 3K1
(416) 499-8412
1 800-387-6192 (Canada)

U.S. Offices
230 Fifth Avenue, #1607
New York, NY 10001
1-800 803-8488 (United States)

Printed and bound in the United States by R.R.
Donnelley Co.

ISBN 0-888383-00-3 (25 volume series)
ISBN 1-888383-21-6 (Volume 21)

Library of Congress Cataloguing-in-Publication Data

XXIII Olympiad : Los Angeles 1984, Calgary 1988.
       p.   cm. -- (The Olympic century : V.21)
    "1st Century Project is a cooperative effort between
World Sport Research & Publications Inc. and the United
States Olympic Committee to research and celebrate the 100
year history of the modern Olympic movement" -- T.p. verso.
  Includes bibliographical references (p.180) and index.
  ISBN 1-888383-21-6
  1. Olympic Games (23rd) : 1984 : Los Angeles, Calif.)
2. Winter Olympic Games (15th : 1988 : Calgary, Alta.)
I. World Sport Research & Publications Inc. II. United
States Olympic Committee. III. Series.
GV722.1984A17. 1995
796.48--dc20

CONTENTS

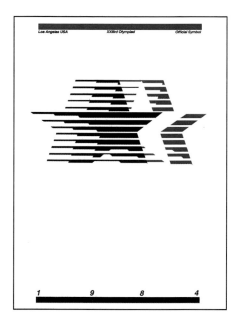

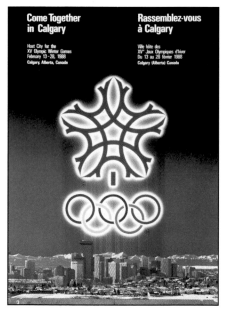

GLITZ AT THE GAMES

Olympic organizers promised an extravaganza to open the Los Angeles Games, and they delivered in grand Hollywood style: lavish size, lavish sounds, and, of course, a cast of thousands. Produced by filmmaker David Wolper, the 41-minute musical program that kicked off the celebration featured a 300-member choir, an 800-piece marching band, and more than 2,000 dancers, not to mention 84 baby-grand pianos (above) that boomed forth a crashing rendition of George Gershwin's "Rhapsody in Blue." At the end of the production number, spectators were cued to hold up cards that turned the Los Angeles Memorial Coliseum's stands into a waving tapestry of national flags.

Despite a boycott by the Soviet Union and most of its Eastern bloc allies, a record 140 countries participated in the Parade of Nations. President Ronald Reagan officially opened the Games—the first American head of state ever to perform this honor—and 11 more Americans, all former Olympians, hoisted the Olympic flag to the top of its 65-foot pole. In the final act of the traditional segment of the program, American hurdler Edwin Moses took the athlete's oath. As Moses returned to the American delegation, the International Children's Choir sang the "Ode to Joy" from Beethoven's Ninth Symphony. Then the 2,000 dancers returned to the field, and the four-hour ceremony ended with the singers, dancers, spectators, and athletes all swaying to an emotional rendering of the pop tune "Reach Out and Touch."

THE SELLING OF THE GAMES

LOS ANGELES 1984

Peter Ueberroth stood in the hallway of a Century City office building, a set of useless keys dangling from his hand. The keys failed to fit the door to what was supposed to be his new office, the one where he would hold sway as president of the Los Angeles Olympic Organizing Committee. The 47-year-old Ueberroth was avid to get on with the job; there were mountains of problems to solve if Los Angeles were to have any hope of successfully hosting the Olympic Games in the summer of 1984. One problem—getting into his new LAOOC office—appeared a logical place to start. Yet there he stood, stranded. It seemed an evil metaphor. So much had gone wrong.

No one could have blamed Ueberroth if he privately wondered on that June morning in 1979 whether the controversial Los Angeles Olympics would ever get off the ground. From the moment he had taken on the job only three months before, he had found himself caught in assorted cross fires—between politicians, foreign and domestic; Washington bureaucrats; the International Olympic Committee (IOC); various other sports establishments; and a large and hostile body of fellow Californians opposed to squandering one cent of the taxpayers' money on the Games. This last group apparently included the office building's landlords. They had, it seemed, decided to show their distaste for his mission by tearing up Ueberroth's lease, then sending someone over in the dead of night to change the locks. It was a sneaky bit of sabotage, but by no means the worst protest he had encountered, nor the worst to come.

As Ueberroth and his assistants fumed in the hallway, telephones—installed in the new office a few hours before the locks were changed—started ringing. It was just conceivable that some of the callers might want to offer help for the task at hand, but for the moment all aid was maddeningly out of reach, as distant and tantalizing as the dream of staging a world-class

Peter Ueberroth, President, Los Angeles Olympic Organizing Committee, July 28, 1984

THE GAMES AT A GLANCE

	July 28	July 29	July 30	July 31	August 1	August 2	August 3	August 4	August 5	August 6	August 7	August 8	August 9	August 10	August 11	August 12
OPENING CEREMONY	■															
ARCHERY												■	■	■	■	
ATHLETICS (TRACK & FIELD)							■	■	■	■	■	■	■	■	■	■
BASKETBALL		■	■	■	■	■	■	■	■	■	■	■				
BOXING		■	■	■	■										■	
CANOEING												■	■	■	■	
CYCLING		■	■	■	■	■	■									
DIVING												■	■	■	■	■
EQUESTRIAN SPORTS		■	■	■		■		■				■	■			■
FENCING					■	■	■	■	■	■	■	■				
FIELD HOCKEY		■	■	■	■	■	■	■	■	■	■	■	■	■	■	
FOOTBALL (SOCCER)		■		■	■	■	■		■			■		■	■	
GYMNASTICS		■	■	■	■	■		■					■	■	■	
JUDO								■	■	■	■	■	■	■	■	
MODERN PENTATHLON		■	■	■	■											
ROWING					■	■	■	■	■							
SHOOTING		■	■	■	■	■	■	■								
SWIMMING		■	■	■		■	■	■								
SYNCHRONIZED SWIMMING										■			■	■		
TEAM HANDBALL					■	■	■	■	■	■	■	■	■	■	■	
VOLLEYBALL	■	■	■	■	■	■	■	■	■	■	■			■	■	
WATER POLO					■	■					■	■		■	■	
WEIGHTLIFTING	■	■	■	■	■	■		■	■	■	■	■				
WRESTLING		■	■	■	■	■					■	■	■	■	■	
YACHTING			■	■	■				■	■	■			■	■	
CLOSING CEREMONY																■
DEMONSTRATION SPORTS																
BASEBALL					■	■	■	■	■	■	■	■				
TENNIS										■	■	■	■	■	■	■

sports spectacle. To Peter Ueberroth, the ringing phones must have sounded like the knell of doom.

Five years later, however, the sounds in Ueberroth's ears would be very different: roars of ecstatic crowds, victory fanfares and national anthems, shouts of triumph—and the silvery song of clinking cash registers. For against all odds, Ueberroth not only would make Los Angeles 1984 happen but would preside over the most successful Games since the modern Olympics began, and—according to some reckonings—the most profitable sporting event in history.

Ueberroth's approach to staging the Games

Freeways and urban murals, both Los Angeles staples, ushered spectators toward the 1984 Games. Organizers commissioned 10 works of street art such as Frank Romero's aptly titled *Going to the Olympics* as part of the Olympic Arts Festival.

would fuel furious debate: Was he the capitalist demon who sold out the Olympics or the pragmatic angel who saved them? Motives and methods aside, though, it was hard to argue with the results. The Games of the XXIII Olympiad would unfold over 16 unforgettable days before the eyes of an estimated 2.5 billion people, watching from coveted stadium seats or, via television, from every corner of the earth. And those who watched would see wonders: Men and women would challenge time, defy gravity, and all but take flight—America's Carl Lewis rocketing down the track and soaring in the long jump, Edwin Moses airborne above the hurdles, Greg Louganis diving with a gull's grace, tiny Mary Lou Retton grinning her engaging way through the arduous vaults and contortions of gymnastics, Brazil's young Joaquim Cruz besting some legendary veterans in the 800-meter run, Britain's breezy Daley Thompson dueling with Jürgen Hingsen, the "German Hercules," in the decathlon. Epic battles would rage, not only among rival athletes but between determined individuals and their personal demons: injury, illness, poverty, prejudice. Champions would rise from slums or sickbeds to reach golden apogees in Los Angeles.

When it came to drama, Hollywood would seldom do better.

Before the glorious cavalcade could roll, however, Peter Ueberroth would have to run an obstacle course that made the nerve-shattering Olympic steeplechase look like an evening stroll—not that most of the hazards weren't predictable.

Since the very beginning of the modern Olympics in 1896, prophets of doom had hovered over the Games, crying disaster. As each Olympiad began, these Jeremiahs promised it would be the last. They were always wrong. Organizational problems, financial woes, economic depression, and two world wars never quite dealt the death blow to the ideal of a truly global sporting event that celebrated exuberant youth and promoted world peace through friendly competition. But by the end of the 1970s, it looked as if the doomsayers were about to have their day.

The Munich 1972 Games became the setting for a blood-soaked massacre when Palestinian terrorists burst into the Olympic Village and seized members of the Israeli team in a nightmare that ended in death. Montreal 1976 brought bad news of a different kind. Those Games were a spectacular fiscal failure, running up a tab that would take generations to settle. In fact, only two modern Olympics, Los Angeles 1932 and Oslo 1952, had ever turned a profit.

It was small wonder, then, that potential host cities had begun to see the Games as a poisoned chalice. When, in 1977, the International Olympic Committee opened bidding for the Games of the XXIII Olympiad, it wasn't exactly swamped with eager contenders. Teheran submitted a lukewarm bid and then withdrew it, leaving Los Angeles the winner in a contest with no other entries. Angelenos themselves were less than joyous about this dubious victory. While many of them favored hosting the Olympics, they objected to putting taxpayers' money to that use. In a referendum held in November 1978, city citizens voted 475,930 to 170,897 to forbid any outlay of public funds to subsidize the Games.

But even before the vote, true believers were working on alternatives to public funds. One of the proponents was an aptly named lawyer called John Argue, who appealed to the IOC to suspend Rule 4 of the Olympic Charter. This rule specified that the Games had to be staged by the host city's government in collaboration with the country's national Olympic committee, in this case the United States Olympic Committee, or USOC. But the Los Angeles bidders now offered a revolutionary proposal: to run the Games as a private enterprise. The idea was redolent of commercialism—an aroma the IOC officially abhorred. Nevertheless, the masters of the Games were over a barrel: Either relax Rule 4 or

face the prospect of no Olympics in the summer of 1984. Argue won his case.

The victory popped champagne corks in the homes of Olympic boosters, but many other Los Angelenos were dour. "It's the worst thing that ever happened to this city," lamented one Los Angeles businessman. Many of the media, local and national, agreed, evoking the grim specter of Munich, the fiscal debacle of Montreal, the threat of foreign terrorists and homegrown criminals on the rampage. The Games, argued the naysayers, would also be choked by traffic, if not by smog.

One of the doubters—he had voted no in the referendum—was Peter Ueberroth, a prosperous businessman who reasoned that no sporting event, however august, deserved subsidy from the hard-pressed public purse. On the other hand, Ueberroth was a risktaker, a gambler who liked impossible jobs for the interesting odds they offered. Playing it safe wasn't his style. So it was that when the board members of the Los Angeles Olympic Organizing Committee asked him to head up the world's first purely private enterprise Games, it was an offer he couldn't refuse.

Ueberroth was, in many ways, the classic American success story. He had come from a modest background, worked his way through college in assorted jobs, starred in collegiate water polo, then parlayed his energy, wit, and instinct for a good opportunity into big-time business success. At the age of 24 he had started his own travel company on a shoestring, representing a collection of small independent airlines. When, some 18 years later, he retired from the business to devote himself to the Olympic project, his First Travel Corporation was the second-largest player in the industry, giving the giant American Express a run for its money.

Most observers figured that Ueberroth had made a fool's bargain—not to say lost his mind—trading the comforts of a smoothly running business empire to steer an enterprise as shaky and

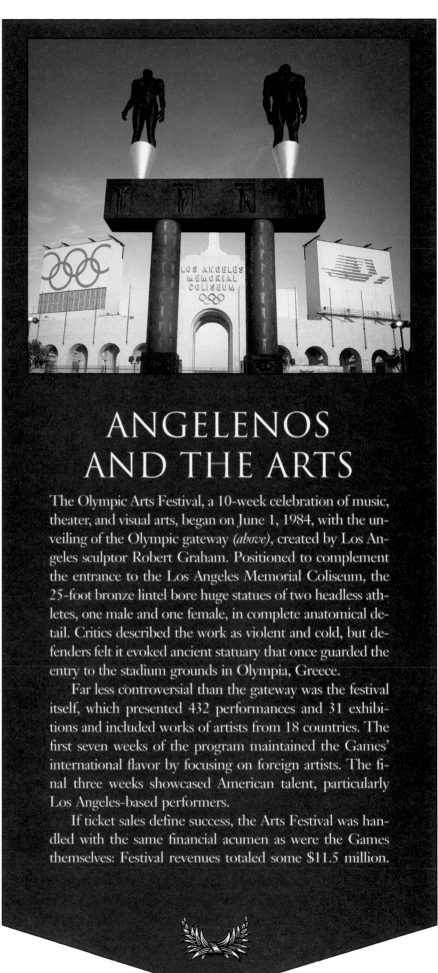

embattled as the Olympic Games. And indeed, Ueberroth himself confessed in his autobiography that his first instinct was to turn down the job. But there was appeal in the challenge of the thing, the new world to conquer. He likened the task to creating a Fortune 500 company from scratch, getting it up to speed from square one in five years flat. And, hardheaded businessman though he was, Ueberroth had his own brand of idealism. If the project succeeded, it would demonstrate to all the world the virtues of the American way of doing business.

He seemed the right man for the job. Ueberroth had stamina, flexibility, agility, and brains. An elegant tactician, he could nevertheless break his own rules if situations demanded a seat-of-the-pants management style. He had a gift for dealing, a knack that would stand him in good stead through five years of cajoling, liaising, and sparring with foreign heads of state, local cops, Olympic mandarins, militant zealots, scalpers, bureaucrats, and apparatchiks of all breeds and creeds. Moreover, he was a canny headhunter and team builder, taking pride in spotting the maverick talent that more hidebound employers might turn away. And, he backed up insight with chutzpah. Close friends and business associates whose abilities he coveted were coaxed, bullied, or charmed until they put their own careers on hold to join his team.

With the right people assembled—and new offices procured—Ueberroth's first priority was to find money. The USOC was underwriting the project with a $5-million guarantee, but that sum mostly amounted to moral support. Ueberroth reckoned it would take between $450 million and $500 million to produce an Olympic festival worthy of the name. The usual sources for financing the Olympic Games were government funds, supplemented by lotteries and charitable donations. But these conventional avenues were closed, since voters had locked the public exchequer. California law at the time banned lotteries,

ANGELENOS AND THE ARTS

The Olympic Arts Festival, a 10-week celebration of music, theater, and visual arts, began on June 1, 1984, with the unveiling of the Olympic gateway (*above*), created by Los Angeles sculptor Robert Graham. Positioned to complement the entrance to the Los Angeles Memorial Coliseum, the 25-foot bronze lintel bore huge statues of two headless athletes, one male and one female, in complete anatomical detail. Critics described the work as violent and cold, but defenders felt it evoked ancient statuary that once guarded the entry to the stadium grounds in Olympia, Greece.

Far less controversial than the gateway was the festival itself, which presented 432 performances and 31 exhibitions and included works of artists from 18 countries. The first seven weeks of the program maintained the Games' international flavor by focusing on foreign artists. The final three weeks showcased American talent, particularly Los Angeles-based performers.

If ticket sales define success, the Arts Festival was handled with the same financial acumen as were the Games themselves: Festival revenues totaled some $11.5 million.

and Ueberroth's own team had decided against soliciting donations. "Considering the general ill will that already existed," he explained, "it would've been insensitive and ill-advised to compete against churches, synagogues, hospitals, YMCAs, Girl Scouts, and all the other worthy organizations that rely on charity for survival."

There remained only three targets: commercial sponsorships, television revenues, and ticket sales for the Games themselves. A glance at the track records of previous Olympic organizing committees wasn't reassuring: None had ever earned more than $75 million from these sources.

Undaunted, Ueberroth forked over $100 from his own pocket to open an LAOOC checking account, then announced that the committee was ready to take bids for the television rights to the Games. To enter the auction, a bidder would have to ante up a refundable deposit of $750,000. ABC, NBC, CBS, a cable network, and an independent production company put down their markers: The bank interest earned on their deposits was enough to get the committee up and running. In the end, the rights went to ABC for a record $225 million. The deal was signed in September 1979.

The next step was the search for sponsors. Marketing expert Joel Rubinstein suggested the team home in on a small, elite group of corporations with massive advertising budgets. In exchange for a minimum contribution of $4 million, members of this exclusive club could look forward to the media exposure and global prestige associated with the Olympics. They would also enjoy the right to use official Los Angeles 1984 Olympic markings on their products, packaging, and advertising. The bidders flocked in, a roll call of commercial giants. Soft-drink rivals Coke and Pepsi dueled for the privilege of seeing their products star as the exclusive official beverages of the Games. Kodak and Fuji arm-wrestled for the honor of becoming the approved film stock for Olympic photographers. IBM provided

the information technology, Xerox the copiers, Atlantic Richfield the fuel for all vehicles connected with the Games. McDonald's fast-food empire built the pool at the University of Southern California for the swimming events. The owners of the 7-11 convenience stores—mindful that many customers arrived at their outlets on bikes—funded the cyclists' velodrome.

For all the good news, there was no shortage of trouble, most of it political. In May 1979, even though the voters had proclaimed their opposition to public funding, Los Angeles mayor Tom Bradley asked Congress for a grant of $141 million toward the Olympics. Bradley also announced an ambitious project to revamp the Los Angeles Coliseum, home of the 1932 Games, to welcome the world in 1984, as well as an enormous new land- and water-sports center at the Sepulveda Basin, with facilities for rowing, canoeing, and other events.

Opponents of the Games went into overdrive. They warned anew that the city would be bankrupted, blighted by Olympic-related construction projects, and would otherwise live to regret the impending Games. Anti-Games politicians urged cancellation of the event and called for yet another referendum, this one on a proposition to ban any kind of public funding—city, state, or federal. (This was overkill; even without benefit of a referendum, Congress turned down Bradley's request.) The residents of the Sepulveda Basin inveighed against any new sports complex slated for their community; Olympic oarsmen, archers, and the rest would have to find another place. On the East Coast, the *New York Times* weighed in, reporting claims that "official deception and cost overruns" were already afflicting plans for the Games.

Ueberroth and his family came under ugly personal attack. At an anti-Olympic rally in their neighborhood, an activist distributed leaflets with Ueberroth's home address. An hour after the demonstration, the family's two dogs nearly died from poisoned food that an ill-wisher had

WHERE THE GAMES WERE PLAYED

Olympic Velodrome

Los Angeles Memorial Coliseum

Lake Casitas

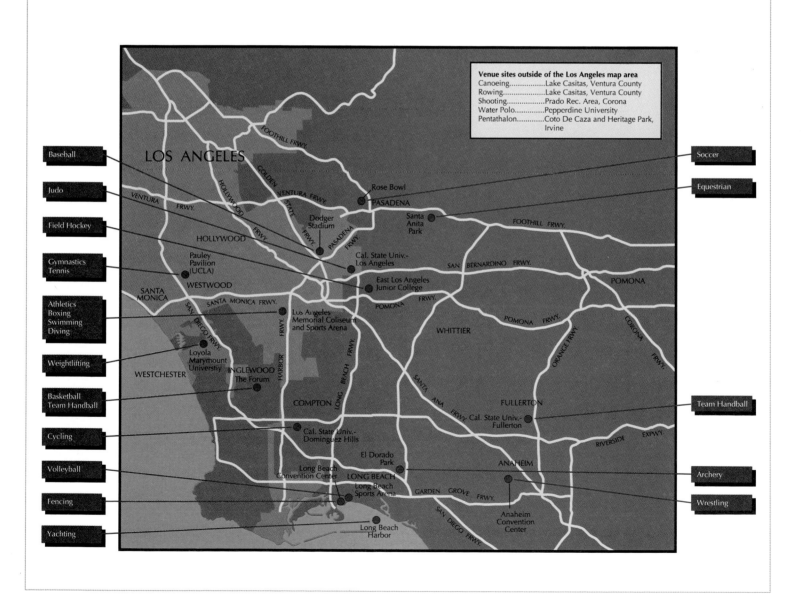

Venue sites outside of the Los Angeles map area
Canoeing.................Lake Casitas, Ventura County
Rowing....................Lake Casitas, Ventura County
Shooting.................Prado Rec. Area, Corona
Water Polo.............Pepperdine University
Pentathalon............Coto De Caza and Heritage Park,
                                Irvine

Baseball
Judo
Field Hockey
Gymnastics
Tennis
Athletics
Boxing
Swimming
Diving
Weightlifting
Basketball
Team Handball
Cycling
Volleyball
Fencing
Yachting

Soccer
Equestrian
Team Handball
Archery
Wrestling

LOS ANGELES
FOOTHILL FRWY.
GOLDEN STATE FRWY.
VENTURA FRWY.
VENTURA FRWY.
HOLLYWOOD FRWY.
Rose Bowl
PASADENA
Dodger Stadium
Santa Anita Park
FOOTHILL FRWY.
HOLLYWOOD
PASADENA FRWY.
Pauley Pavilion (UCLA)
Cal. State Univ.- Los Angeles
SAN BERNARDINO FRWY.
WESTWOOD
East Los Angeles Junior College
POMONA
SANTA MONICA
SANTA MONICA FRWY.
POMONA FRWY.
SAN DIEGO FRWY.
Los Angeles Memorial Coliseum and Sports Arena
HARBOR FRWY.
WHITTIER
POMONA FRWY.
ORANGE FRWY.
CORONA FRWY.
Loyola Marymount Universtiy
INGLEWOOD The Forum
LONG BEACH FRWY.
COMPTON
SANTA ANA FRWY.
FULLERTON
WESTCHESTER
Cal. State Univ.- Fullerton
Cal. State Univ.- Dominguez Hills
RIVERSIDE EXPWY.
El Dorado Park
ANAHEIM
Long Beach Convention Center
LONG BEACH
Long Beach Sports Arena
GARDEN GROVE FRWY.
Anaheim Convention Center
Long Beach Harbor
SAN DIEGO FRWY.

MEDALS OF LOS ANGELES

The winners' medals for Los Angeles 1984 adapted a design created by Florentine artist Giuseppe Cassioli and used at every Games since Amsterdam 1928. The front shows a seated Nike, Greek goddess of victory, holding a laurel wreath; on the back, a champion is borne away in the arms of his fellow athletes. American artist Dugald Sturmer altered the design slightly, adding more definition to Nike and modifying the features and musculature of the athletes on the reverse to suggest ethnic diversity.

tossed into the yard. Ueberroth hired round-the-clock security guards, and after a family conference, persuaded those of his four children not yet away at college to move temporarily to the safe haven of boarding schools.

The ugliness ranged from personal to global, for thousands of miles away from Los Angeles, the Cold War was wreaking its own anti-Games havoc. As a mark of disapproval against the Soviet invasion of Afghanistan, President Jimmy Carter had effected an American-led boycott of the 1980 Games in Moscow. Retaliating, the Soviets persuaded their allies to join the USSR in shunning Los Angeles 1984. Ueberroth, along with the IOC, became embroiled in shuttle diplomacy, trying to keep as many countries as possible in the Games. He even traveled to Cuba, smoking cigars and talking baseball with Fidel Castro, vainly hoping to coax the bearded dictator into breaking ranks and sending his athletes to California. Despite these efforts, the boycott went ahead: Apart from Romania and Yugoslavia, the Soviets and their socialist friends stayed home. The official line was that the Eastern bloc countries couldn't guarantee the security of their athletes in hostile, trigger-happy Los Angeles.

Nevertheless, four-fifths of the world's nations prepared to join the party, including a 200-strong team from the People's Republic of China, a country that hadn't participated since 1952. With most of the world thus convinced that Los Angeles 1984 was a worthwhile idea, there remained only for Ueberroth and his team to persuade their fellow Los Angelenos. Slowly but surely, through a long campaign of careful public relations, they began changing local hearts and minds. Some 50,000 volunteers, the largest force of its kind ever mustered in peacetime, participated in the onslaught to make the Games as perfect and palatable as possible.

The logistics were boggling, Ueberroth conceded, "tougher than staging 10 Super Bowls a day for 16 straight days." The venues for Olympic events—27 different stadiums and sports facilities—lay scattered across an area 200 miles long and 50 miles wide, and their owners and managers didn't automatically throw open their doors. Ueberroth pushed his negotiating skills to maximum strength to secure leases on the best possible terms in exchange for percentages of parking revenues, souvenir and refreshment sales, and other incentives. The object was to ensure that all parties went away feeling like winners.

Some events, by their very nature, burst out of the venues and into the streets. The trick in such cases was to minimize inconvenience, soothe tempers, and if possible, turn doubting citizens into willing conspirators in making the Games a success. Miraculously, Ueberroth persuaded authorities in his expressway-mad city to close down an entire freeway and block off roads for cycle racing and the marathons. Residents in affected areas were bombarded with letters of gratitude for their anticipated cooperation. And, although only heaven would have the final say on the weather, Ueberroth politicked hard for local industries to undertake antipollution measures to combat the city's notorious smog.

It was, on the whole, a herculean effort, but not everyone applauded. Purists in the

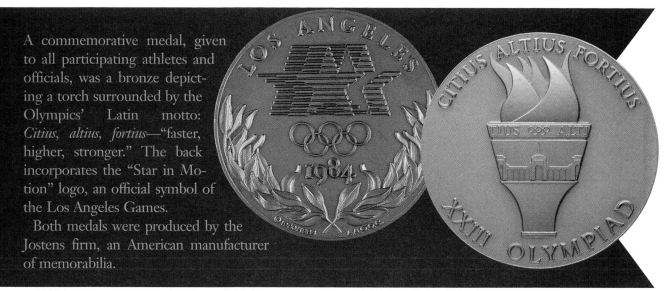

A commemorative medal, given to all participating athletes and officials, was a bronze depicting a torch surrounded by the Olympics' Latin motto: *Citius, altius, fortius*—"faster, higher, stronger." The back incorporates the "Star in Motion" logo, an official symbol of the Los Angeles Games.

Both medals were produced by the Jostens firm, an American manufacturer of memorabilia.

Olympic movement perceived Ueberroth as Mephistopheles, stealing the Olympic soul and corrupting it forever.

"You, Mr. Ueberroth," declared Sir Reginald Alexander, British-born IOC delegate in Kenya, "represent the ugly face of capitalism and its attempt to take over the Olympic movement and commercialize the Games." But, detractors notwithstanding, Peter Ueberroth was opening a new chapter in Olympic history.

If some members of the sports community thought the Los Angeles Games symbolized the ultimate sellout of Olympism, others felt that 1984 marked the moment when the Olympic movement finally faced up to the harsh economic realities of modern life. Traditional theory held that the celebration of athletic excellence shouldn't be contaminated by commercialism, but theory and reality had been at odds for quite some time; in truth, Mammon had long been a guest at the Games. No matter how lofty the Olympic ideal of sport for sport's sake, ideals alone could not pay the ever-increasing costs to stage the competitions, bring athletes from the four corners of the earth, provide the venues, print the tickets, or stamp the medals.

Besides, the members of the IOC could hardly pass themselves off as financial virgins in the marketplace. For decades they had debated among themselves such thorny issues as commercial sponsorship and amateurism. Financial contributions from the world of business might be welcome, but maybe not if the gifts entailed letting donors profit from their generosity by advertising their connection with the Games. Similarly, the IOC had struggled from its inception to define

amateurism and control just how and when—if ever—an athlete could profit from his talents. On both questions, over the years, the purists had grudgingly but steadily ceded ground.

The money changers definitively entered the Olympic temple in the 1960s, when television became a key player in the Games. Beginning as a trickle and swelling steadily to a torrent, the sale of broadcast rights would eventually mean hundreds of millions of dollars for the official Olympic bodies. The broadcasters, in turn, recouped their costs many times over by selling advertising time. The astronomical sums cast a huge shadow, big enough to largely eclipse the moral dilemma of purity versus profit.

For individual athletes, too, much was at stake. According to Baron Pierre de Coubertin and other founders of the modern Games, a champion should follow in the footsteps of the original Olympians, spurning any reward save the crowd's acclaim. Unfortunately, this vision of fiscal chastity in antiquity owed as much to wishful thinking as it did to historical accuracy. In the latter days of the ancient Games, winners went home from Olympia with generous prizes, and the heroes' proud hometowns sometimes accorded them lifetime financial benefits.

In fact, the rigid division between an amateur, who competed purely for the love of sport, and a professional, who played for money, had less to do with classical ideals than with Anglo-Saxon social snobbery. The 19th-century English class system strictly distinguished between the well-born gentleman, who played for the love of the game, and the rough-handed workingman or street entertainer who wrestled, boxed, or raced

HISTORY FOR SALE

Ever on the prowl for revenue, Los Angeles organizers seized on the idea that the torch relay could be used to raise money to support sports programs for American youth. The plan was to charge would-be torchbearers $3,000 each for the privilege of carrying the flame along one kilometer of its U.S. route. Americans liked the concept; Greeks, who regard the torch-lighting ceremony at Olympia as an almost religious event, were appalled. They were particularly alarmed by a report that a Lake Tahoe casino planned to buy a block of 50 kilometers and use them in a raffle for patrons. The Los Angeles Olympic Organizing Committee denied the report and reassured all and sundry that far from being defiled, the torch would be casting light for a good cause.

The Greeks weren't entirely appeased; nevertheless, on May 7, 1984, the torch was lighted at Olympia as scheduled, then flown to New York City. The following day it began its 82-day trip across America, spanning 33 states and the District of Columbia. Gina Hemphill, granddaughter of Olympic legend Jesse Owens, ran the first leg of the relay; later, she would also carry the torch into the Memorial Coliseum. Rafer Johnson, decathlon gold medalist at Rome 1960, had the honor of running the last lap and igniting the fire in the Olympic cauldron.

In all, 3,636 runners carried the flame, most of them paying customers. The total take for the venture was almost $11 million.

The torch (below) that American decathlete Rafer Johnson used to light the Olympic flame was made of aluminum with an antique brass finish. It was 22 inches long and weighed 34 ounces. After climbing a stairway in one of the stadium's gateway arches, Johnson touched the flame to a gas-filled tube that carried the fire through the Olympic rings and from there to the cauldron on top of the arch.

for a reward. Heaven forfend that these different breeds should meet on the same playing field—especially if the plebeians won the day. Thus in the early days, athletes who accepted money for their sporting efforts were strictly barred from taking part, and if they entered, won, and were later found out, were retroactively stripped of their medals.

Then came television, a medium that manufactures instant celebrities. Stars whose hard-won glory entitled them to dip into the bottomless honey pots of endorsement money weren't likely to turn down overnight riches for the sake of ideals that many considered outworn. Over time, payments once made under the table grew more and more open—more blatant, said some; less hypocritical, said others. By the early 1970s the issue of amateur status had become so complicated that the IOC gave up trying to legislate it, allowing the international federations that governed each Olympic sport to make their own individual rules. The result was a thicket of contradictions. Track and field athletes, for instance, might earn thousands of dollars in prize money at track meets, but woe betide them if they played any other sport for money: A few dollars earned playing professional baseball for the humblest minor league team would suffice to strip them of their amateur status.

Los Angeles 1984 helped end the confusion and the hypocrisy. In the heartland of free enterprise—or, some would say, rampant commercialism—market forces marched out of the closet for good and all. Gold medalists in the most glamorous sports, such as track, would unblushingly scoop up all manner of glittering prizes: lucrative advertising contracts, luxury cars, fat bonuses from the makers of the running shoes that had carried them to victory. Meanwhile, those athletes who had dedicated themselves to such low-profile events as archery or rowing would still play for love rather than money, whether they liked it or not. The ghost

of Coubertin might smile on their purity, but the television cameras would focus elsewhere.

Courtesy of these same cameras, the Los Angeles Games would be seen worldwide by an estimated 2.5 billion viewers, representing more than half the population of the planet. Emanating from the home of the Hollywood dream factory, the official opening of the Games had to be an unforgettable extravaganza. Masterminded by producer David Wolper, the event combined Olympian ceremony, American exuberance, and Southern California glitz. (Some European commentators decried the event as "Disney culture" tackiness, but such sneers were hardly novel in traditional Old World attitudes toward brash America.)

The rites began with the arrival of the Olympic torch after its voyage from Greece and its hand-to-hand odyssey across the United States. The torch was borne into the stadium by Gina Hemphill, granddaughter of Jesse Owens, hero of the 1936 Berlin Games. (Owens, incidentally, was a man who had made woefully little money from his own superb talents.)

Watching as the torch made its last lap, Peter Ueberroth could at last begin to relax. The crowd was cheering, spirits were high, natives were happy, most of the best athletes in the world were on hand. And money was in the bank—profits that, when the exact amount was announced some months hence, would stagger even the most optimistic backer of the controversial Games. Producing the world's greatest sports festival had been a titanic struggle, but Ueberroth had evidently enjoyed it; he now looked forward to his next assignment, as the new commissioner of major league baseball. Knowing the political and financial troubles brewing in that beloved national sport, most people considered him a glutton for punishment. After effecting a dazzling flurry of deals—most notable, a billion-dollar contract with CBS and ESPN for the rights to televise major league

American Carl Lewis leans into the curve near the end of the 200-meter dash. Though he competed at the distance infrequently, Lewis owned four of the best times ever recorded over 200 meters.

baseball—he would resign, in September 1988, and return at last to private business. By the mid-1990s he was managing partner of a Southern California business-management firm called the Contrarian Group.

Peter Ueberroth had made his point: The Olympic Games could pay their own way, and a good deal more. The rest of the world saw the future at Los Angeles and liked the look of it. Once as bereft of suitors as a dowager at a debutante ball, the IOC could now pick and choose among cities clamoring for a chance to host the Games. If the Olympic movement had finally lost its innocence, at least it had gotten a good price.

If money was the medium for saving the Olympics themselves, it was also conspicuously inspirational for some individual Olympians. Los Angeles 1984 demonstrated as perhaps never before that Olympic gold—in some sports and for certain extraordinary performers—meant not only medals around the neck but deposits in the bank.

Men's track events, especially, were fertile ground for superstars. Leading the pack as both a winner of laurels and a moneymaker was the phenomenally talented Carl Lewis. Matching the achievement of his boyhood idol, Jesse Owens, Lewis scooped up gold medals in four events: the 100-meter and 200-meter sprints, the 4 x 100-meter relay, and the long jump.

No one who witnessed Lewis sprinting down a track or striding through space in the long jump could deny his artistry. But long before he touched the Coliseum's starting blocks, the 23-year-old megastar was a controversial figure. Lewis's talents had brought him fame, fortune, and—according to his detractors—arrogance. Not every sportswriter at the precompetition press conference believed him when he declared, "My object is to be the role model, not the rich man."

A passion for sports had come early to Lewis,

who was born into a family of athletic achievers. His father had excelled at both track and football, his mother had been a hurdler at the 1951 Pan-American Games, one brother won laurels as a runner, a second was a soccer star, and his sister Carol was the first woman in the United States to clear 23 feet (7 meters) in the long jump. Growing up in the Philadelphia suburb of Willingboro, New Jersey, Carl had been the runt of this energetic litter until a growth spurt at age 15 helped him discover his potential as a sprinter.

Coaches and professional talent scouts soon noted the teenager's potential. While still in high school, Lewis found himself juggling offers of college scholarships and considering other material inducements from all directions, including those dangled by running-shoe manufacturers such as Puma and Adidas. (The whole Lewis family was sporting gear from both companies before Carl ever graduated from Willingboro High.) The University of Houston won the Lewis collegiate-inducement sweepstakes. Enrolling there in 1979, the brash young freshman—by now no stranger to commercial possibilities—announced to track coach Tom Tellez, "I want to be a millionaire, and I don't ever want a real job." Under Tellez's tutelage, Lewis soon qualified for the U.S. Olympic track and field team. He was thrilled to be an Olympian, even though America's boycott of Moscow 1980 meant that there was one set of medals that Carl would never win. While awaiting his chance for glory in the next Games, he set about gathering championships at a string of U.S. and European meets.

In 1984 Lewis arrived in Los Angeles trailing clouds of controversy because of his belief that the huge sums he now earned in appearance fees and sponsorship deals—an estimated $750,000 a year—were the just reward for his hard work and undoubted talent. "Track is my livelihood, not a hobby," he declared. Like many of his fellow athletes, he felt that the Olympic ideal of amateurism was pure pretense, and he scorned

even to pay it lip service. (With ironic tongue in cheek, perhaps, he would one day title his autobiography, *Inside Track, My Professional Life in Amateur Track and Field*.) A resentful Lewis also felt in 1984 that the media were out to smear him, falling like vultures on such details as his expensive clothes, his luxury car, and his insistence on staying in a rented house with his parents instead of sharing the U.S. team's more spartan quarters at the Olympic Village.

But even those who carped at Lewis's alleged bad attitude had to admit themselves awed by his achievements on the track. In his first race, the 100 meters, he came out of the blocks in an unpromising start. But then—halfway through the distance—he loosed an incredible burst of speed that pushed him past the front runner, Sam Graddy, and opened a gap that no one could hope to close. Lewis, who later admitted that he had feared this event more than any other, said that the sudden explosion of energy made him almost drunk with joy.

Launching into a victory lap, he seized a huge American flag from a member of the crowd and bore it aloft as he circled the track. Some journalists implied afterward that the flag snatching had been a prearranged trick, a charge that both Lewis and the banner's owner—a 50-year-old sports fan from Louisiana—hotly denied.

A victory lap with an American flag was Lewis's way to celebrate his 100-meter title. After the race, which gave him his first gold medal of the Games, a confident Lewis would declare his pursuit of Jesse Owens's record of four gold medals "60 percent over."

Carl Lewis floats over 28 feet on his second attempt in the long-jump finals. Because he could regularly make that distance, fans expected him to challenge the long-jump record set by Bob Beamon in 1968.

Debate grew even fiercer over Lewis's conduct in his next event, the long jump. Each contender was allowed six jumps; Lewis took only two. In the first round he performed his elegant airborne stride to achieve a distance of 28 feet 1/4 inch (8.54 meters). Although the leap didn't break the fabled world record of 29 feet 2 1/2 inches set by Bob Beamon in 1968, it was a dazzling achievement in its own right: Only three other jumpers in history had soared so far. In the second round, possibly hampered by the failing evening light, Lewis fouled and didn't score. Thereafter, he stood aside and refused to take his turn in the four rounds that followed. Nevertheless, after his 11 competitors had made their attempts, Lewis's distance for his single successful jump still outstripped all others by a substantial margin, and he won the gold.

Despite the impressive victory, when Lewis mounted the podium to receive his medal he was booed by some members of the crowd. The detractors—perhaps ignorant of the fine points of the long jump or the rules of competition—felt shortchanged. They had paid at least $50 per ticket to see the megastar of track perform. They wanted their money's worth—not a measly couple of jumps. But more knowledgeable track aficionados scoffed at this reaction: Lewis, they knew, wasn't required by the rules to make the extra jumps, and there was no compelling reason to make them, since his one good jump had been a clear winner. Indeed, there were good reasons not to gild the lily: Lewis was entered in two more events after the long jump. There was no logic in risking injury in pointless additional leaps.

On August 8, four days after the long jump, Lewis again took a gold, this time in the 200 meters. Even running against a headwind, he covered the distance in an Olympic-record 19.8. To the great delight of the mainly American crowd, Kirk Baptiste and Thomas Jefferson, who came pounding home behind him for the silver and the bronze, respectively, were also on the U.S. team. To finish his Olympic winning streak, Lewis anchored the U.S. squad in the 4 x 100-meter relay. This shared gold medal was the final step toward the completion of his personal Olympic dream: to duplicate the spectacular Olympic quadruple triumph of Jesse Owens. And, despite the cynicism of journalists who dismissed him as a flash in the pan, Lewis would go on to gather still more Olympic gold in later years.

Unlike Carl Lewis, American hurdler Edwin Moses seemed able to capture both gold medals and hefty financial rewards without antagonizing the sporting press and public. When Moses entered the stadium on August 5, he got a standing ovation, the warmest applause granted any star athlete in the Games—this despite the fact that his link to amateurism was just as tenuous as Lewis's. The crowd knew full well that Moses, like Lewis, was one of track's richest men. In 1983 the hurdler had unabashedly declared his own earnings, from the usual sponsorship deals and advertising and appearance fees, as $457,000. "Amateur athletics is just a play on words," he proclaimed in a *Time* magazine interview. "No one can run hurdles as fast as I can. No one can run the 100 as fast as Carl Lewis. We're the professionals in our fields."

Disarmed, perhaps, by Moses's directness and his engaging gap-toothed grin, the fans in Los

Angeles seemed far less concerned with his wealth than with rooting him on to perpetuate his spectacular seven-year winning streak. Moses had first burst into the public consciousness at the age of 21 as the unexpected victor of the 400-meter hurdles at Montreal 1976. One hundred and five contests later, he still held exclusive claim—apart from one single setback in 1977—to the gold medal in his chosen event.

Behind his stunning successes lay a remarkable physical aptitude, coupled with rigorous self-discipline. If ever there was a man genetically adapted to hurdling, it had to be Moses, a lanky 6-foot-2 speedster with a stride measuring an incredible 9 feet 9 inches. Where less advantaged hurdlers laboriously jumped the barriers, Moses seemed to float over them. "Compared to Ed," said one hurdling coach, "everyone else looked like roosters with their tails on fire."

But even before Moses had come into his full physical powers—he, like Lewis, was on the small side until he blossomed in late adolescence—he was gifted with uncommon energy and intellect. The son of two educators, the thin and bespectacled young Edwin spent his childhood in Dayton, Ohio, pursuing a wide range of interests, from science to music and art. When he entered Atlanta's Morehouse College it was indeed on a scholarship—but for academics, not track. Nevertheless, Moses, by then willowy and well-muscled, went out for the track team and made it. He was soon known among his fellow athletes as the Bionic Man because his studies in physics and civil engineering helped him develop a systematic, highly detailed approach to monitoring and perfecting his performance. In training sessions then and later he bleeped and bristled with electronic gadgetry providing readouts on his lap times, as well as such vital physiological data as heartbeat and respiration.

Along with his remarkable physique and intellect, Moses also seemed psychologically suited to

America's Edwin Moses glides over a barrier in a heat of the 400-meter hurdles. His dominance in the event was unchallenged. In his career he had already run the race in under 48 seconds 27 times. Only three other athletes in history had clocked a time that fast, none of them more than three times.

A heat of the 400-meter hurdles brings a familiar sight: Edwin Moses in front. Moses was aiming for his 90th consecutive hurdles title at the Los Angeles Games.

the strains of competing on the Olympic level. Although he once claimed that the pressure of sustaining a seemingly endless winning streak meet after meet was "like going to your execution 14 times a year," he also conceded that stress was what he fed on. "The way I get the best out," he explained, "is by not expecting an easy race. It's easier when there's pressure. You get emotional and you go out and perform."

Fortunately for Moses, there was pressure aplenty at Los Angeles. At the very moment the finals of the 400-meter began, he was almost disqualified for jumping the gun, mistaking the loud click of a nearby camera for the starter's pistol. His victory—a graceful 47.75-second soar over the hurdles—didn't break his own 47.02 world record, but it gave him the prize he was after, his second Olympic gold. Nor would Los Angeles 1984 see the end of his unbroken chain of victories. That day would have to wait until almost a decade after the winning streak began,

until June 1987, when Moses was finally bested by Danny Harris, the U.S. teammate who had captured the silver medal at Los Angeles.

Although Los Angeles 1984 was, to be sure, a showcase for big moneymakers, it was also a stage where actors whose main currency was heart played out moving human dramas. There were, for example, the men of the middle-distance runs. The 800-meter and 1,500-meter races saw the rise of a new young star from an entirely unexpected quarter, the surprise comeback of an ailing champion who had been written off as yesterday's hero, and the courageous—and losing—battle of a wounded champion.

The new star was a 21-year-old Brazilian named Joaquim Cruz, who had grown up in poverty in the town of Taguatinga, near the capital city of Brasilia, where his father labored in the steelworks. To help feed himself and his four siblings, young Joaquim had sometimes

worked as a shoeshine boy and helped his father peddle oranges at a local fair. Cruz was something of an oddity among his compatriots. In the shantytowns of Brazil, most boys grew up dreaming of stardom on the soccer pitch rather than the running track.

The mentor who made the difference for Joaquim was a school coach named Luiz de Oliveira, who recognized the boy's enormous potential. Cruz himself, who preferred the camaraderie of the school basketball team, was at first a lukewarm convert from court to track. "Running," he would recall later, "was boring and lonely." On the other hand, it brought quick success. At the age of 15, Joaquim ran the 800 meters in 1 minute 54 seconds and the 400 in 48.7 seconds. Realizing that he had a prodigy on his hands, Oliveira forged a working partnership with Cruz. Three years later, after Cruz had established a world junior record at a race in Rio de Janeiro, the pair left Brazil and traveled north to the United States to perfect Cruz's gifts.

Oliveira applied himself to the science of middle-distance training. He saw that the crux of the problem for runners at this distance was oxygen debt, the shortfall that occurs when an athlete burns more oxygen during a race than he can take in. So the coach trained Cruz to hold his breath for part of each circuit. The payoff was Cruz's enhanced endurance and his ability to run at phenomenal speeds without fatigue.

In the 800 meters at Los Angeles, Cruz claimed the gold medal in a run of 1:43. His streamlined and seemingly effortless pace disconcerted such formidable rivals as the 1980 gold medalist, Steve Ovett, and the celebrated Sebastian Coe. "Clocks have nothing to do with Cruz," said Coe. "This man doesn't worry about the speed he's running. He is a supreme champion."

Back home in Brazil, sports fans were ecstatic. The boy from Taguatinga had gained the only Olympic gold medal ever won by a Brazilian runner. Authorities wanted to award Cruz a homecoming victory parade, but the new hero modestly declined, asking that the parade money be used instead to help upgrade track and field facilities throughout Brazil. The formerly reluctant runner had acquired a missionary zeal. "In my country," Cruz told journalists, "soccer is first, then volleyball. Track and field is last. I hope this will change something."

As Cruz had worked toward his inspired

Moving to the front of the pack, Joaquim Cruz heads for a decisive victory in the 800 meters. Cruz was Brazil's first track and field gold medalist since Adhemar da Silva, the triple-jump champion at Melbourne 1956.

Olympic debut in 1984, British runner Sebastian Coe was pursuing the year of the comeback. Coe had enjoyed brilliant success on the track in the late 1970s, amassing a dozen world records before winning the gold medal in the 1,500 meters at Moscow 1980. The streak had come to a painful end, however, when Coe was felled by a debilitating and life-threatening disease. His illness and recuperation had taken up most of 1983, losing him months of precious training time. Various members of the press announced that the hero had fallen. "Based on 1983," prophesied one journalist, "I'd write Coe off completely."

But the detractors failed to factor into their auguries Seb Coe's near-obsessive dedication to his craft. Ever since he was 13 years old, running had been the focus of his life. His father, Peter, had recognized the boy's abilities and had channeled his own considerable energies into coaching Sebastian, who would later be lauded by some sportswriters as the greatest middle-distance runner in history. By 1981 the younger Coe had become one of the sport's high earners, gleaning appearance fees of nearly $20,000 per event, and his income for the year following Moscow topped $300,000. Money, however, was not the sole incentive. "I want to run for myself," he said in his 1981 autobiography, "for the pure fun and exhilaration of running at speeds that have not been run before."

In the early 1980s, Coe, along with his countrymen Steve Ovett and Steve Cram, had come to symbolize a golden age of British middle-distance running. Yet his struggles with toxoplasmosis had seemed—to onlookers, if not to Coe himself—to put a full stop to his career. Grimly determined to make up for the time lost during his illness, he trained hard enough to qualify for the 1984 British Olympic team.

The schedule for the Games would be grueling. Between heats, semifinals, and finals of the 800- and 1,500-meter contests, Coe faced an assault course of seven races in nine days. His aspirations were hardly modest: As well as hoping to match or exceed the silver medal he had gained in the 800 at Moscow, he resolved to do what no middle-distance Olympic champion had ever managed before: to match the gold medal he had won in Moscow with a second, consecutive gold in the 1,500 meters.

The 800-meter race came first in the schedule. Coe felt he had a chance until Joaquim Cruz outstripped him to win by five meters. Bearing his silver medal and soothed by the knowledge that the world record he had set for this event

was still intact, Coe seemed philosophical. "I was beaten by a guy who was younger and stronger," he said. "I'm not leaving dissatisfied."

For Coe's British teammate Steve Ovett, however, the disappointment cut deeper. Since the mid-1970s, Ovett had been one of the most exciting and versatile runners in international track. His hallmark was an explosive finish, a kick that withered the competition. When Ovett won the 1977 world championship 1,500 meters in Düsseldorf in 3:34.5, his compatriot Seb Coe described the race as the finest example he had ever

seen of 1,500-meter running. Between 1977 and 1983, Ovett set a dozen British records at distances from 800 to 2,000 meters, twice broke the world record for a mile, and defeated all comers in a long succession of international and European championships. At Moscow he had claimed the gold medal for the 800 meters, and he might have regained it in 1984. But at Los Angeles a bout of serious bronchial trouble sabotaged Ovett's chances. In the qualifying heats for the 800 meters, he flung himself across the finish line to achieve the fourth place that would gain him

Medics come to the aid of Great Britain's Steve Ovett, the defending 800-meter champion, who crumpled to the ground at the finish of the race. Against doctor's cautions, Ovett would compete two days later in the 1,500-meter race.

entry to the semifinals. Ignoring his doctor's warnings against running the race at all, he forced himself as far as the finals, struggled around the track behind every other competitor, and finally collapsed. He was carried off the field on a stretcher and spent two days in the hospital.

To everyone's amazement, Ovett was back in the picture for the 1,500-meter heats, and astonishingly, he once again made it to the finals, along with Sebastian Coe. But Ovett's breathing problems returned with savage intensity as the race progressed. Coe, meanwhile, was back in form as never before, running what commentators would dub the perfect race, to gain the gold—for an unprecedented second Games in succession—and set an Olympic record of 3:32.53. In a gesture of triumphant defiance, Coe turned toward the British press corps and roared, "Who says I'm finished?" Ironically, as Coe took his victory lap, Ovett lay gasping on the grass alongside the track, where he had fallen during the final lap, waiting for the paramedics to carry him from the field.

Another British lion, however, was ready to roar. Daley Thompson, victor in the Moscow 1980 decathlon, had come to Los Angeles primed for a second successive gold medal. London-bred Thompson, half-Scottish and half-Nigerian, had discovered his passion for

track at a boarding school for children with behavioral problems, where he had been sent when he was seven years old by his hard-pressed mother. Sports provided both the discipline and the outlet for his prodigious energies. By his mid-twenties the irrepressible Daley would find himself laden with laurels and commanding hundreds of thousands of dollars per year in appearance fees and endorsements.

However breezy his attitude, Thompson knew that Los Angeles would be no pushover. The Games would bring him face to face with the only other decathlete who had ever shaken his confidence: West Germany's Jürgen Hingsen.

After Thompson swept the field at Moscow, he was jolted to find that his world record for total points had been shattered by Hingsen, a towering 6-foot-6 3/4-inch Teuton nicknamed the "German Hercules." In the years leading up to Los Angeles, Thompson had won every time the two men had confronted each other. Thus Hingsen's rise to stardom came as a shock. "I'd never considered him a rival," Thompson reflected. "I was surprised when he broke my record, and I was even more surprised when he kept on doing it."

Whatever qualms he might have had, Thompson greeted the press in Los Angeles in an upbeat and characteristically cheeky mood. Asked about Hingsen's chances, the Briton announced,

Catapulting skyward, Great Britain's Daley Thompson takes command of the decathlon with a soaring vault.

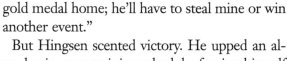
The Netherlands' Stephan van den Berg maneuvers around a buoy during the sailboarding competition in Los Angeles. The five-time world champion added a gold medal to his laurels.

BREEZY BEGINNINGS

When California surfer Hoyle Schweitzer attached a mast with a pivoting rig to his surfboard in 1967, he had no idea how quickly his invention would sail to international success. Cheaper than traditional sailing and easy to learn, sailboarding became an instant sensation: More than 100,000 boards were plying the world's waters within three years of Schweitzer's Windsurfer patent. By 1980 the International Yacht Racing Union (IYRU), the governing body for sailing, had won unanimous approval from the International Olympic Committee for an Olympic boardsailing event.

It was then that windsurfing sailed into controversy. The IYRU decreed that Olympic entrants would all use the same brand of sailboard in order to assure that competition would test skill, not equipment. Vying to supply the boards were two rivals: Schweitzer's Windsurfer and a West German firm's Windglider. Most aficionados thought the Windsurfer faster, more maneuverable, and more durable than its competitor. Nevertheless, the IYRU gave the nod to the Windglider, explaining that it alone met the criteria of being uniform, readily available, comparatively inexpensive, and suited to all sizes of competitors.

A Schweitzer lawsuit to keep the Windgliders out of the United States was unsuccessful, and the first Olympic boardsailing races were held in Long Beach harbor as scheduled, beginning July 31. Sailboarders competed on a nine-stage triangular course identical to the one used by traditional Olympic boats—a course that did not play to the strengths of the much lighter, quicker, more versatile boards.

Despite its problems, the inaugural race drew 38 competitors from 38 countries. At the conclusion of the series of seven races, Holland's Stephan van den Berg became the first Olympic boardsailing gold medalist.

"There are only two ways he is going to bring a gold medal home; he'll have to steal mine or win another event."

But Hingsen scented victory. He upped an already-rigorous training schedule, forcing himself to end each session with one last extra lap. "This one's for Daley," he explained.

The two rivals had different strengths and weaknesses. Hingsen, an austere perfectionist, was a better jumper than a runner; Thompson was a stronger runner than a jumper. An athlete combining the best of both men, Thompson mused, would be a formidable creature indeed: "His body and my speed—wouldn't that be interesting?"

"Interesting" was pure British understatement. Throughout the two days of their confrontation, Thompson and his German rival Hingsen would keep the crowds—and themselves—on tenterhooks. Although there were 22 other excellent decathletes in the running, the real battle was fought between these two men.

The first event on Day 1—the 100 meters—was Daley's, as he burst across the finish line in 10.44 seconds. Hingsen was 0.47 of a second behind him. Hingsen might have expected to get his own back in the long jump, but Thompson—in the best of three tries—soared 26 feet 3 1/2 inches (8.01 meters), outstripping the German Hercules by 8 1/4 inches (21 centimeters).

Hingsen's hopes rose with the shot put; he sent it flying 52 feet 3/4 inches (15.87 meters), comfortably beyond anything Thompson had yet managed. Then Thompson surprised everyone with a new personal best of 51 feet 7 inches (15.72 meters)—a shorter throw than his rival's, but much closer than expected. He was still well ahead of Hingsen on points. Hingsen's spirits—and score—rose when he crested at 6 feet 11 1/2 inches (2.12 meters) in the high jump, far better than anything the shorter, stockier Thompson could have managed, and clawed back 77 points for himself. But the day ended with Thompson winning the 400 meters and standing 114 points ahead of his foe.

Said Aouita of Morocco displays his national pride after winning the 5,000-meter race. To honor the achievement, Morocco's king Hassan II gave Aouita a villa in Casablanca and named an express train after him.

The second day began with the 110-meter hurdles, and here the long-legged Hingsen took the lead, edging ahead by a tight 0.04 of a second. Next, for the first of three tries in the discus throw, he launched the dish to a sky-skimming personal best of 166 feet 9 inches (50.82 meters). Thompson's two initial efforts were poor enough to threaten his hold on first place. But his third try was a lifetime best of 152 feet 9 inches, or 46.56 meters. He had succeeded in keeping his lead, though it had narrowed to 32 points. Hingsen knew that if he did well in the pole vault, and kept the pressure on in the javelin throw, he would be in a very strong position for the final event—the 1,500 meters. "If it comes to the 1,500 meters," the German had predicted earlier, "I'll blow him away."

But once the pole vault began, Hingsen found himself literally sick with nervous tension, vomiting twice while awaiting his turn. His first two tries were so poor that he was almost disqualified for not making the height. The crowd could hardly believe its eyes: One of the world's leading decathletes seemed to be caving in on himself, performing like a high school freshman. Hingsen marshaled all his forces for the last, crucial attempt, clearing the bar by the merest sliver of space. Thompson, delighted, knew he had him. After vaulting 16 feet 4 3/4 inches (5 meters), he celebrated with a cocky grin and a back-flip on the landing pad. The dispirited Hingsen went on to make a poor showing in the javelin throw, a dismal 23 feet short of his previous best effort.

The 1,500-meter race was, in effect, Daley Thompson's victory lap. His finishing score of 8,798 was two points short of a world record, but he had bested Hingsen by 125 points. "I was just running on feeling," he told the press later. "I was having a good time."

Another 1984 gold medalist who, like Thompson, raced his way from a deprived background to an athletic apex at the Olympic Games was Morocco's Said Aouita. Aouita had grown up in a crumbling, medieval quarter in the city of Fez, supplementing the family income by working as a street vendor. His prospects seemed as narrow as the winding alleys where he worked, but he burned with ambition. Disappointed by a mediocre report card, he informed the teacher, "What I will not get through the pen, I will get with my legs." His speed matched his determination, and he would find on cinder tracks the path to his boyhood dreams of glory, for himself and his country. Aouita made it clear that he saw himself as a child of destiny. "Everything I do is out of duty for Morocco," he told interviewers. "I am a Moroccan warrior who has to do battle."

Patriotism aside, Aouita also liked a good scrap for its own sake, and his competition in the 5,000-meter race at Los Angeles was more than worthy. Some of the event's strongest contenders were absent, among them the world champion, Ireland's Eamonn Coghlan, because of injury, and a number of Eastern bloc athletes because of the boycott. Nevertheless, at the contest's end, commentators agreed that no other 5,000-meter had ever been run at such prodigious speeds.

All six of the front runners, in turn, broke the Olympic record of 13:20.34 set in a preliminary heat by the United Kingdom's Brenden Foster at Montreal 1976. The punishing pace was set by two Portuguese runners, Antonio Leitão and Ezequiel Canario, but both were bested in the final stretch by Swiss runner Markus Ryffel and Said Aouita. The last 100 meters belonged to the Moroccan, who felt confident enough of his victory to wave to the crowd during his sprint to the finish, leaving Ryffel 10 to 12 yards behind. Aouita's winning time was 13:05.59.

Once his lap of honor was run, the ecstatic gold medalist spoke on the telephone to his most important patron, King Hassan II, who had given Morocco's Olympic track and field competitors $30,000 each to subsidize their training. Apparently pleased with his investment, the king would soon reward Aouita with the gift of a Casablanca villa. "He protects us and loves us," said the runner of his royal sponsor, "as if we were his own children."

Thanks to Aouita and Ryffel, Portugal had seen the gold and silver medals slip from its grasp in the 5,000 meters. But on the following day—Sunday, August 12—the men's marathon would bring surprising compensation.

Some sports journalists deemed the field the best collection of marathon runners ever gathered, and knowledgeable fans argued over the likely winner. Some put their faith in Australia's Robert de Castella: In the three and a half years leading up to 1984, Castella had run in only four marathons, but he had won them all. Other pundits opted for another resident of the Pacific Rim, Japan's Toshihiko Seko. Back in 1979, Seko had, it was true, once lost a marathon; since then he had come first in each of the five he had entered. Alongside these favorites stood another quintet of runners who had all completed the race in less than 2 hours 9 minutes.

The day of the marathon turned out hot and humid, but Castella and the other prime contenders made a strong start. The Australian held his position inside a leading pack of a dozen powerful runners and kept pace when four of them fell away. At the relief post on the 20-mile mark, he paused for a swift cup of water, then found himself contemplating the heels of the last of the lead pack, a full 55 yards ahead of him. Try as he would, Castella could never manage to close that vital gap. By the next mile marker, Toshihiko Seko had also disappeared from among the front runners.

Charles Spedding of Great Britain held his place at the head of the line, setting a punishing pace in the sticky heat. The only two men who could match it were Ireland's John Treacy, running his very first marathon, and Portugal's Carlos Lopes, silver medalist in the 10,000 meters at Montreal, and now, at age 37, the grand old man of this marathon. In the last stage of the run, Lopes gathered himself for a final burst, shaking free of his last two challengers and covering the last three miles in 14:33 to win the gold. Treacy claimed the silver and Spedding the bronze. Castella finished fifth, while Seko crossed the line in a disappointing 14th place.

Lopes's triumph was doubly surprising. Not only was he among the older competitors ever to win an international marathon, but he was still

bearing the marks of injuries he sustained when
he was hit by a car a mere 15 days before the
race. While on a training run in Lisbon, he had
suddenly found himself sprawling across the
hood of a large Mercedes with his elbow poking
through a shattered windshield. Lopes had to be
hospitalized, losing four days of vital training
time, but the wounds had proved fairly minor.

While the Portuguese champion was rejoicing
over his medal, a small, secret drama played itself out at the farthest end of the straggling line
of marathoners bringing up the rear. The very
last man to struggle into the stadium was the
Haitian runner, Dieudonne Lamothe. His only
previous claim to Olympic fame had been his

performance in the 5,000-meter race at Montreal 1976, where he had clocked one of the slow-
est times in the history of the modern Games.
Now, two Olympiads later, he was back. The
few Los Angeles spectators who noticed him at
all may have wondered why he didn't simply
give up the effort as a total loss and drop out before the humiliating limp across the finish line
43 minutes after the race had been won.

At the time, Lamothe said nothing, to the
press or anyone else. Only later, after the fall of
the Haitian dictator Jean-Claude "Baby Doc"
Duvalier did Lamothe explain what had happened in Los Angeles. Officials within the Haitian regime, he said, had threatened to kill him if

World record holder Zhu Jianhua leans into a qualifying high jump. Zhu's best leap of 7 feet 7 inches (2.31 meters) was only good enough for a third-place finish—a disappointment, but still a milestone for Chinese track and field athletes.

he didn't stay the course and finish the race. Lamothe wasn't dreaming of Olympic glory; he was running for his life.

Even without the murderous breath of a dictator's hit squad on his neck, an Olympic competitor may feel that the anxious attention of his fans back home is a burden as well as an inspiration. High jumper Zhu Jianhua from the People's Republic of China confessed to an interviewer, "When I jump, I jump with one billion people on my shoulders."

Zhu, a 21-year-old from Shanghai, had come to Los Angeles bearing the world high-jump record of 7 feet 10 inches (2.39 meters). A gangling 6 foot 4, Zhu was exceptionally tall for a Chinese, although he looked frail, even emaciated. He had been only 10 years old when he attracted the attention of a talent scout for a special sports training school for gifted young athletes. The recruiter had to take considerable pains to persuade the boy's anxious mother that the act of jumping over a bar onto a mat wouldn't shatter the bones of her precious youngest son.

Reclusive China lacked the sophisticated training techniques and equipment available in the West, and in his early meets outside his homeland, Zhu's inexperience showed. Trips to competitions in the U.S. and Europe were marred by injury, illness, shattered concentration. Even so, in late spring of 1983, Zhu set a world record of 7 feet 9 1/4 inches (2.37 meters) at a meet in Peking. A few months later, in Shanghai, he broke his own record, leaping 7 feet 9 3/4 inches (2.38 meters). In the spring of 1984 the shy young Chinese reached his 7-foot-10-inch (2.39-meter) pinnacle—not among familiar surroundings in his homeland, but far away in Eberstadt, West Germany, against world-class competition. When the Chinese team arrived in Los Angeles, Zhu was reckoned by many the man to

beat for the gold. The experts figured that the silver would be a battle between lanky West German Dietmar Mögenburg, a former world record holder who had finished second on the day of Zhu's epic jump in Eberstadt, and two-time Olympic bronze medalist Dwight Stones of the United States.

But it was not to be. In the early rounds, Zhu seemed unbeatable; as the bar rose higher, so did the Chinese champion. Mögenburg, also in fine form, was giving Zhu a run for his money. With the bar standing at 7 feet 7 inches (2.31 meters), only four jumpers were still

Chinese free-pistol champion Xu Haifeng celebrates his victory during the medal presentation ceremony. The Los Angeles Games marked the return of mainland China to Olympic competition after a 32-year hiatus. Xu's gold in shooting was the first medal awarded at the Games.

France's Pierre Durand leads Jappeloup de Luze over a jump in the Prix des Nations competition at Los Angeles. Durand fell from his mount during the round, knocking the French team out of medal contention. American riders won team and individual honors.

in the hunt: Zhu, Mögenburg, Stones, and Sweden's Patrik Sjöberg. At a bar height of 7 feet 7 3/4 inches (2.32 meters), Zhu tallied his first miss. He was just about to try again when disaster struck.

At that moment in the crammed Olympic schedule, the Los Angeles Coliseum was hosting more than one event. As the high jumpers made their tries, the runners in the 1,500 meters were pounding around the track, with the crowd roaring its acclaim as Seb Coe made a crucial move on the backstretch. Already disconcerted by the noise, perhaps, Zhu found his concentration shaken further as the ailing Steve Ovett collapsed right on the edge of the high-jump apron.

Zhu, who had built up a head of steam and had been bursting for his second try at 7 feet 7 3/4 inches—a height that should have been no problem for him—stood anxiously by while medics bent over Ovett. As the time ticked away, so did Zhu's focus, and with it his chance for the gold.

He decided to pass on a second try at 7 feet 7 3/4 inches, then missed twice at 7 feet 8 1/2 inches. His billion compatriots had to content themselves with his bronze medal. The first prize went to Mögenburg, who, after long experience with the hurly-burly of huge international meets, had found his own strategy for coping. "I was lucky this time," he told journalists. "I was mentally prepared for the noise. I just tried to concentrate and block everything out." Sjöberg took the silver. Stones finished fourth.

Zhu's disappointment at the high jump was matched by the frustrated hopes of U.S. favorite Henry Marsh in the 3,000-meter steeplechase, a demanding and dangerous sequence of 35 different obstacles ranging from hurdles to a water jump. If there were any such creature as a typical high-living athlete, Marsh would invert the stereotype. He was a 30-year-old lawyer, a pious Mormon and devoted family man. A frustrating succession of

mishaps and injuries had snatched more than one gold medal from his grasp. Still, many admirers rated him as the greatest American steeplechaser in history, mainly because of his trademark, a killer finishing kick.

When his day of opportunity arrived at Los Angeles, Marsh knew he was far below his physical peak, weakened by a prolonged viral infection and undermined further by an injury sustained during a practice session. But he battled his way into the finals, determined to prove himself.

As if the steeplechase didn't afford enough threats to equilibrium, during the race the runners were suddenly thrown off balance when a daredevil spectator burst onto the track. The intruder, waving a flag, plunged into the water jump and darted off in pursuit of the legitimate entries. Stunned security staff managed to wrestle the misbehaving fan back into the stands, only to see him wriggle out of their grasp and onto the track once more before he was captured once and for all.

Marsh, who had needed every scrap of focus and will simply to push his weakened body over the obstacles, had nevertheless managed to gain second place behind Kenya's Julius Korir late in the race. In the end, though, the American crossed the finish line in fourth place, collapsed, and had to be carried away on a stretcher. The gold medal he had yearned for went to Korir, the silver to Frenchman Joseph Mahmoud, and the bronze to Marsh's U.S. countryman, Brian Diemer.

While the steeplechase intruder had been an unwelcome glitch in the smooth-running Games, it seemed that for every such mischance in Los Angeles there came some compensatory unexpected pleasure. Officials of the 20,000-meter walk, for instance, found small but significant satisfaction in the fact that, for the first time in Olympic history, not a single walker was tossed out of the event for improper form.

Ordinarily, the long-distance walking races, with their peculiar gait and punctilious rules for technique, tend to get overlooked by track and field fans drawn to flashier events. Not so in Los Angeles, which has more citizens of Mexican descent than any town save Mexico City itself. The Mexican team was favored to win both walking races, and both events drew large, enthusiastic crowds.

As expected, the Mexicans prevailed—and in fine style—with world champion Ernesto Canto and his teammate Raúl González winning gold and silver, respectively, in the 20,000 meters, and González coming back eight days later to capture the 50,000-meter gold medal. Each of the two winners gilded his victory with an Olympic record, Canto with a time of 1:23:13 in the 20,000 meters and Gonzáles at 3:47:26 in the 50,000. As well as gratifying their fellow citizens back home, Canto and González were joyously feted by Los Angeles's proud Mexican-American community.

Ernesto Canto holds off the field at the finish of the 20-kilometer walk. Canto took the lead for good in the race after 10 kilometers to initiate a Mexican sweep in the walk races.

A bespectacled Rolf Danneberg grimaces as his discus sails 218 feet 6 inches (66.6 meters). The West German was an unexpected champion in an event diminished by the absence of boycotting athletes. Danneberg's winning throw was more than 17 feet (5.18 meters) short of the world record.

Meantime, however, the host city's primary home team—the U.S. contingent—wasn't always doing as well as expected. Before the Games, pundits had predicted that the discus throw would yield not only an American gold, but likely even an American sweep of all three medals. Certainly the U.S. teammates themselves anticipated a strictly intramural contest. They were thus amazed to find themselves outstripped after six suspense-filled rounds by an upstart outsider, a bearded dark horse in sunglasses. He was West Germany's Rolf Danneberg, a competitor who, despite years on the scene, had never achieved top international ranking. But in Los Angeles, to the loud acclaim of an astonished crowd, Danneberg managed a distance that had been bettered by only three discus throwers in modern Olympic history. His winning toss was 218 feet 6 inches (66.6 meters). U.S. favorite Mac Wilkins took the silver with a throw that fell a foot behind Danneberg's. John Powell of the U.S. won the bronze. "I feel terrific, yet terrible," said a bemused Wilkins after the contest. "I did everything right except win."

Whatever their personal tribulations, track and field athletes at Los Angeles could confidently expect to make money, as long as they had enough talent—and specialized in events with plenty of box-office allure. In certain other sports, the rules of national or international governing bodies required the

athletes to maintain a strictly amateur status while in competition, but the stars knew full well that they were playing to a gallery of checkbook-waving agents, managers, and professional promoters, all ready to sign them up once the Games ended.

Amateur boxers in the United States were permitted by their national governing body to accept sponsorship money—from a shoe manufacturer, for instance, or from a maker of boxing gloves. The boxers were barred, however, from any agreement, such as a contract with a sports promoter, that would carry over into a professional career. Even so, no one had any illusions about the long-term plans of most Olympic contenders. "After I get that gold medal," announced U.S. lightweight champion Pernell Whitaker, "I'm turning pro." His words could have served as the motto for the U.S. team.

Boxing events took place at the Los Angeles Memorial Sports Arena. Under its roof, the Olympic ideals of good sportsmanship and international amity were, bout after bout, blown sky-high.

Every competitor fighting under a foreign flag faced the hostile jeers of a chauvinistic American crowd. Exposed to an atmosphere that might have seemed familiar to Christians facing lions in the Roman Coliseum, one foreign pugilist after another fell to his U.S. opponent, and there were mutinous mutterings about the bias of judges and referees. "The Americans are getting whatever they need to win these fights," claimed Tongan boxer Tevita Taufoou. And, however formidable the array of homegrown talent, U.S. chances were not harmed by the boycott-induced absence of powerful boxers from the Soviet bloc, especially the hard hitters from Cuba.

One American fighter, however, did not leave the ring crowned in glory—and most of the boxing world felt he had been cheated of his rightful gold. Light heavyweight Evander Holyfield, a 21-year-old from Atlanta, had knocked out his first three opponents and was about to dispatch a fourth in the same way when something peculiar happened. Just before the end of the semifinal second round, Holyfield lashed out with a right

Disappointed by a disqualification in his semifinal match, American Evander Holyfield can't look as the referee signals that New Zealand's Kevin Barry is the winner of the light heavyweight bout. Holyfield would later see most decisions go his way as a professional heavyweight champion.

BAD CHEMISTRY

The Soviet-led boycott had a huge impact on weight-lifting events at Los Angeles, but the sport took an equally big hit from drugs.

Ever since Munich 1972, Olympic officials had tested athletes for anabolic steroids, the synthetic male hormones that can help maximize muscle mass. Even so, pressure to win pushed several athletes at Los Angeles to tempt fate. Eleven of them, the most since testing began, were disqualified for steroid use. Weight lifters were among the worst offenders; three of their number—Austrian super heavyweight Stefan Laggner (*right*), Swedish heavyweight Göran Pettersson, and Lebanese flyweight Mahmood Tarha—were disqualified. In addition, two Canadian lifters were sent home for drug-related reasons before the competition started.

None of the medal-winning lifters was disqualified, though the top two finishers in the middleweight class, West German Karl-Heinz Radschinsky and Canadian Jacques Demers, found themselves battling steroid possession charges in court within a year after the Games.

Drugs aside, the weight-lifting competition at Los Angeles was flawed, since more than 90 percent of the world's top-ranked lifters didn't take part. The missing champions showed their worth at the 1984 Friendship Games in Varna, Bulgaria—an alternative games for boycotting athletes—by bettering the totals of every 1984 Olympic gold medalist.

to the body, followed by a left hook that sent New Zealander Kevin Barry clanging to the canvas. The Yugoslavian referee counted Barry out, but then disqualified the American, saying Holyfield had thrown the left after being ordered to stop. Videotape of the fight would show that Holyfield did indeed hit late, but it would also confirm that before the last dubious blow, he and Barry had already thrown four late punches each.

Even Barry evidently thought the decision was fishy. When the referee announced his ruling, the New Zealand fighter raised Holyfield's hand into the air, telling him, "You won the fight fair and square." Sharing that view, the audience pelted the referee with generous lashings of invective, and police had to usher him out of the arena to safety.

Exacerbating the incident was a subsequent ruling that Barry, having been declared a knockout victim before Holyfield's disqualification,

would not be allowed to fight for 28 days. This meant the gold medal went by default to the winner of the other semifinal, one Anton Josipović. Josipović—like the controversial referee—was from Yugoslavia. Barry took the silver medal and Holyfield the bronze. Serenaded by boos during the medals ceremony, Josipović nevertheless made the generous gesture of pulling Holyfield up to join him on the top dais. "I am a bit disappointed that the audience doesn't realize that this is not the way I wanted it," the young student from Bosnia sorrowfully mused later. "I took the opportunity to have Holyfield join me on the top step because I believe the Olympics are the spirit of friendliness and goodwill."

The American team as a whole could hardly have been disappointed by the overall results: 9 U.S. golds of the dozen top spots available. As for Evander Holyfield, whatever wounds he

suffered in Los Angeles were doubtless salved when, as a professional, he won the world cruiserweight championship and then went on in 1990 to deck Buster Douglas in the first round to become heavyweight champion of the world. Holyfield lost the title to Riddick Bowe in 1992 and regained it a year later.

Cyclists, like boxers, weren't reluctant to push the boundary separating amateur from professional. Since the 1970s, bicycle racers had been allowed to win up to $2,500 in prize money per race without sacrificing their amateur eligibility. And the prize money was plentiful: Cycling had

benefited from an upsurge in sponsorship by bicycle manufacturers eager to display their latest state-of-the-art equipment in the hands of champion racers.

"My job is to ride," said American Steve Hegg, the gold medalist in the 4,000-meter individual pursuit, happy to add that the Raleigh company paid the freight for his air travel and hotel bills. "We're almost at the stage now where we're being taken care of by corporate sponsors the way the Eastern bloc governments take care of their athletes," Hegg told an interviewer.

Corporate generosity was largely responsible for

The technologically impressive bike Steve Hegg used in the 4,000-meter team pursuit didn't give the Americans a winning edge. Australia finished first. Hegg had enjoyed better luck two days earlier when he won the 4,000-meter individual pursuit.

Exulting in victory, Alexi Grewal becomes the first American to win the cycling road race. Grewal was fortunate to have a shot at the milestone. A positive drug test 10 days before the Games made U.S. Olympic officials drop him from the team. Uncertainty about the results forced his reinstatement.

the unaccustomed success of U.S. cyclists in 1984. Until the Los Angeles Games, American riders had never even sniffed an Olympic medal, nor any other kind, since some long-forgotten race back in 1912. Watered by the wellspring of manufacturers' money, however, the 1984 U.S. men's team garnered three gold medals, two silvers, and two bronzes—unheard-of results in a sport so long dominated by Europeans.

The machines the U.S. team rode to glory stood at the cutting edge of cycle design and had cost approximately $1 million to develop. Their features included small front wheels and solid, spokeless rear wheels made of Kevlar, the substance used in bulletproof vests. Experts estimated that the high-tech rear wheels shaved off one to three seconds per kilometer in a race. In the team pursuit event, the Americans were bested by Australians using classic spoke-wheeled machines. Still, the seven-medal American shower after so long a drought was pure elixir, to riders and fans alike.

The success helped enhance domestic fascination with cycling—and not just because of the flashy bikes. The U.S. team also featured some unusually colorful individuals. Sprinter Nelson Vails, for instance, was one of 10 children growing up in a cramped ghetto household in Harlem; he honed his cycling skills as a bicycle messenger on kamikaze runs through the traffic hell of midtown Manhattan. Mark Gorski was a shrewd entrepreneur of the cycle track, picking up lucrative sponsorship deals and extolling

them as a great way to raise the sport's profile and commend it to fitness seekers and fashion mavens alike. Road racer Alexi Grewal was the son of a Punjabi Sikh who had emigrated to America and reared a family of cycle-mad sons in Colorado. Alexi was a temperamental figure—by turns difficult and brilliant—who was briefly thrown off the U.S. team by his coach before returning, reprieved, to win a gold.

Unfortunately, the team's technological experiments were not restricted to cycle design. After

United States commemorative stamps honoring the 1984 Los Angeles Games.

the Games ended, it came to light that certain members of the squad had engaged in the ethically shady practice known as blood doping. Usually, this dubious technique begins several weeks before a race when an athlete has from one to two pints of his own blood removed and its red cells isolated and stored. The body soon replenishes the lost blood. Shortly before the race, the stored red cells are injected into the athlete's bloodstream. Since red cells carry oxygen, the presumed upshot of the procedure is to significantly boost the competitor's endurance.

Varying the method in a potentially dangerous way, the Americans used not their own blood, but that of close relatives with similar blood types. Fortunately, the offenders avoided any illness that might have occurred with a blood mismatch, and they also avoided official sanction: Blood doping wasn't illegal at the time, although the IOC had condemned it and has since outlawed it. Still, news that the Americans had dabbled in this unsavory practice considerably dimmed the U.S. team's luster.

The tempting sponsorship deals offered to medal-winning athletes who used equipment such as bicycles or running shoes were rarely available to water-sports competitors. Swimmers and divers made their appearances barefoot, wore nothing but modest scraps of fabric, and used no apparatus other than their own finely tuned muscles, bones, and nerves. But sometimes physiology could outshine technology, especially in the case of swimming's West German giant, Michael Gross. This 20-year-old world champion, rising to a height of 6 feet 7 1/2 inches, had been nicknamed the Albatross because of his giant wingspan; his arms, outstretched, measured 7 feet 4 inches from fingertip to fingertip.

Gross arrived in Los Angeles with his well-deserved reputation preceding him. In 1982 at the world championships in Guayaquil, Ecuador, he had shaken the confidence and snatched the world records of two reigning U.S. champions. Then he had swept the board at the 1983 European championships in Rome, taking four gold medals and a silver and smashing three world records in a breathless five-day blur.

In two of his Olympic contests, Gross lived up to expectations, winning both the 200-meter freestyle and the 100-meter butterfly, setting world records in both. But the event that many observers considered Gross's strongest suit, the 200-meter butterfly, delivered a major upset. At first, all eyes focused on the center lanes, where the Albatross battled U.S. favorite Pablo Morales, reckoned as the German champion's only serious challenger. Then the audience realized that an even hotter competition was taking place off to the side, in lanes 6 and 7, between Australia's Jon Sieben and Canadian Tom Ponting. At the halfway mark in the race, dark horse Sieben had been in seventh place; with only 30 meters to go, he accelerated like a killer shark scenting a shipwreck, bursting ahead of the pack of higher-rated competitors to beat them all in a world record time of 1:57.04. The rest of an incredibly fast field slammed in just behind him. Four swimmers achieved times below 1:58, and six came in under 2 minutes. Until he turned around and faced the scoreboard, 17-year-old Sieben didn't realize that he had won. The crowd, abandoning its habitual home-team chauvinism, rose up and roared with one voice. Even the mighty Gross, secure in the ownership of gold medals elsewhere, seemed to share the collective delight at this unexpected outcome.

Like swimming, diving had its world-class

superstar in the 1984 Games in the sleek form of Greg Louganis. Half-Samoan and half-Swedish, Louganis grew up in the home of his adoptive parents in Southern California, and at an early age he began to entertain himself by practicing spectacular gymnastic dives into the family's backyard pool. In spite of a comfortable home environment, however, Louganis had more than his share of childhood troubles: bouts of asthma, learning difficulties caused by undetected dyslexia, and racist bullying by schoolmates because of his Polynesian coloring. Under stress, the boy turned for a time to both alcohol and drugs.

For Louganis, the diving board became both an escape from problems and the platform for developing his unique abilities. At the age of 11, taking part in the Junior Olympics in Colorado, he ambushed the attention of legendary diving coach and former Olympic champion Dr. Sammy Lee, who recalled his first thoughts on watching young Greg's performance: "My god, that's the greatest talent I've ever seen." Coached by Lee, Louganis would at 16 win his first Olympic medal, a silver, at Montreal.

By the time he climbed onto the board at Los Angeles, Louganis had collected 33 titles in international, Pan American, and national competitions. He had also gathered his share of battle scars in a sport more dangerous than many onlookers imagine. In 1979 he had injured himself in a collision with the platform, blacking out during his 33-foot plunge into the water. He had also seen a fellow diver killed in 1983, slamming into the platform during the same exceedingly perilous triple-somersault maneuver that he himself would undertake in 1984.

At Los Angeles, Louganis showed impeccable form, moving through the air like a swooping seabird to awe the crowd and compel the judges to award him the gold in springboard and platform

With his prodigious wingspan in perfect butterfly motion, West German Michael Gross leaves little doubt why he was called the Albatross. After he won four out of five races at the European swimming championships in Rome in 1983, experts thought Gross capable of an Olympic performance to equal the seven-medal record tallied by Mark Spitz at Munich 1972.

Hovering in space, American Greg Louganis seems gracefully indifferent to gravity. Many consider him the greatest diver in the history of the sport.

events alike. He was the first male Olympic diver in more than half a century to win both sets of laurels, and he would repeat the same double success at Seoul in 1988. Asked by an interviewer how he achieved an aerial performance that seemed impossible for earthbound humans, Louganis explained, "You just follow your instincts. When you're in the air, you have something like a cat's sense. You're aware of where your body is going, and your peripheral vision tells you how high off the water you are, so you can plan your dive and your entry. If you are diving well, you have all the time in the world to attend to the details."

Like swimmers and divers, Olympic gymnasts might enter the competition as amateurs, but the small elite of superstars, such as U.S. teammates Peter Vidmar and Bart Conner, also had managers waiting in the wings with professional contracts in their pockets.

Until Los Angeles the elegant, technically demanding tests of skill, style, and strength in floor exercises and on the various apparatus—horizontal bar, parallel bars, long horse vault, pommeled horse, and rings—had never been an American strong point. Now, for the first time since 1904, the U.S. men's squad won the gold medal for the team competition in a rapid-fire, edge-of-the-seat duel against previous world champion China. Conner and Vidmar brought home the first individual golds the United States had seen since 1932.

The gold medal for individual all-around performance, however, went to Japan's Koji Gushiken. In a sport dominated by agile adolescents, Gushiken was—at the age of 27—a veritable Methuselah. Bad luck, injuries, and Japan's participation in the Moscow 1980 boycott had all conspired to keep him out of Olympic competition. Thus 1984 was his first, and presumably last, opportunity to show the world what he could do. He set about the task with mystical intensity, proclaiming his credo of "self-perfection to break through the barriers."

Placing only fifth after the preliminaries,

Gushiken nevertheless came from behind to edge past Peter Vidmar in the Games' closest all-around contest in more than half a century. Vidmar probably realized what he was up against when, several hours before the last round of competition, he walked into the gym to find Gushiken sitting alone, performing an intensely private Buddhist-style precontest ritual. Whether it was a murmured mantra, the intense desire to seize his single chance, or merely skills honed to a sword's edge, Gushiken succeeded in beating Vidmar to the gold by a microscopic 0.025 of a point, 118.7 to 118.675.

Tense and riveting as it was, the men's gymnastic competition suffered from the conspicuous absence of the boycotting Soviets, who along with the Japanese had loomed large in the sport for decades.

In all, Japan would garner 10 gold medals in Los Angeles. One notable triumph came in judo, a

Peter Vidmar whips through a routine on his favorite apparatus, the pommeled horse. Vidmar achieved perfection on his final routine to gain a tie with China's Li Ning for the gold medal in the individual event.

America's Bart Conner dismounts from the parallel bars. Conner would earn a 10 for his routine on the bars during the team all-around competition, becoming one of four Americans awarded perfect scores.

martial art indigenous to Japan. But, although the Japanese invented judo, they had not held sole copyright on Olympic gold in the event. They may have dominated the sport in the Tokyo 1964 Games when judo first entered the Olympic lists, but subsequent Games had seen stars emerge from such far-flung quarters as the Netherlands and the Soviet Union. In the 1984 open division, however, Yasuhiro Yamashita—at 5 foot 11 and 280 pounds a giant among Japanese—seemed unbeatable. He was in his eighth year of a winning streak, with 194 victories to his credit since 1977.

The streak seemed in serious peril, however, when in his second match, against West Germany's Arthur Schnabel, Yamashita tore a calf muscle. The Japanese champion won that match, but the near-crippling injury seemed likely to rupture his chance to win the gold and run his victory string to 195. Ten seconds into the final match, Egypt's Mohamed Ali Rashwan, abiding by the classic rule of attacking an opponent's

weak spot, made straight for Yamashita's injured leg. Despite his own agony, Yamashita sidestepped a charge by Rashwan, who flew off balance, fell, and found himself pinned down on the mat by Yamashita for a decisive 30 seconds.

If judo is fairly new among Olympic forms of combat, a speciality known as Greco-Roman wrestling claims descent from ancient times. In this sport, contact is limited to the upper body, with no holds permitted below the hips. At Los Angeles, the hero above all others in the Greco-Roman lists was U.S. super heavyweight Jeff Blatnick.

History—Olympic history and his own—didn't favor Blatnick. No U.S. contender in any division had ever won an Olympic medal of any color. Although the native of Niskayuna, New York, might have been at the top of his form in 1980, the Moscow boycott had lost him a chance to compete. Any hope of future Olympic success seemed to be eradicated two years later when Blatnick was diagnosed with Hodgkin's disease, a

Gold medalist Koji Gushiken holds a perfect iron cross on the rings. His most impressive performance came in the individual all-around: Standing only fifth after the preliminary round, Gushiken moved into first following an outstanding series of final exercises.

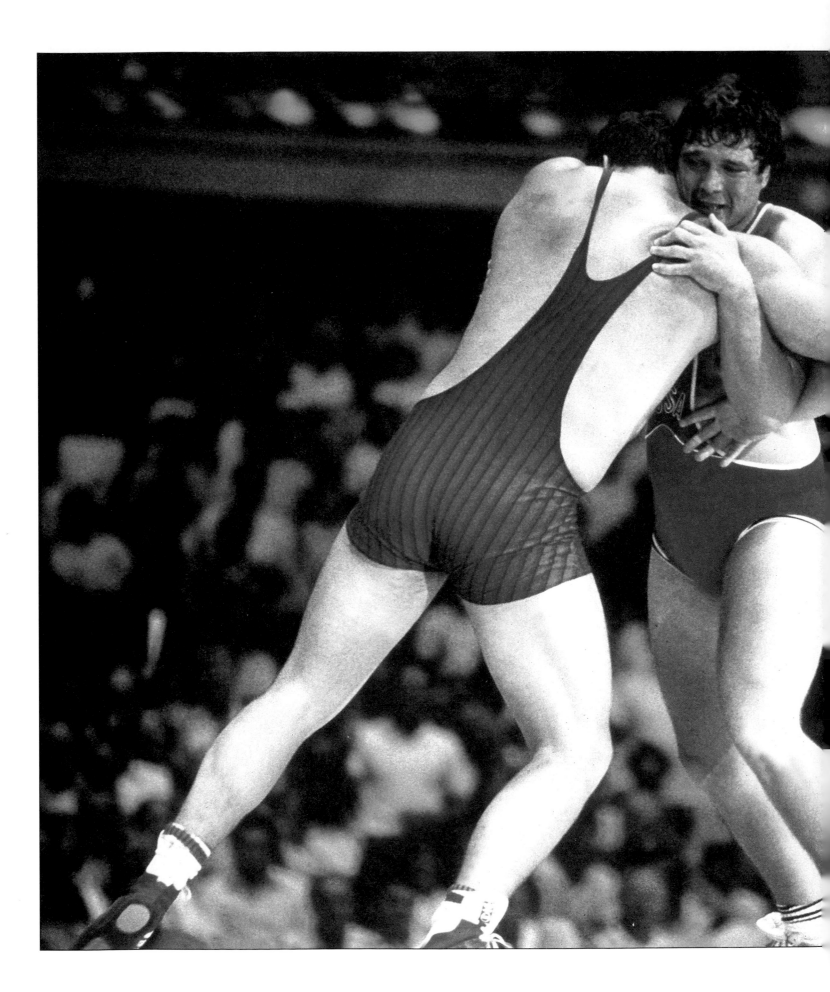

form of cancer that attacks the lymphatic system, liver, and spleen. The burly wrestler lost his spleen and appendix to the illness, then had to endure an aggressive course of radiation treatments. Grueling as it was, the radiation put him into remission, and Blatnick ignored his doctors' warnings and started training for Los Angeles.

Approaching the Games as a decided underdog, Blatnick nevertheless made an impressive debut in his first match, upsetting the gold medal favorite, Yugoslavia's Refik Memišević. The gritty American lost his second match to Panayotis Pikilidis of Greece, but against all odds Blatnick managed to end up as a finalist in his four-man draw when Memišević defeated the Greek in another semifinal match.

Knowing his hard-luck story, the crowd at ringside held its breath as Blatnick fought a dogged battle against Sweden's Thomas Johansson, who outweighed him by more than 35 pounds. The matches were divided into two three-minute segments with one minute in between. Almost five minutes into the action, neither man had tallied a point. Then, with just over a minute left, Blatnick took down the big Swede twice to score in rapid succession. Spectators

Proud parents congratulate an emotional Jeff Blatnick following his final match. Blatnick's gold medal also symbolized a more important conquest, his defeat of life-threatening cancer.

Pertti Karppinen wears the third gold medal of his Olympic career. The 6-foot-7 Finn won his third consecutive single sculls title at Los Angeles, equaling the record of Soviet rowing great Vyacheslav Ivanov, whose reign ran from Melbourne 1956 to Tokyo 1964.

counted down the final decisive seconds along with the referee. When the matches finally ended, Blatnick, weeping, fell to his knees in prayer. Tears seemed epidemic in the audience, too, as the crowd roared its admiration, as much for the new champion's great heart as for his brawn and talent.

Unfortunately, Blatnick's battles weren't quite over. A recurrence of his cancer required a new and longer series of radiation treatments before he once again went into remission.

One of the lowest-profile sports in the Olympics, pursued by some of the most purely motivated amateurs, is rowing. By its very nature, rowing has little telegenic appeal and offers scant hope of individual glory. All the casual observer sees is the swift passage of boats along a stream, with a quick glimpse of anonymous crews straining at the oars. Seldom is stardom at stake, and few lucrative contracts or fat endorsement deals lie across the finish line. Most rowers are impelled solely by their passion for their sport, and they live in a closed world of fellow enthusiasts who appreciate the dedication and agony that their discipline entails. One member of the American Olympic crew calculated that he spent at least 600 hours in training and 475 hours of hands-on rowing every year, in preparation for no more than 130 minutes of racing. The Olympics, a crew's only chance for real media exposure, might afford at best a slender seven minutes in the public eye.

In the 1984 Games, rowing seemed even more orphaned than usual, though the reasons had more to do with the geography of Greater Los Angeles than with any deliberate marginalization by the organizers of the competitions. The 1984 rowing events took place far from the Olympic mainstream, some 85 miles northwest of downtown Los Angeles. Lake Casitas, despite its scenic charms, was notorious for capricious winds; so races began at 7:30 a.m., when the lake was generally at its calmest, to ensure that the boats were off the water well before noon. Despite the remote location and the early start, the rowers drew an atypically fine turnout: Some 10,000 spectators gathered on Sunday, August 5, to watch a pair of U.S. underdogs, Brad Allen Lewis and Paul Enquist, win a gold medal in the double sculls.

The single sculls competition, on the same day, was a furious battle between two highly ranked favorites and long-time rivals, Peter-Michael Kolbe of West Germany and Pertti Karppinen of Finland. Each represented a different style of rowing: Kolbe the technical perfectionist, Karppinen the muscular powerhouse, who conceded "My success is more based on my physical abilities than my technique." Victory at Lake Casitas went to Finnish brawn; Karppinen, in the last 100 meters, surged past Kolbe to win the race and his third Olympic gold medal.

Karppinen's proud compatriots expressed their delight by offering him a new job back home in Finland. Instead of working long hours as a fireman at an oil refinery in Turku, the rowing hero became vice president of a local bus company. The best part of the job was that it entailed no actual duties—apart from training as much as he liked in his chosen sport. Even for rowers, the occasional perquisite could be had.

A few scraps of metal and ribbon, some fleeting applause, an offer of safer, easier labor, and the leisure to explore more fully one's passion for perfecting strength and skill. The rewards meted out at Lake Casitas that August were meager, perhaps, compared with the golden harvest reaped by a Carl Lewis or a Daley Thompson. But, however modest, the accolades underscored the fact that in at least one small and noble branch of the Olympic family, classic amateurism—sport for the love of sport—still survived.

THE YEAR OF THE WOMEN

LOS ANGELES 1984

Speeding into the tunnel that led the way to the Los Angeles Coliseum, American marathon runner Joan Benoit said to herself, "Once you leave this tunnel, your life will be changed forever." This close to the finish she was alone, even though the field of competitors toiling behind her included 10 of the best women marathoners in the world. Benoit herself could not have counted the miles of practice that had brought her to this point, nor could she have tallied the fare paid in pain and discipline. It didn't matter anyway. All that mattered now was that winning was inevitable, and she knew it, and winning would give her a unique place in the history of sport.

Benoit ran on, her pace smooth and unlabored, as though the 26 miles of hot pavement behind her had been no more than the welcoming terrain of a neighborhood park during a morning jog. Sunlight blazed at the end of the tunnel and she swept into it, a tiny figure that the crowd could easily identify because of the white painter's cap that she habitually wore. She circled the track, her slight body still energetically upright, borne along now by the roar of 77,000 spectators.

The tape snapped across her chest, and, beaming, Benoit began an exultant victory lap. Her time had been excellent: 2 hours 24 minutes 52 seconds. But the time mattered little compared to the real import of the achievement. Joan Benoit had just won the first women's marathon in the history of the modern Olympic Games.

Benoit did not take her victory lap alone. At her side, in spirit, ran every woman athlete who had ever struggled against prejudice, fought exhaustion, honed her muscles, faced down pain, tested her own limits and then transcended them. These were the legions of sportswomen who, since the modern Games began, had had to fight for every inch of Olympic ground they occupied.

Joan Benoit, Olympic gold medalist, 1984

Virtually every sport required a battle of its own. Event by event, the Olympic godfathers' cherished assumptions about the supposed physical frailty and mental delicacy of womankind were challenged and chipped away. But the last great male bastion to fall was the marathon, that most sacrosanct of Olympic races. Encrusted with myth and tradition, the 26-mile course still resounded with the footsteps of a lonely soldier, straining every sinew to bring home to Athens news of the decisive Greek victory over the Persians at Marathon in 490 BC. Small wonder, then, that Joan Benoit was greeted not only by the cheers of the Coliseum crowd but by the triumphant shouts of women around the world.

The marathon was not the only proof that women were, at long last, claiming equal rights to Olympic glory. On many fronts, the Los Angeles Games gave women reason to celebrate. The program offered new challenges for female athletes. On the track, women could now prove themselves in the 3,000-meter race and the 400-meter hurdles. The old pentathlon—a five-event test of all-around athletic versatility that was the women's counterpart to the men's decathlon—was elevated into the heptathlon by the addition of two new events, the 200-meter dash and the javelin throw. And, for the first time in Olympic history, female cyclists broke the gender barrier with a road race of their own.

But the real excitement for women at Los Angeles lay in the dazzling performances delivered by so many female athletes, in individual exhibitions and closely contested duels. In the first women's heptathlon, home-team favorite Jackie Joyner joined in a tense and passionate two-day battle with Australia's Glynis Nunn. High drama unfolded in the 3,000 meters when two of the world's top middle-distance runners—a barefoot Afrikaner teenager named Zola Budd and America's Mary Decker, the star Budd idolized—tangled on the track in a literal and tragic way. Pint-sized American gymnast Mary Lou Retton

achieved the sporting equivalent of pop-star status with a pair of perfect vaults and a highly telegenic grin.

Also in these Games, sprinter Valerie Brisco-Hooks, raised in Los Angeles's Watts ghetto, attained heights in her hometown never before scaled by any other Olympic runner, male or female, while her teammate Evelyn Ashford dashed into the record books as the fastest woman ever in the Olympic 100 meters. And, from a land far removed in miles and mores from the track mecca of the United States, came the first female athlete from the Arab world to win a gold medal: When Moroccan Nawal el-Moutawakil glided over the barriers in the 400-meter hurdles, the hurdles stayed upright, but an entrenched set of sexual and cultural stereotypes seemed to collapse like a house of cards.

To Baron Pierre de Coubertin and most of his like-minded end-of-the-century colleagues, such unseemly goings-on as scantily clad women careening around cinder tracks would have been abhorrent. In his vision of the Games, the father of the modern Olympics saw women only as spectators. As medieval ladies had encouraged jousting knights in the age of chivalry, so a grandstand full of admiring females might spur modern athletes to deeds of glory. In his own explication, Coubertin defined the Olympic ideal as "the solemn and periodic exaltation of male athleticism with internationalism as a base, loyalty as a means, art for its setting, and female applause as reward."

In comparison with the ancient Greeks, though, the baron might have deemed himself a liberal, if not an outright feminist, for the first Olympians barred women even from watching their Games, on pain of death. And although the Greek women had a sporting event of their own, a sprint race known as the Heraean Games, Coubertin saw no reason to revive it, or to come up with any substitute. Neither did the modern

Corseted archers compete at London 1908. Olympic officials in those days deemed genteel sports such as archery and tennis the only acceptable competitions for females.

Greeks, who hosted the first of the latter-day Olympics, Athens 1896—an all-male festival. About a month before those historic Games, when men were running trial marathons in preparation for the event, a woman decided that she, too, wanted to participate. Only three salient facts survive about her: Her first name was Melpomene; in March of 1896 she did complete a trial run from Marathon to Athens, in a time of 4 hours 30 minutes; and officials did bar her from running the Olympic marathon.

At the chaotic 1900 Games in Paris, the gender issue passed out of the hands of Coubertin and his colleagues. These disorganized Olympics were part of a larger event, a world's fair, and officials of that exposition had the final say in who could take part. The upshot was that women made their official Olympic debut, a rather inauspicious bow as members of mostly male teams in yachting and ballooning. Ladies had their own archery competition at St. Louis 1904, followed four years later in London by tennis, figure skating (there were no Winter Games then), and a modest exhibition of gymnastics. But the last wasn't modest enough: Loud protests were heard from several moral guardians, including Pope Pius X, and the American Olympic Committee (AOC, a precursor of the U.S. Olympic Committee) huffed in an official statement to the *New York Times*, that it would never countenance "women taking part in any

Canada's Jenny Thompson *(second from left)* is first off the line in the debut of the women's 800-meter race at Amsterdam 1928. Germany's Lina Radke *(third from right)* would win; Thompson finished fourth. Several exhausted runners fell to the ground after crossing the finish line of the 800 meters, arming critics who claimed that women had no place in track and field.

event in which they could not wear skirts." Indeed, when the skirts came off at Stockholm 1912 for women's swimming and diving events, the AOC stood aloof and sent no team.

Still, Olympiad after Olympiad, female athletes and a few male allies chipped away at official resistance. Yielding to pressure—and looking over their shoulders at the alarming success of a rival "women's Olympics" which had gathered an audience of 20,000 spectators—members of the IOC reluctantly introduced five women's track and field events in the 1928 Games at Amsterdam. When it came to endurance races, however, both the IOC and the International Amateur Athletic Federation (IAAF), world governing body for track and field, remained adamant against female participation.

Some official heads stayed planted in the sand even after the fitness boom of the late 1960s and 1970s attracted athletes of both sexes in equal numbers. Women, the mandarins of sport insisted, had neither the strength nor the stamina for endurance running events. And who knew what effects such efforts might have on their mysterious female anatomies? Still, the doubts grew ever fainter in the thunder of pounding female feet as women flocked to a growing

number of non-Olympic meets. In the 5,000- and 10,000-meter races and in marathons, women began to pare down their times dramatically, showing rates of improvement that left their male counterparts standing still.

Of all the endurance running events, Olympic and otherwise, the marathon was the toughest nut for women to crack. In 1966 an art student named Bobbi Gibb gate-crashed the prestigious men-only Boston Marathon by jumping from behind a bush to join the pack after officials had barred her from the starting line. When she completed the race, these officials questioned whether she had actually run the course.

One year later, the guardians of the same marathon tried to manhandle Katherine Switzer off the course, even though she was a legitimate entrant with an official number: Allegedly unaware that the Boston Marathon was single sex, since there were no written rules excluding women, she had filled out an entry form listing herself only as K. Switzer. Furious at her treatment, she became a leader in the fight for change. Running clubs began welcoming women into their road races, and the official bodies of the great sport bureaucracies—after insisting on elaborate medical reports about the

An official tries to pull Katherine Switzer from the men-only Boston Marathon in 1967. The race would open up to women five years later.

risks faced by female long-distance runners—finally capitulated in 1972. The first International Women's Marathon was held in Waldniel, West Germany, in 1974, and the long, hard road to an Olympic race lay open at last.

That road opened just in time for Joan Benoit, who, it seemed, had been born to explore its reaches. For her, sports—all sports and any sports—were in the blood.

Growing up in coastal Maine, in an exuberantly athletic family that hoisted its skis onto the car's roof at the sight of the first snowflake, Benoit had resolved by eight or nine that she would someday ski in the Olympics. At that young age, running didn't seem a reasonable goal; she thought of it as a mode of transportation rather than a sport. But even then she showed signs of what was to come. Visiting some eight-year-old cousins in Connecticut, she tagged along to a junior track meet, where

she signed up for every event available. An overheard remark about an older participant's talents—"Look at the way he carries his arms"—inspired her to study the high-school track star in question, to figure out why he looked so good and what made him move so fast. When it was her turn to run, she faithfully copied his style, holding her arms close to her sides, hardly moving her head and upper body, putting all her energy into her legs. To her cousins' intense irritation, little Joan came away with five blue ribbons.

Benoit began running in earnest as a high-school freshman, finding in the quiet back roads of Maine the perfect scope and solitude for training. A leg injury in a skiing accident ended her ambition to be a champion skier, so she turned her attention to endurance runs such as the 880 yards and soon set her sights on the mile and beyond. By the time she had graduated from Bowdoin College and taken a job coaching women's

MIXING IT UP

Given that men generally have an athletic edge over women in terms of sheer muscular strength, the two sexes compete separately in most Olympic events. But in equestrian, yachting, and shooting, the two sexes contend side by side. An equalizing element in these sports is the fact that athletes don't perform them unaided: Sailors use boats, shooters use guns, equestrians use horses. The international equestrian federation integrated competition at Helsinki 1952. Yachting allowed women as early as 1908 on some classes of boats, and shooting included them for the first time at Mexico City 1968.

Women have had the least success on water. No all-female yachting crew has ever competed against men, but mixed-gender British crews won gold medals at London 1908 and Antwerp 1920 in the since-discontinued event for seven-meter-class yachts. Only two of the 305 yachting competitors at Los Angeles 1984 were women. The disparity would narrow at Seoul 1988 with the addition of a women's event in yachting's 470 class. A women's sailboard event would join the program in Barcelona 1992.

Females have fared better in shooting. The top

Karen Stives leads her mount, Ben Arthur, over an obstacle during the show-jumping portion of the three-day equestrian event at Los Angeles. Stives' steady riding won her an individual-event silver medal and helped America to the team gold.

track at Boston University, she had become dedicated to long-distance running.

"I run because I love to run," she declared, and nothing could stop her. Stuck in a massive traffic jam on the way to the 1979 Boston Marathon (now welcoming runners of both sexes), she jumped out of the car and ran the two remaining miles to the starting line. Warmed up by this little preliminary jaunt, she broke out of a huge pack, finished first among the women, and did so in the women's world-best time of 2:22:43.

Benoit's success lay in part with her punishing practice schedule. In 1983, with the Olympics looming, she customarily ran more than 100 miles a week. But in the spring of 1984, it appeared for a time that all the effort had been useless: Pain in her right knee became too bad to ignore, and she had to have arthroscopic surgery

to remove its source, an inflamed mass of fibrous tissue. The operation was done just 17 days before the Olympic trials.

Determined that nothing would keep her from running at Los Angeles, Benoit started training again, as best she could, the day after the surgery. She was still confined to her hospital bed, but an exercise bike was installed above it, to be hand-pedaled with the aim of rebuilding her strength. Two days later she graduated to a treadmill, and before the week was out she had run a mile, swum, cycled, and worked out with weights. No less relentless than her determination was the pace she set at the Olympic trials in Los Angeles. She not only qualified, she won, with a time of 2:31:04.

On August 5, with the big event itself only a few minutes away, Benoit was feeling ready, both single performance was American Margaret Murdock's second-place finish in the small-bore rifle event at Montreal 1976. In spite of Murdock's achievement, rules limiting the number of competitors make it hard for women to get a spot on Olympic teams: Only five females were among the 248 shooters at Moscow 1980. In an effort at equity, the Olympic shooting program added three women-only events at Los Angeles: standard rifle, air rifle, and pistol.

Women's greatest success in mixed-gender competition has come in equestrian events, where females were quick to make their mark. The first time out, at Helsinki, Denmark's Lis Hartel won a silver in individual dressage. Horsewomen's participation has grown ever since, but men equestrians still outnumbered the women by almost three to one at Los Angeles. Even so, the women had a big impact, winning at least a share of nine of the 18 medals in contention.

Three-time yachting gold medalist Paul Elvström of Denmark stands on the Long Beach Shoreline Marina dock with shipmate and daughter Trine Elvström. They finished fourth in the Tornado-class yachts at Los Angeles.

physically and psychologically. She had told reporters earlier that anticipation and excitement at the prospect of participating in the first women's Olympic marathon had evaporated all sense of pressure. "The Los Angeles race doesn't seem like it will be an ordeal," she said, "so much as a prize."

That prize was in her sights as Benoit and her fellow runners assembled at Santa Monica College, but the race shaped up as a close contest. In the field of 50 starters were 11 of the 14 fastest female long-distance competitors in history. In addition to Benoit, hot prospects included Norway's Grete Waitz, rated No. 1 in the world. Waitz, who lived in the United States, was the most famous of all women marathoners and had done much to popularize the sport. Whippet-thin and a shrewd tactician, she had won all seven

marathons that she had completed. She was also a veteran of two Olympic 1,500-meter races, and she had outstripped Benoit at varying distances on 10 of the 11 occasions that they had met. Also on hand was Waitz's teammate, Ingrid Kristiansen, the second-swiftest female in long-distance racing history.

The Norwegians and other serious competitors from cooler countries had trained zealously to accustom themselves to hot-weather running, but to their relief the race began under overcast skies with the temperature standing at 75 degrees Fahrenheit (24 degrees Celsius)—balmy by Los Angeles standards. It would shortly rise to 80 degrees, however, and the smog would thicken into an oppressive atmospheric soup.

Whatever the rigors to come, a sense of the significance of the moment seemed to infuse the

Joan Benoit doffs her cap as she crosses the finish line to become the first women's Olympic marathon champion. Benoit was not a stranger to benchmarks: She owned the world's best time in the marathon and had won the Boston Marathon twice.

runners, as well as the thousands of spectators already lining the marathon route. Barely 7 minutes and 2 kilometers into the race, Olympic history was made. Never before since the Games began had women run as long a distance.

Seemingly by consensus, the mass of runners sustained a fairly cautious pace in the early going. But it felt too tortoiselike to Benoit. She had no desire to push ahead too soon, only to find herself burned out and bypassed later, but she knew she could keep up a stronger speed. So, three miles out, she broke away from the others. At first her principal rivals, well aware of the recent knee operation, seemed unworried. "I knew she had been hurt," admitted Ingrid Kristiansen, "and I hoped she'd break down and come back to us."

But Benoit never came back. As mile followed mile, on a route that skirted the shoreline of the Pacific Ocean and then snaked along freeways and through city streets, her lead increased. For a time she found herself in the surreal situation of running all alone down the middle of a completely empty freeway. She was puzzled by the silent space behind her—no sign of the pack. Had it not been for spectators and camera crews, she might have suspected that the world had somehow come to an unheralded end during her solitary journey. She kept up a steady pace—and a fast one: 5 minutes 40 seconds per mile. But she felt inexplicably strong, free of fatigue, confident that she had plenty of energy in reserve.

Benoit's lead at the 19-mile point was a stunning 1.51 minutes. Then Grete Waitz made her move, upping her pace to close the gap. Her pale, sharp-featured face, tight with the effort, could be seen in close-up on the Coliseum's giant television screens, which relayed the progress of the race to the crowd. With Waitz's concerted move, Benoit's victory suddenly seemed less a sure thing, and tension mounted as the audience waited for someone to appear at the mouth of the stadium tunnel. But Waitz, despite slicing 30

seconds off the distance between them, could not or would not push herself further.

About one half mile from the Coliseum, Benoit ran past a huge mural depicting her, much larger than life, at the moment of her triumph in the Boston Marathon. Her sponsor, Nike, had commissioned the painting. Benoit gave it only a brief glance. She was a reserved and private person; that kind of hoopla embarrassed her. She ran on, plunging into the brief darkness of the tunnel, treasuring one last sliver of solitude before the real ballyhoo began. Emerging into the glare on the other side, though, she gave herself to the moment. She tore the painter's cap off her short, sweat-drenched black hair and started to wave. The crowd responded with new levels of cheers as she made her circuit of the track and crossed the finish line.

"I was so charged up," Benoit recalled of that final moment, "that when I broke the tape, I could have turned around and run another 26 miles." This was not mere vainglory; she realized, to her own amazement, that she had never had to push as hard as she had anticipated. "It was kind of like following the yellow brick road," she said. "I don't know how to say this without sounding cocky, but it was a very easy run for me."

It had not been so easy for Grete Waitz, who finished 86 seconds behind Benoit. "I could perhaps have run faster," the Norwegian star mused later, contemplating her silver medal, "but because of the heat I was afraid of dying." Despite her hard training, Waitz had apparently failed to fully acclimate to the porridge of heat and smog that was Los Angeles in August.

Behind Benoit and Waitz were other women in the historic marathon who savored shares of victory. Portugal's Rosa Mota overtook Ingrid Kristiansen to gain the bronze with a personal-best performance of 2:26:57. Great Britain's Joyce Smith finished only 11th, but she was a big winner just the same: At 46, she was the oldest track and field athlete of either

Winners at Los Angeles received a diploma to document their achievements. A separate certificate went to arts festival participants *(left)* in recognition of their involvement with the Games.

sex at the Games. And to many observers, the most heroic battle of the marathon was waged not by the front runners, but by 39-year-old Swiss runner Gabriele Andersen-Schiess, who—dazed and contorted with pain, dehydration, and heat prostration—managed to complete the course. Waving off help, she took almost six minutes to cover the last few yards. She lurched and staggered, sometimes almost falling as she fainted on her feet, collapsing at last into the arms of waiting medics. Television cameras recorded every agonizing moment.

Despite their grim attention to Gaby Andersen-Schiess's ordeal, the cameras don't usually focus on also-rans. They stay with the winners, ever attentive to the all-important moment of triumph. But if ever there was an exception to this rule, it came during the women's 3,000 meters at Los Angeles, where a few dramatic seconds midrace so gripped the world's attention that the contest's final outcome was almost forgotten.

This Olympic event, above all, was supposed to have been Mary Decker's ultimate moment of triumph. The 26-year-old U.S. middle-distance runner had long been a legendary figure in the world of track. Her action-packed career was a saga of dramatic highs and lows, fraught with injuries, bad luck, fierce struggles, and Hollywood-style comebacks. Now, observers agreed, her odds for taking the gold were about as good as odds ever get.

Mary Decker was only 11 when she first learned about the joys of running—almost by accident. Had there been any other distractions on a certain lazy weekend in Garden Grove, California, in 1969, it might never have happened. "It was out of boredom," she would recall years later. "In the sixth grade, my best friend and I were sitting around one Saturday saying, 'What can we do?' We had a flyer from the parks department and saw there was 'cross-country' that day. We didn't know what cross-country was. We went down and found it was running, so we ran. My friend dropped out. I won—by a long ways. I don't remember its being very hard."

Shortly afterward, as she took part in various local races and won a county-wide contest, Decker came to the notice of racing coach Don DeNoon of the Long Beach Comets club. Working with DeNoon, and encouraged by her mother, Decker plunged into strenuous training and ran virtually every race that came her way.

At 12, for instance, in one memorable week she ran a marathon, a 440-yard and an 880-yard race, a one-mile race and a two-mile race. The morning after the last contest, she underwent an appendectomy. The doctor in attendance inquired if she had been under any unusual stress.

Young Mary didn't regard her race-laden schedule as stressful, or even unusual. "I was born to be a runner," she would say. "I simply love to train." But some adult friends and admirers wondered if she was not being pushed too far, too early.

At 13 she ran a 4:55 mile. At 14 she was breaking records and amassing medals and personal bests. She toured Europe and Africa with the U.S. track and field team and was lauded as the best female half-miler in America. In those days—the early 1970s—she was hailed on the track circuit as a child prodigy. The most formidable adult contenders suddenly found themselves outrun by a teenager weighing less than 100 pounds. "Little Mary," as she was soon universally known, specialized in coming from behind, when least expected, to steal the race from her elders.

But by the end of 1974, Decker had begun to suffer from a sequence of stress fractures and other injuries. At first she tried to face down the mounting agony, and then she tried a variety of treatments and strategies—any and every treatment and strategy, anything to keep her running. "I rested," she said. "I had all kinds of therapy. I tried different shoes. I only ran on the grass. Nothing worked."

As the 1976 Olympics drew ever closer, it was clear that Decker would never be able to compete. She moved from California to Colorado to escape pressure from well-meaning friends demanding to know why she wasn't competing at Montreal. Despite the pain she endured every time she ran, she persisted as best she could with her training. She began running with the University of Colorado track team, and once more she started winning medals. "She did it for the team," recalled her Colorado coach, Rich Castro, "but, lord, was she sick afterward, and of course every time she ran fast the pain blossomed."

X-rays had revealed the source of Decker's troubles to be a mass of tiny, imperfectly healed stress fractures in her shinbones. Impervious to treatment, the minuscule cracks threatened to abort her career. But then Decker met a New Zealand runner, Dick Quax, who had found relief from the same condition through a simple operation. Decker underwent the surgery, and a month later she was running again, pain-free for the first time in years.

Decker soon rejoined the ranks of world-class runners, collecting such laurels as the 1,500-meter gold medal in the Pan American Games and a world record of 4:21.7 for the mile. But clouds were gathering, on personal and political horizons. There were new pains from new strains and injuries; and although she qualified for the

1980 U.S. Olympic track team, the American boycott of the Games quashed her hopes of winning the contest every great runner dreams of.

Two years later, after more surgery, Decker made a second spectacular comeback. Her triumphs included a long, unbreached string of victories, an assortment of world records, the 1982 Jesse Owens Award as America's best track athlete (she was the first woman ever to win this honor), and the Women's Sports Foundation titles as 1982 and 1983 Amateur Sportswoman of the Year. By the end of 1983 she owned world indoor records at 880 yards, 1,500 meters, and the mile, as well as world outdoor records in the mile, 5,000 meters, and 10,000 meters.

At 26, fitter than she had been for more than a decade, Mary Decker awaited her chance at Olympic glory. But during her years of struggle, a new child star, Zola Budd, had entered the firmament. The inevitable duel between them shaped up as one of the most exciting clashes at Los Angeles.

Like Mary Decker, young Zola Budd had the eyes of the world on her—though the attention was not solely because of her ability. Budd was a native of South Africa, a nation banned from the world athletic community for its apartheid policy. To take part in the Games at all, she would have to tread a path strewn with more obstacles than any Olympic steeplechase.

Budd grew up in an Afrikaans-speaking family on a farm near Bloemfontein, surrounded by ostriches, rabbits, dogs, and a cherished pet parrot. She was something of a loner, shy with children apart from her own siblings, but she loved to run. And, like most rural South African children, she preferred to run barefoot.

By the time she was 11, Budd was dazzling spectators with her speed in school races. In one four-lap race, for instance, she beat the nearest competitor by an entire lap. Her father, convinced of her exceptional talent, persuaded Pieter Labuschagne, a coach at a nearby school,

WONDER WOMAN

America's Cheryl Miller soars for a layup against China. Miller scored 12 points during the 91-55 U.S. victory.

Alas for fans of team sports, the classic battle at Los Angeles 1984 was the one that didn't happen. Because the Soviets boycotted the Games, the world missed a basketball battle between an established dynasty and one in the making. The absent Soviet women's team was the two-time defending Olympic champion; the Americans were a power on the rise. What fans did get to see was the Americans overwhelm the six-team field, winning its six games by an average margin of 32.7 points.

They also got to see one of the greatest female players in history, All-American Cheryl Miller of the University of Southern California. A 6-foot-3 forward, Miller led the Americans in points (16.5) and rebounds (7), as well as in assists and steals.

Miller began playing basketball with her three brothers when she was seven and continued to compete with boys through her teens, often beating them. That early training helped her develop a fast, aggressive style that improved as she matured. As a California high-school student, she set national records for career scoring, points in a season, and most points in a game—an eye-popping 105, scored in a match that also saw her become the first woman ever to dunk the ball in regulation play. Recruited by virtually every college in America, she enrolled in USC in 1983. There she guided the Lady Trojans to two consecutive NCAA titles and won nearly every major basketball award available to collegiate women. After graduating in 1986, Miller played on the international circuit for two years, winning more accolades. Injuries forced her to miss Seoul 1988 and a chance at a second Olympic gold medal. She retired after that season. The Basketball Hall of Fame inducted her into its ranks in 1995. She was only the sixth woman the Hall has honored,

to help with her training. The coach found his new pupil a more than willing subject. "Her determination came across like an army of safari ants on the march," he said. "She was the most dedicated runner I had ever seen."

Unlike Decker, Budd was encouraged to develop her talents slowly. Labuschagne took a gradualist approach to her training, helping her build up distance and endurance before concentrating on speed. Instead of hitting every race on the calendar, she began to work slowly but carefully toward participation in 1,500-, 3,000-, and 5,000-meter events. As she moved through the age groups, she carried off whatever prizes

The favorites—America's Mary Decker, Great Britain's Zola Budd, and Romania's Maricica Puica—run 1-2-3 early in the finals of the 3,000-meter race. The capable Puica, who had already clocked the fastest 3,000 of the year, thrived in obscurity while attention focused on her two front-running peers.

Despite Budd's star quality—her talent, her appealing elfin looks, her quaint insistence on continuing to run barefoot—there was no way she could enter the 1984 Olympics unless she emigrated from South Africa. And this, with the encouragement of London's *Daily Mail*, is precisely what she did. Because her father had been born in England, Budd had a lawful claim to citizenship in the United Kingdom. However, many thousands of applicants stood ahead of her on the waiting list for naturalization: If she went through the regular bureaucratic channels, the Games would come and go long before she acquired the right to run for her newly adopted country. The *Daily Mail* pulled some strings, however, and Budd raced through the red tape in a mere 10 days—a speed that overshadowed her most astounding efforts on the track. But this particular world record did not delight the hordes of immigrants forced to wait years for naturalization or the many Britons opposed to immigration policies they considered racist. Moreover, there were critics who said that the young athlete had distanced herself from her white supremacist homeland only by the width of her passport. Budd soon found herself the target of political demonstrations and angry protests, on and off the track.

"I'm just a runner. I am not a politician," was her only comment on the subject to the press.

Since she was indeed a runner, the political uproar was probably far from Budd's mind on the afternoon of August 10, 1984, when she, Decker, and 10 other contenders came to the starting line of the first women's 3,000-meter race in Olympic history. Some 800 meters into the contest, Decker, in the lead, was blazing a pace that approached world-record speed. At 1,400 meters the race's first collision occurred, when Portuguese runner Aurora Cunha and American Joan Hansen made contact. Hansen tripped and fell, but quickly recovered and set off to rejoin the pack.

The pace, fast to begin with, grew even hotter.

were available. She ran the fastest times ever achieved by a female runner in the under-19 group for 1,500 and 5,000 meters, and she broke Decker's own world record at 5,000 meters, whittling almost 7 seconds off the mark. All the while, Budd kept a poster of Decker on her bedroom wall. Mary was her inspiration.

Grazing the back of Zola Budd's bare foot, Mary Decker begins the catastrophic fall that would knock both women from contention. Decker would try the race again at Seoul 1988, and Budd would compete at Barcelona 1992 as a member of the South African team, but neither champion would ever win an Olympic medal.

Ahead of the rest, four front runners—Decker, Budd, Romania's Maricica Puică, and Great Britain's Wendy Sly—were jammed together, vying for position. Into the race's fourth turn, Budd and Decker were in front, Budd with about a half-pace advantage, running at Decker's right shoulder. This was a peculiar situation for both women; each was accustomed to running alone, well in front of the pack. Somewhere around the 1,700-meter mark, Decker first made contact with one of Budd's legs, jarring her slightly. The two kept moving for another five strides. Then, 4 minutes 58 seconds into the race, the decisive collision happened.

It would take long, hard scrutiny of the videotapes before officials could begin to understand what actually took place at this point: Perhaps still reacting to the first impact, Decker and Budd again became entangled. Budd's left foot brushed Decker's thigh, and the younger runner lost her balance; her left foot lurched into Decker's path, and Decker's spiked shoe came down hard enough to draw blood on Budd's ankle, just above the heel. In close-up the pain showed on Budd's face, but she kept her equilibrium and kept moving.

Decker, now off balance herself, screamed and fell forward, flailing wildly for a support and

NO DISABILITY

The very word Olympian evokes the notion of physical perfection, but that image blurred when Neroli Fairhill wheeled herself onto the Los Angeles Memorial Coliseum track for the opening ceremony as a member of the New Zealand women's archery team.

Fairhill lost the use of her legs as the result of a spinal-cord injury suffered during a motorcycling accident when she was 24. Rather than curse her fate, she determined that life in a wheelchair would not slow her down. She spent the next three years learning to get around on wheels, then entered a competition for paraplegics as a shot-putter and discus thrower. Poor showings made her switch to archery. She excelled as a wheelchair archer, winning her first medal at the 1974 Commonwealth Paraplegic Games. That taste of success gave her the confidence to take on athletes who were not physically challenged. She took up archery full-time and in 1980 won the New Zealand national title for the first of four times. Recognized as one of her country's best archers—ambulatory or otherwise—she made the 1984 New Zealand Olympic team.

When Fairhill took part in the one women's archery contest at Los Angeles, she became the first paraplegic athlete to participate in an Olympic Games. She would finish in 35th place, well behind gold medalist Seo Hyang-soon of South Korea, but an undisputed winner all the same.

New Zealand's Neroli Fairhill lines up a shot during the women's archery competition in Los Angeles.

catching hold of the number on Budd's back. It ripped off and stayed clutched in Decker's fingers as she crash-landed on the grass, her left hip slamming into the ground. Dazed and shocked, she lay prone for a few moments, struggled to rise, then fell, as if paralyzed, to watch the pack flying off without her.

Budd, in tears, lost her place among the leaders and finished seventh, shocked and devastated by what had happened. The gold medal went to the Romanian, Maricica Puică, who had always been a formidable—if less publicized—contender. Puică's time was an Olympic-record 8:35.96. Budd's teammate Wendy Sly took the silver medal, and Lynn Williams of Canada won the bronze.

As the last of the runnners crossed the finish line, a medical team helped the grief-stricken Decker from the field. She had suffered a badly bruised left hip and thigh. Weeping with pain and disappointment, she vowed to "raise a protest." When Budd approached her, mortified and desperate to express her sympathy, Decker bitterly waved her away.

The collision set the stage for a fresh battle, this one off the track and between U.S. and British

PINMANSHIP

Collecting and trading Olympic pins first became a popular pastime at the 1976 Games in Montreal but popularity exploded into frenzy at Los Angeles 1984. Visitors who'd never seen an Olympic pin before suddenly caught the fever to create a set of unique souvenirs. Pin trading areas got so crowded at times that mounted police were needed to control the hordes.

Like any collectables, some pins were more valuable than others. Sponsors' pins—those produced by corporations that were backing the Games financially—appreciated in worth the fastest, often selling for hundreds of dollars. For example, the pin of Sam the Eagle holding a Coke

bottle (top center), rejected for use by the Los Angeles Olympic Organizing Committee but traded anyway, was selling for $1,000 by the end of the Games.

The other pins shown below: Los Angeles 1984 banner pin (center), one of the miniatures of the many banners decorating city streets during the Games; an Olympic pin depicting the U.S. flag (center right); the ABC sheriff's badge (bottom left), one of several highly coveted media pins; McDonald's Sam and Ronald pin (bottom right); a team pin worn by Taiwanese athletes (top left); the U.S. judo team pin (center left); and two pins designed by the LAOOC for donors (top right) and volunteers handling housing (center right).

officials. An on-field official monitoring the race—an American—disqualified Budd on the grounds that she had impeded Decker's progress; the British lodged a protest against this decision. A four-man appeals jury met to adjudicate, studying tapes of the race from four different angles, concluding that the disqualification was unfair and should be overruled. Other observers felt that Decker had been the more culpable of the two, desperate to hold back Budd's advance.

Gold-medalist Puică viewed the shambles with equanimity and, seemingly unaware of Decker's injuries, expressed regret that the fallen American had not forced herself to rise and finish the race. Puică herself, after making Olympic history as the winner of the Games' first-ever 3,000 meters for women, would go on the very next day to win the bronze in the 1,500. But even in victory she was upstaged by the disaster that had overtaken her defeated rivals: In sports mythology, the first Olympic women's 3,000 meters would belong, however disastrously, to the tragically enmeshed Budd and Decker.

Other women's track events brought their own surprises, though none as fraught with trauma as the ill-starred 3,000 meters. In the women's heptathlon—another Olympic first—five powerful favorites, led by America's Jackie Joyner, found themselves upstaged by a comparative outsider from a country that hadn't garnered an Olympic track and field gold medal in 16 years.

Like the men's decathlon, the women's heptathlon presented the ultimate challenge to athletic all-arounders, the Renaissance women of track and field. Heptathlon competitors had to accumulate points in seven events over two days: the 100-meter hurdles, the high jump and long jump, the shot put, the javelin throw, and races of 200 and 800 meters. Before 1984 the women's heptathlon had been the pentathlon, its contests consisting of a hurdles event and a

race (distances for both varied over the years), along with the long jump, high jump, and shot put. At the expanded version in Los Angeles, predictions were that all three medals would wind up, in one combination or another, in the hands of the United States, West Germany, or just possibly Great Britain.

The outsider who upset these forecasts was Glynis Nunn, an Australian from the Queensland town of Toowoomba. From her earliest years, Nunn was a sports-mad tomboy in a terrible hurry. "I was always first through the door," she recalled, "first up the stairs, first to the fridge. I was always falling over, knocking myself about, cutting myself. Mum used to say she owed the school so many packets of Band-Aids it wasn't funny."

At nine, to her family's relief, Nunn began channeling her prodigious energy into athletics at a local club. The club's sports program was unpretentious; parents helped with the coaching, and equipment was, to say the least, modest. Hurdles, for instance, were improvised from pairs of vertical sticks, with a third stick placed precariously on top; it took no more than a good gust of wind to blow the contraption down. The club's training ground was a grassy slope in the town park. "Even the long jump," Nunn remembered, "was uphill."

By the time she was 17, Nunn had acquired a string of national titles, and the Australian press had nicknamed her the Prima Donna of Track—presumably because of her stellar talent, rather than for any operatic fits of temperament. But, like Mary Decker and so many others, Nunn would find the road to the Olympics littered with setbacks. After attaining seventh place against a galaxy of international greats at the 1983 world championships in Helsinki, Nunn gave up a much-loved job as a physical education teacher in order to devote herself solely to Olympic training. And—rare indeed among the top athletes of her era—she trained

A midfield steal by the New Zealand women prompts an abrupt change in the action during a field hockey match against the Netherlands. In the end, though, the Dutch team dispatched the Kiwis 2-1 on the way to the gold medal.

as an amateur. Devoid of sponsorships and endorsements, she survived on a combination of state unemployment benefits and modest grants.

Despite Nunn's dedication, knowledgeable observers predicted that she might, if all went well, aspire to a chance at the bronze. She was reckoned too much of a lightweight for the heptathlon, shorter and slighter than most other contenders. But Nunn found ways of making up the difference. She made sure to arrive in the United States well in advance of the Games, and she warmed up with a number of pre-Olympic meets, faring well enough in them to boost her confidence.

Lifting her spirits even higher was a dream that Nunn reported having on the night before the heptathlon. With extraordinary clarity, she saw herself running 13.01 seconds in the 100-meter hurdles—a full 0.16 of a second faster than her personal best. In the next part of the dream she was laden with congratulatory bouquets. Bolstered by these omens, she also relied on her personal gastronomic talisman: For breakfast on both days

of the heptathlon, she ate a pavlova, an Australian meringue and fruit confection. She had consumed this sugary delicacy before her most crucial races back home, and it had rarely failed her. Without doubt she would need it this time.

Of all the strong competitors that Nunn faced in Los Angeles, the most daunting was Jackie Joyner. Born and raised in a close-knit family on the mean streets of East St. Louis, Illinois. Joyner and her older brother Al had supported and encouraged each other in nurturing their shared athletic talents. Together they would mature into one of America's first families of track and field: Both Jackie and Al, as well as Al's future wife, glamorous sprinter Florence Griffith, would take part in the 1984 Games.

By 12, Jackie could leap more than 17 feet in the long jump, and she soon expanded her interests into the pentathlon, volleyball, and basketball. Basketball won her a scholarship to UCLA, where she enjoyed considerable academic success along with her sports triumphs. But, like Glynis

Nunn, Joyner put most of her life on hold during the pre-Olympic year to perfect her skills in readiness for the Games.

No multievent athlete is merely a jack- or jill-of-all-trades: Each has particular loves and hates, strengths and weaknesses, in the various events. Both Nunn and Joyner looked forward to the long jump; both were wary of the javelin throw and the 800-meter run. Joyner was nursing a hamstring injury that threatened to undo her on the track, while Nunn found the 800 meters so loathsome that she had even worked with therapists and tried hypnosis to get over the mental block: For some reason, the notion of crossing a finish line and then having to run the circuit again drove her almost to a frenzy.

The heptathlon began with the 100-meter hurdles, and Nunn made a spectacular entrance, chalking up the fastest time ever recorded by a woman in an Olympic multievent— 13.02—not quite as good as she had dreamed, but close enough. (The scoreboard had indeed flashed 13.01 initially but had corrected the time later.) Joyner's time was 13.63. Both Nunn and Joyner leaped 5 feet 9 inches (1.80 meters) in the high jump, but Joyner heaved the shot 47 feet 2 inches (14.39 meters), besting the rest of the field. The American was 8 points ahead of Nunn for the last test of Day 1, the 200 meters. There, Joyner's time of 24.05 was a scant 0.01 of a second faster than Nunn's. The end of the day found Joyner getting the best of the duel, but just barely. And, surprisingly, both women were trailing Great Britain's Judy Simpson, who, although she had no standout event, had a solid day all-around. The standings for Day 1 were: Simpson 3,759 points, Joyner 3,739, Nunn 3,731.

Day 2 began with a surprise setback for Joyner in one of her strongest events, the long jump, when a fine leap of 22 feet 4 1/4 inches (6.81 meters) was ruled to be a foul—one of two on her initial tries. Jarred into excessive caution on her third and final attempt, she jumped only 20 feet 1/2 inch (6.11 meters), far below her usual standard and good enough only for fifth in the field.

The last two events were make-or-break time. Joyner gave the javelin throw everything she had, flinging the missile nearly 30 feet (8.9 meters) farther than Nunn had managed, and leaving Simpson well to the rear. At this point, Joyner was, by 31 points, the front runner: If Nunn hoped to wrest the gold medal from her, she

Australia's Glynis Nunn stretches for every inch of a long jump during the debut of the Olympic heptathlon. Nunn had decided before the Games to retire from track and field after Los Angeles. Her last meet was her greatest.

Glynis Nunn *(No. 17)* stays in front of American Jackie Joyner in the 800-meter race. Nunn wouldn't finish first in the event, but she would beat Joyner by 3.5 seconds—all she needed to capture the heptathlon title. Nunn's victory would make her the first Australian track and field champion of either sex since Mexico City 1968.

would have to do it by slaying her own bête noire—winning the 800 meters.

"It was like racing at the bottom of a teacup," the Australian would relate later. "There was no way to get out, no matter how hard I tried. I kept going round and round. And there were all these people sitting round the teacup."

It took Nunn 2:10.57, a personal best, to run her way out of the teacup. Joyner's time was 2:13.03. Nunn assumed that her margin of victory hadn't been wide enough to close the gap and put her ahead of Joyner in overall points. But, thanks to the byzantine complexities of heptathlon scoring, the competitors had to cool their heels for a tense 25 minutes before the official results were announced—and Nunn discovered to her profound amazement that she had won, beating silver medalist Joyner by a hair's-breadth 5 points. Joyner would have her own golden moment four years later, but for now, the gold medal for the first women's Olympic heptathlon was headed for Australia. The bronze went to Sabine Everts of West Germany. Judy Simpson, who had fared badly in the javelin and the 800 meters, faded to fifth.

Unlike Glynis Nunn, U.S. runner Valerie Brisco-Hooks arrived at the Olympics as a likely winner—especially in the absence of the strong sprinters from the Eastern bloc. The Coliseum's computerized scoreboard, unable to accommodate all the letters of her name, listed her as Brisco-Hoo, which track fans jauntily converted to "Brisco-Who?" But that was a joke: Everybody knew who she was.

Valerie Brisco was born in Mississippi but raised—along with nine brothers and sisters—on the fringes of the troubled Watts district of Los Angeles. Although young Valerie showed natural talent on the track at school, she didn't seem very interested in the hard training that might shape it. "I used to come home and break down and not work out," she would remember. "I didn't like the pain. I was really lazy." But two events shook her out of her complacency: Her beloved older brother Robert died in a classic urban American tragedy, felled by a stray bullet while jogging on a high-school track. The second factor, less traumatic, came in the form of a homework assignment: A perceptive teacher directed Valerie to read a biography of Wilma Rudolph, the graceful African-American runner from Tennessee, who had sprinted to Olympic immortality at Rome 1960. In Rudolph's story, Brisco found inspiration.

More concrete help would come in 1979, when Brisco began training with coach Bob Kersee at the World Class Track Club in Los Angeles. With Kersee she worked as much as seven hours

American sprinter Valerie Brisco-Hooks helps her son, Alvin Jr., over a hurdle. Motherhood poses a unique challenge to women athletes. Even so, many Olympians, like Brisco-Hooks, have been both parents and gold medalists.

a day, five days a week, the sessions ending with two or three hours of weight lifting, topped off with 250 push-ups and 1,000 sit-ups.

There was a brief hiatus in Brisco's progress when she married pro football player Alvin Hooks in 1981 and moved across the country to Philadelphia, where he had been drafted to play for the Eagles. The following year, after a knee injury took Hooks off the team, the couple returned to Los Angeles and Valerie gave birth to a son.

But the lure of the track was too strong to resist. In 1983, as soon as Alvin Jr. was old enough to sit in a stroller and watch from the sidelines, Brisco-Hooks undertook a rigorous exercise program to shed the 40 pounds she had gained in pregnancy. That done, she returned to competition.

By the next year, in time for the Games, Brisco-Hooks had honed her skills to their finest edge ever. Rather than slowing her down, the rigors of childbirth and motherhood seemed to have made her faster and stronger. Unlike many other runners, who shied away from competitions too close to the Olympic trials for fear of injury, she ran at a meet a week, setting a U.S. record of 49.83 for the 400 meters. Her personal best at 200 meters was 22.16 seconds, a little less than 0.5 off the world record of 21.71 held by East Germany's Marita Koch.

In the 400 meters at Los Angeles, Brisco-Hooks's principal rival was teammate Chandra Cheeseborough, who had broken Valerie's pre-Olympic 400-meter national record just a week after it had been set. Moreover, Cheeseborough had come from behind to beat Brisco-Hooks in the Olympic trials. But the big race itself saw a turnabout: For the first half Cheeseborough looked unbeatable. Then, coming around the turn, Brisco-Hooks flew into the lead and held on, finishing in an Olympic-record 48.83, a full 2 meters ahead of silver medalist Cheeseborough. Running just three miles from the spot where her brother had been killed a decade before, the kid from Watts had won a gold medal—her first of three.

Three days later, on August 9, Brisco-Hooks found herself up against a tough trio of veteran favorites for the 200 meters. Even without the world-beating runners who were boycotting, the field was strong, dominated by Jamaica's Merlene Ottey-Page, Kathy Cook of Great Britain, and Valerie's flamboyant teammate Florence Griffith. (Griffith would come into her own four years later in Seoul. In Los Angeles, however, she stood out less for her speed than for her beauty—not to mention her spectacularly long fingernails, patriotically painted in stars and stripes.)

As the gun sounded the start of the 200, Brisco-Hooks stumbled coming off the blocks. But she made a quick recovery and soon turned her second race of the Games into an abbreviated version of the first. Coming around the turn, she stepped hard on her own accelerator, pulling power from her high-swinging right arm. As those around her began to flag, she held on, pounding steadily across the last meters and across the finish line in a time of 21.81, a U.S. record.

"I was very determined, but I didn't feel I had anything to prove," Brisco-Hooks told reporters shortly after she had hugged fellow competitors, husband, baby, and coach Bob Kersee in a joyful victory leap that had knocked him flat. "I had a lot of people supporting me and I wanted to win it for them. I'm just happy it's finished."

But it wasn't quite finished. Brisco-Hooks not only had become the first athlete of either gender ever to win Olympic gold in both the 200 and 400 meters, but she would go on two days later to take another jet-propelled turn—this one in the 4 x 400-meter relay—helping teammates Lillie Leatherwood, Sherri Howard, and Chandra Cheeseborough to victory. With three golds to her credit, Brisco-Hooks had equaled the record of her idol, Wilma Rudolph, for the greatest number of gold medals won by an American woman in a single Olympic Games.

The celebrated Rudolph was also a role model for sprinter Evelyn Ashford. Louisiana-born Ashford was an army brat whose family's peregrinations ultimately took her to Roseville, California. There she achieved an unusual kind of high-school stardom: Hearing tales about the girl's phenomenal speed, her math teacher set up a race between Evelyn and the fastest boys in the school. Evelyn won, seemingly without effort, and was promptly invited to join the hitherto all-male track team. She ran in numerous meets, and she generally beat the boys hands down.

But raw speed alone wasn't enough to make Ashford the world's fastest female sprinter; she needed training. She acquired it in 1975 when she entered UCLA on an athletic scholarship and began working with women's track coach—and three-time Olympian—Pat Connolly. Connolly was dazzled by Ashford's potential. When the freshman ran her first time trial, Connolly thought her stopwatch was broken: No one could have run that fast.

The two women entered into a long-term collaboration that would launch Ashford on her path to the winner's podium at Los Angeles. Connolly provided encouragement, discipline, and technical expertise; Ashford brought her own unique combination of physical strength, elegant movement,

Valerie Brisco-Hooks dashes to one of her three victories at Los Angeles. Brisco-Hooks is the only athlete, male or female, to win both the 200- and 400-meter races in the same Games.

A gold medalist at last, Eveyln Ashford listens to "The Star Spangled Banner" after winning the 100-meter dash. Her winning time of 10.97 made her the first woman to break the 11-second barrier over 100 meters in an Olympic Games.

and a sense of purpose so powerful that even her coach found it daunting. "Evelyn's strongest attribute as an athlete," said Connolly, "is her ability to concentrate. I would hate to have to compete against her, in anything. Her intensity is so fierce." By 1979 this intensity had carried Ashford into the top class of international runners. In both the 100 and 200 meters at the World Cup races in Montreal, she outran the two East German stars, Marita Koch and Marlies Göhr, and set her sights on Olympic gold at the forthcoming Moscow Games. She trained with an almost mystical concentration, until President Jimmy Carter's call for the United States to boycott the Games. "The boycott ripped out my soul," Ashford said. "I had put all my emotional eggs in that one basket, and when it was yanked away from me, I felt totally empty."

But more was injured than her morale. A damaged hamstring muscle took Ashford out of competition for most of 1980. The problem recurred in 1983 when she ran the 100 meters at Helsinki, causing a disastrous midrace collapse. The hamstring caused trouble yet again during the 1984 Olympic trials in June, and she feared that, once more, her chance of participating in the Games might be jinxed. But a therapy and massage program helped her heal in time.

The years of struggle came to a climax almost too fast to see: Ashford, with the grace of a leopard and the power of a truck, took only 10.97 seconds to dash the 100 meters into the record books. As well as setting an Olympic record, she became the first woman in the history of the Games to run the distance in less than 11 seconds. Yet when she broke the tape, she was almost the last to realize what she had just achieved. "When I first crossed the finish," she said, "I was mad at myself because I thought it wasn't a fast time. Then the Olympic record of 10.97 was announced, and I thought, 'Is that all there is to it? What was all the anxiety about all those years? Let's do it again!'"

And, in a way, Ashford did do it again. Six days later, on August 11, she carried the baton in the final leg as the U.S. team won the 4 x 100-meter relay.

Ashford, Brisco-Hooks, and other American female runners at Los Angeles enjoyed a certain edge: Their nation had a tradition of producing great track stars, of molding them with the best facilities and coaching available. And, comparatively, their culture afforded approval of their athletic talent. Not all women were so lucky.

In some Islamic communities, a strict interpretation of religious law prohibits women from taking part in any sport that requires them to expose any part of their bodies: The bare arms and legs of a female runner would utterly violate the rules dictating female modesty in dress. Women in Iran, for instance, are restricted to sports such as shooting, which can be done by participants veiled from head to toe.

But Nawal el-Moutawakil, an entry in the first-ever women's Olympic 400-meter hurdles, came from Morocco, where these restrictions are not universally applied. Growing up in Casablanca, and running races against her brothers on the beach, she showed natural speed and agility. Her family, especially her father, encouraged her to develop these gifts.

"My father always supported me," el-Moutawakil recalled. "He always encouraged me, and I listened only to him. I didn't care what anyone else in our society said. He always told me I could be a champion, first Moroccan and then African and then an Olympic champion."

Before long, el-Moutawakil's potential was recognized even by King Hassan II of Morocco, who subsidized her athletic training. In search of tougher competition and better coaching, she traveled to the United States and enrolled at Iowa State University. A relative unknown when the Los Angeles Games began, she was not the

Morocco's Nawal el-Moutawakil breezes over a hurdle in a race full of milestones. Though she finished almost a second and a half faster than her closest competitor, the victory was clouded: Many of the best women's hurdlers did not compete because of the Eastern bloc boycott.

town well-wishers surging into the streets in Casablanca, and the winner got a congratulatory phone call from the king. She would return to a heroine's welcome, with thousands of fans mobbing her at the airport and sackfuls of mail from women all over Africa, thanking her for an achievement that not only made them proud but gave them hope for the future.

Two days later, on August 8, an Olympic first of a different stripe took place in the Coliseum as a remarkable pair of Olympic veterans, West Germany's Ulrike Meyfarth and Italy's Sara Simeoni, vied with each other in the high jump.

Meyfarth had debuted on the Olympic scene 12 years earlier, at Munich 1972, when at 16 she became the youngest Olympic track and field gold medalist in history. She was lionized by her country, but her popularity plummeted at Montreal 1976 when she cracked under pressure and fumbled her chance for a fresh Olympic medal. Any hopes she might have nursed for recovering her reputation four years later were quashed when West Germany joined in boycotting the Moscow Games. Now, though at 28 she was a senior citizen by high-jump standards, she resolved to try for gold just one more time.

Remarkably, Meyfarth's chief rival for the prize was even older. Sara Simeoni, who had won the high jump in the Games denied to Meyfarth at Moscow, came out of semiretirement to compete again at Los Angeles at the age of 31. Her motivation, she said, was not only to defend her title but to experience once again the Olympic magic. "The Olympic Games," she said, "have always given me very beautiful emotions—emotions that are very hard to experience elsewhere."

The high-jump bar started at 5 feet 8 inches (1.73 meters) and, as always, rose round by round. As it went up, more challengers went down. Apart from Simeoni and Meyfarth, the last to fall was American Joni Huntley, who had been written off by the experts as the U.S. entry least likely to win a medal. Huntley was eliminated by

favorite in the field. Nevertheless, when the starting gun fired, she came out fast and stayed fast, moving lightly over the hurdles and giving all her competitors a good view of her disappearing heels. Her personal-best 54.61 was good enough for a gold medal—the first ever won by a woman from an Arab country.

El-Moutawakil mourned the fact that her father had died six months before his dreams for her came true at the Games. But all Morocco, it seemed, had stayed up half the night to watch her win. (The event was televised live there at 2 a.m.) El-Moutawakil's triumph brought home-

missing her try at 6 feet 5 1/4 inches (1.96 meters), but she was delighted at surprising everyone with a bronze. With the bar at 6 feet 6 3/4 inches (2 meters), both Meyfarth and Simeoni cleared on their first attempts, floating over backward with easy grace. Then, at 6 feet 7 1/2 inches (2.02 meters), Meyfarth glided over, but Simeoni failed to clear the bar.

Simeoni was pleased enough to end her sparkling career with an eminently respectable silver medal. As for Meyfarth, she enjoyed a unique distinction: She was not only the youngest woman ever to win the high jump but, three Olympiads later, also the oldest.

Italian track fans who had pulled for Simeoni were able to console themselves with the success of Gabriella Dorio in the 1,500 meters. The disastrous Decker-Budd collision the day before in the 3,000 meters was fresh in everyone's mind, and the 1,500 got off to a slow, cautious start. Even at the plodding pace, Dorio kept herself in the back half of the pack until, 600 meters from the finish, she opened the throttle and charged forward to take the lead. She lost it to Romanian Doina Melinte, then seized it back in the home-stretch and held on to grasp the gold. In victory Dorio was disarmingly modest: "I'm always afraid of my adversaries," she said, "so I tried to stay ahead of them."

One country with very specific Olympic high hopes went away from Los Angeles disappointed. Finnish men had been a power in the javelin throw for years: Their small northern nation of five million people had nurtured half a dozen

Arching over the bar, Ulrike Meyfarth clears 6 feet 7 1/2 inches. The height set an Olympic record. After winning the event, Meyfarth made three attempts to set a world record but came up short.

Running a tactical race, Italy's Gabriella Dorio *(No. 226)* sprints to the front of the 1,500-meter pack. Dorio, learning from her fourth-place finish in the 800 meters five days earlier, conserved her energy for a winning surge in the final 100 meters of the longer race.

world-record holders and five Olympic gold medalists in the sport. Even so, no Finnish woman had ever won an Olympic gold in the javelin. Tiina Lillak seemed likely to fill that void. Lillak had secured her status as a national heroine when she won the gold medal at the 1983 world championships in Helsinki. The day after her success, every sporting-goods store in the land sold out of javelins, and young would-be Lillaks turned to their homeland's boundless forests to cut down saplings and fashion them into spears.

But Lillak's hopes for the Olympic gold medal at Los Angeles were undone by Tessa Sanderson, a Jamaica-born member of the British team. In the first round Sanderson hurled the slender shaft 228 feet 2 inches (69.56 meters) for an Olympic record that no one in the competition would better. Lillak, in her second round, came closest to it,

with a distance of 226 feet 4 inches (69 meters). But as she completed the throw, she was betrayed by an old injury: Her right ankle, heavily taped after a stress fracture sustained in the spring, suddenly gave way again. A suffering Lillak retired from the fray, not quite consoled by the fact that her last throw would bring her the silver medal. "I am sure that without the injury," she lamented, "I could have won. I cannot say I am satisfied." For Sanderson, however, it was a set of firsts: She was the first Briton and the first black to win any Olympic throwing contest.

In women's field events, as in track, Eastern bloc athletes were sorely missed. The shot put, discus, and long jump all suffered from the loss of some top-quality competitors. But one sport particularly hard hit by the Moscow-led pullout in the end provided one of the most

spectacular duels of the Games—a contest between the darling of the host country and a tiny prodigy from Romania, the only Eastern bloc country to ignore the boycott.

Ironically, gymnastics had the Soviets to thank for its astonishing surge in popularity. In the 1970s their young Byelorussian superstar, Olga Korbut, had persuaded a generation of agile little girls from Omsk to Oklahoma that the path to glory lay along the balance beam and the uneven parallel bars. But on the night when Romania's Ecaterina Szabó waged a fierce private war with America's Mary Lou Retton for the individual all-around gold medal, the boycotters were completely forgotten.

In spite of growing up several thousand miles apart, the two rivals had something more than their diminutive height—4 feet 9 inches—and their gymnastic abilities in common. Both had experienced the unorthodox training methods of the same powerful, innovative coach: Bela Karolyi, a mustachioed 6-footer from Transylvania. Karolyi had been the prime mover behind Romania's emergence as a world-class gymnastic power, nurturing a host of international

champions. His star protégé was the legendary Nadia Comaneci who, at Montreal 1976, entered Olympic history as the first woman to score a perfect 10. By the end of the competition, she had seven perfect scores to her credit. (Comaneci would be in Los Angeles as a front-row spectator.)

In 1963, as a young graduate of a physical education college, Karolyi set up a small gymnastics school in Vulcan, a remote and grimy coal-mining town in western Romania. His approach to the sport was radical—and deeply shocking to those who believed that women's gymnastics should be no more than a slightly athletic version of ballet.

Karolyi's own sports specialties had been the hammer throw—he was a national champion—and handball. He wanted gymnastics to convey the same intensity and power as those muscular sports. As far as he was concerned, women's gymnastics as he found it was "all these cute, delicate girls, just sort of kicking up their heels and going 'la, la, la.' Nobody had ever thought of turning them into little bombs."

So Karolyi developed his little academy into a

Upset-minded Tessa Sanderson of Great Britain prepares to launch her javelin. In Moscow 1980, Sanderson, a favorite, failed to qualify for the finals. She turned the tables in Los Angeles, beating highly favored Tiina Lillak of Finland for the javelin title.

Canada's Alexandra Barre and Sue Holloway take the lead in a heat of the women's 500-meter pairs kayak. Barre and Holloway would finish second in the finals to the Swedish team of Agneta Andersson and Anna Olsson.

gymnastics munitions factory with a rigorous training regimen that stressed agility, strength, and energy. He believed in starting his girls young, and he demanded fierce dedication and hard work even from seven-year-olds. Critics said that his methods sometimes amounted to outright torment. But his pupils repaid him by winning almost every competition they entered. Romania's gymnastics establishment, which had initially dismissed him as a maverick, soon greeted him with open arms and open coffers.

Within a few years Karolyi's pupils, Comaneci among them, had earned 10 world titles and five Olympic championships for their homeland. But in 1981, visiting the United States with the Romanian team, Karolyi and his wife made a sudden decision to defect. With the enthusiastic help of a number of Texans, they managed to set up a gymnastics school in Houston, run according to the same philosophy that had formed so many young champions back home. Tough as the Romanian's methods were, they still succeeded in attracting the cream of aspiring young gymnasts, including, in 1983, Mary Lou Retton.

Retton was a short but sturdy Italian-American from a West Virginia coal-mining community, Appalachia's equivalent of Romania's Vulcan. From her earliest childhood she was off to a running start, frantically active, the chief lamp smasher and furniture wrecker of a large and loving family. Her mother sent her off to a gymnastics class to let off steam, and the high-energy four-year-old took to it at once.

"From the beginning," Retton would recall in her autobiography, "I never had any trouble relating to the equipment. I just got up and it felt natural. The fear factor was never there, not for me." At eight, lying on her stomach in front of the family TV, she watched Nadia Comaneci's triumph at Montreal, envied it, and began to dream. By the time she was 12 she was competing on a national level, and soon thereafter she was bringing home medals both foreign and domestic.

When Retton met Karolyi, the result was a marriage of true minds. Only 14, Mary Lou left home and moved in with a host family near Karolyi's Houston gym. After only two weeks with the Romanian coach, she scored her first perfect 10 on the vault. In competitions at home and abroad, she began

China's southpaw standout Luan Jujie *(left)* attacks West German Cornelia Hanisch. Jujie would win the bout for the individual foil title; Hanisch would gain a share of the team gold.

outclassing top-ranking U.S. gymnasts and even giving the formidable Eastern Europeans cause for concern.

At Los Angeles, together with fellow Karolyi pupil Julianne McNamara and four other teammates, Retton would help the U.S. team to a silver medal, its first since 1948. The Americans scored 391.2 points, close on the heels of the 392.2 tallied by the winning Romanians. But the climax of Retton's Olympic efforts would come in the competition for the individual all-around title: There she would face another product of the Karolyi school of hard-pounding, do-or-die

gymnastic perfectionism, in its original Romanian incarnation.

Ecaterina Szabó, 17, was described by some sports journalists as a tough little cookie. A pale, delicate brunette, she managed to look ethereal despite her steely gaze and the glittery eye shadow that framed it. She had a string of gold medals and championships and during 1983 she had achieved five perfect scores in the gymnastics world championships at Budapest. The only gymnasts reckoned capable of beating her were the Soviets, and they weren't in Los Angeles. Karolyi, who had known Szabó since she

GET RHYTHMIC

Harmonious movement is the soul of rhythmic gymnastics, a sport accentuating a kind of physical excellence that is distinctively female. Its femininity made the discipline an obvious choice when the IOC decided to add two new disciplines for women to the Olympic program in 1984.

Rhythmic gymnastics in its modern form is relatively new, though its origins date to the 19th century. Like its time-honored acrobatic cousin, rhythmic gymnastics developed as an educational tool. The first great gymnastics theorist was Johan Guts Muths, a Prussian professor whose ideas spread quickly throughout Europe and spawned a plethora of related systems. In most of them, exercises for women stressed dance and rhythm. To these elements, several theorists added devices such as balls, hoops, and ropes, believing that concentration on the props would evoke more relaxed movement. Ball routines were part of women's gymnastics at Berlin 1936, London 1948, and Helsinki 1952. By 1956, however, the Fédération Internationale Gymnastique, gymnastics' governing body, had voted to standardize exercises performed in international competitions: Rhythmic routines didn't make the cut.

Stranded in exile, rhythmic gymnastics developed slowly. Regulations concerning proper moves and the choice of devices were not resolved until the 1970s. Thereafter, however, worldwide interest grew rapidly, and the IOC granted the discipline Olympic status in 1980. It debuted in Los Angeles with one event, the all-around, with each athlete competing in rotation with a ball, hoop, ribbon, and Indian clubs.

America's Valerie Zimring *(left)* throws her pair of Indian clubs in a tricky maneuver.

Doina Staiculescu *(above)* of Romania tries to keep her six-meter ribbon airborne. Letting it touch the ground constitutes an error.

Canadian Lori Fung *(upper right)*, the 1984 Olympic rhythmic gymnastics all-around winner, displays her skill with the ball, one of four devices used in her sport.

Jumping through hoops is a simple order for American Michelle Berube *(right)*.

A graceful leap shows the practiced poise of Romania's Ecaterina Szabó. Without the Soviets, Szabó and her teammates were favored to win the gymnastics competition.

was five and had transformed her from a rural moppet adept at handstands into a precocious star, described her as "a very powerful little kid. Ambitious, clear-minded, and as technically clean as you can be." He acknowledged that his former pupil probably had the edge over Retton in terms of fine coordination, but he assessed that Mary Lou was stronger. (He neglected to add that Retton would also have the advantage of support from a strongly partisan crowd.) Karolyi believed the Romanians had added two years to Szabó's birth date to get her into competitions that she would otherwise be too young to enter. But, whether Szabó was 17 or 15, she was formidable.

In the individual all-around competition, 36 competitors—representing the top three scorers from each national team—were divided into four groups that would take turns at the balance beam, the uneven parallel bars, the floor exercise, and the side horse vault. In this contest, gymnasts retain half the points they contributed in the team events: This meant Retton started off as the front runner, 0.15 of a point ahead of Szabó.

Szabó's first exercise was the balance beam. Even world-class gymnasts often find this four-inch-wide strip of wood, four feet above the floor, their nemesis: They may strive to pirou-ctte, leap, twist, and somersault along it, but sometimes even staying on it is a problem. The little Romanian had herself come to grief on the beam in previous meets, but this time she dazzled the crowd and the judges, cavorting along its length, whirling backward in a rapid-fire quartet of handsprings, and returning to earth with a double-back-somersault dismount. Her score was a perfect 10.

Retton, meanwhile, had tallied 9.85 on the uneven bars. For most gymnasts, in another context, the score would have been a triumph, but in this Olympic showdown it was a serious setback: The two rivals were now neck and neck. After the judges—to Karolyi's fury—awarded Retton

only 9.8 for her turn on the beam, Szabó had clawed away Mary Lou's starting advantage and stood 0.15 of a point ahead.

Ecaterina's floor exercise, which had won her 9.95, had been a punchy routine with a stars-and-stripes musical accompaniment, ranging from Gershwin to "The Battle Hymn of the Republic" and designed to please the U.S. crowd. Retton, ironically, went for a more Slavic sound track, while she defied gravity with a lofty double-back somersault and other airborne marvels. Her resulting perfect 10 was answered by Szabó on the vault. One rotation remained to decide it all.

Szabó's turn would come first, her final test the

A balance beam somersault was one of the daring moves favored by American gymnast Mary Lou Retton. Known for her powerful athleticism, Retton was the standout performer of an unusually strong American women's gymnastics team.

Japanese swimmers Saeko Kimura and Miwako Motoyoshi (*underwater*) demonstrate the beauty of synchrony. The pair would win a bronze medal. Duet and solo synchronized swimming events, for women only, joined the Olympic program at Los Angeles.

uneven bars. They had given her victory in the 1983 European championships, and now she soared between them as if she belonged to some strange arboreal species, swinging elegantly on branches high above a forest floor. Her reward was a 9.9. Retton, now preparing for the vault, would need a 10 to win.

If there is such a thing as an earsplitting silence, it now fell upon Pauley Pavilion. Retton, her face grim, set off powerfully toward the vault, then sprang over it in her own version of a famous leap known as the Tsukahara, a layout reverse somersault culminating in a double twist. The crowd, Karolyi, and Retton herself went wild: The score was, could only be, the desired 10, putting her a vital 0.05 of a point ahead of Szabó. But Retton had a second turn coming, whether she needed it or not. She chose to take it and, for the sheer joy of the achievement, performed the impossible a second time. Afterward, the wholesome grin that had so enchanted a world of television watchers told the story: She had become the first American woman ever to win an Olympic gold medal in gymnastics. And that was not her only reward: The gold and the grin would not go unmarked by purveyors of corporate endorsements, who deluged her with offers once the Games were over.

Another Olympic first-time women's event in 1984 was rhythmic gymnastics, a discipline very different from the muscular exertions practiced by Retton, Szabó, and their ilk. Rhythmic gymnastics entails the use of ribbons, hoops, balls, and small clubs, and it is designed to showcase uniquely feminine beauty and grace. The Bulgarians had come to dominate this exotic specialty, but in their absence the gold medal went to Canada's Lori Fung.

A women-only event with similar aesthetic aims also made its debut: synchronized swimming, once known as water ballet. The sport's formal bow at Los Angeles had a certain poetic justice, since it first came to world attention via Hollywood films of the 1940s starring stunning swimmer Esther Williams. Some members of the athletic community sniffed that synchronized swimming was not a sport at all, but enthusiasts insisted that it required as much fitness, concentration, precision, and skill as any other contest on the Olympic menu. Its gold medalists, Tracie Ruiz and Candy Costie, were both members of the U.S. team.

While synchronized swimming had its detractors, nobody questioned the credentials of yet another Olympic event that opened its doors to women for the first time at Los Angeles: Without doubt, bicycling was a sport. Cycling had been part of the Olympic calendar for men since the very first modern Games, Athens 1896. Now women came pedaling furiously over the horizon in a 49.2-mile (79.2-kilometer) road race from Los Angeles to Mission Viejo.

For men and women alike, cycling had long been a European preserve: The first and only Olympic medal won by an American had been a bronze in the road race back at Stockholm 1912. But the fitness boom that began in the late 1970s had put millions of U.S. cyclists on the roads, and new racers by the thousands had begun to compete, swiftly raising standards in the sport. With the help of former Polish national coach Edward Borysewicz, known to his new American compatriots as "Eddie B," the 1984 U.S. Olympic team emerged, for the first time, as a serious threat.

The hottest prospect on the women's squad was Connie Carpenter-Phinney, who had won the national women's cycling championships 13 times. Now, at 27, she had emerged from virtual retirement to take part in the first Olympic cycling contest for women, calling it "the one last race of my life." One of her rivals in the quest for a medal was her compatriot, 21-year-old Rebecca Twigg, and the media predictably hyped the rivalry between the young challenger on her way

Side by side at the start, Americans Rebecca Twigg *(left)* and Connie Carpenter-Phinney would also be nose to nose at the finish of the first women's Olympic cycling event.

up and the old champion seeking to go out in a blaze of glory.

On July 29, the first day of the Games, 200,000 flag-waving spectators lined the entire route, and for two hard-pumping hours, the racers navigated the hills, flats, and tricky curves of the course. Speed and endurance were the obvious requisites for this tough event, but cycling also requires shrewd tactics and quick responses to changing situations and conditions. Replete with all these virtues, Carpenter-Phinney and Twigg were shoulder to shoulder at the finish, and only a final, lurching thrust pushed the veteran's machine across the line scant inches ahead of Twigg's. The moment, for Carpenter-Phinney, was as golden as the medal. She described it later as "the crowning glory of a long career. It gave me the chance to retire on top, which is what I wanted to do."

Swimming, too, saw a veteran athlete emerge from retirement to claim a gold medal. In the case of Nancy Hogshead, the prize for the 100-meter freestyle was shared with the youngest woman to medal in swimming at the Games, l6-year-old Carrie Steinseifer. The two Americans completed the course in a dead heat, with a time of 55.92 seconds. "This," said Hogshead, "is a great way to end my career." The fact that she ultimately went home with a total of four medals—two other golds and a silver—made for an even more spectacular farewell.

The U.S. women reigned supreme in swimming in 1984. There were double gold medals for Tiffany

Shock and excitement register on the faces of Carrie Steinseifer *(left)* and Nancy Hogshead after they tied for the gold in the 100-meter freestyle. American women would take home 19 medals in the swimming events at Los Angeles.

Zhou Jihong folds into the pike position during the
platform diving competition. The 19-year-old Jihong
maintained her poise throughout her series of
dives—a rarity with the promising but inexperienced
Chinese athletes—to win the event.

Cohen, Mary Meagher, and Tracy Caulkins, who had been the superstar of American swimming since setting a world record of 2:15.09 in the 200-meter individual medley back in 1977. The second most successful nation was the Netherlands, with gold medals for Petra van Staveren in the 100-meter breaststroke and Jolanda de Rover in the 200-meter backstroke, plus a bronze for de Rover in the 100-meter backstroke. The remaining gold medal stayed on the North American continent, in the hands of Canada's Anne Ottenbrite, who gained the prize in the 200-meter breaststroke in spite of a whiplash injury and a pulled thigh muscle suffered only days before the race.

Without doubt, the swimming events in Los Angeles were diminished by the absence of the mighty swimmers of the German Democratic Republic. Showing their prowess at a concurrent meet held for the boycotting nations, the East Germans achieved far better times than the Olympic winners at Los Angeles. Had the East German women attended the Games, pundits asserted, all the top swimmers would have been pushed to better performances.

The diving competitions, however, proved that experts can be wrong. Knowledgeable fans of these perilous leaps through space predicted gold for the United States or perhaps for China, whose athletes, despite inexperience in international competition, were fast approaching championship level.

The springboard diving event caught the sages napping with the victory of Canada's Sylvie Bernier. Bernier had a history of choking at big competitions. In Los Angeles she found a way to soothe the nerves that had previously sabotaged her efforts: She spent the time between dives with a Walkman clamped to her head, distracting herself with music. More relaxed than ever before, she won the gold. The silver medal went to America's Kelly McCormick, the daughter of Pat McCormick, the legendary diver who had won gold medals in women's springboard and platform diving at Helsinki 1952 and Melbourne 1956. In the platform diving at Los Angeles, the prophets proved correct as 19-year-old Zhou Jihong won China its first diving gold medal.

If China's diving medal was a nice surprise, the victory of that nation's volleyball team was a cause for general rejoicing. The surprise triumph caused throngs of Chinese citizens to dance in the streets.

Jolanda de Rover cuts through the water on her way to the gold medal in the 200-meter backstroke. De Rover, who also placed third in the 100-meter, paced a resurgent Dutch women's swim team that trailed only the United States in medal count.

The volleyball final was a fierce contest between the Chinese women and the U.S. team. When the game was aired in China, businesses and factories throughout the vast nation came to a virtual standstill. At the moment of victory, excited supporters detonated scarlet firecrackers and hoisted flags. Factories blew their whistles, storekeepers and their customers celebrated, and according to one Chinese civil servant, "absolute pandemonium broke out in our ministry. Even the vice ministers were shouting and cheering."

The silver medal for volleyball went to the United States. Although the sport had originally been an American invention, it had been adopted

A spike by a Chinese volleyballer eludes the U.S. defense. America had beaten China in a five-set preliminary match. In the finals, however, the Chinese crushed the Americans in straight sets.

and transformed after World War II by Soviet and Japanese athletes. They converted it from a casual rainy-day entertainment at the YMCA into an intense trial of strategy, strength, and skill. A small band of dedicated American sportswomen—led by the inspirational athlete Flo Hyman—devoted their energies to forging a team that would restore the U.S. to preeminence in the game. In Los Angeles their efforts began to bear fruit. After a brave battle against the superior Chinese, Hyman declared, "We accomplished a lot. We're proud of our silver medal."

Tragically, Hyman's own post-Olympic career on the professional volleyball circuit in Japan would end barely 18 months later: She collapsed and died during a match as a result of a congenital heart disorder. In her honor, the Women's Sports Foundation created a prize, the Flo Hyman Award, to be given to the female athlete sharing Hyman's "dignity, spirit, and commitment to excellence." Among its winners was another great African-American Olympian, Evelyn Ashford, who—like Hyman and so many other gifted female athletes—had showed the world what she was made of at the Los Angeles Games.

Flo Hyman (center) consoles her American teammates after their loss to the Chinese. Hyman, at 6 feet 5 inches, was a towering presence and the top player in the tournament.

Fireworks bring the Games of the XXIII Olympiad to an end. The pageantry of the closing ceremony concluded with a stage full of singers and break-dancers, a laser show, and a visit from a purported space alien.

RIVER OF GOLD

THE XXIII OLYMPIAD

On a December day in Los Angeles, city of rumors, the gossip mills were in high gear. Reporters hovered outside the offices of the Los Angeles Olympic Organizing Committee, where auditors had just finished another scrutiny of the books for the 1984 Olympic Games. Soon, the LAOOC's executive vice president, Harry Usher, would emerge to announce the bottom line. The buzz among the waiting men and women of the press speculated that this would be no routine financial report. Everyone already knew that the Games had ended up in the black. Back in September, a preliminary report had predicted $150 million in profits—an astounding sum, given the Olympics' recent years of fiscal travail. But leaks from LAOOC insiders intimated that the total might go even higher.

The irony was sublime: These were the Games that nobody in the world had wanted, including a goodly portion of the citizens of the host city that had won them by default. Moreover,

LAOOC chief Peter Ueberroth had warned every step of the way that the whole enterprise teetered on the edge of a fiscal abyss. Pennies had been pinched, belts tightened, unpaid workers conscripted to labor long and hard. The work and faith and persistence had paid off, as they should: That was the hallowed American way. Still, how high could the payoff be? Leaks from the LAOOC hinted at upward of $200 million, an impossibly stratospheric sum.

After a suitably theatrical delay, Harry Usher emerged to face the press. The surplus, he announced, "amounts to $215 million and may reach $250 million by June." Even as the journalists scribbled down the astonishing numbers, all those dollars, nestled in a warm cocoon of compound interest, were giving birth to still more dollars. In the end, the official final tally of profits from Los Angeles 1984 would fall comfortably within Usher's announced parameters: a cool $222.7 million.

Harry Usher, Executive Vice President/General Manager, Los Angeles Olympic Organizing Committee, 1984

Profits from the Los Angeles Games allowed the Amateur Athletic Foundation to advance sport in Southern California in both practice and theory. Students in a 1986 AAF-rowing clinic learn not to rock the boat.

Several thousand miles east of Los Angeles, in the Swiss city of Lausanne, the ruling powers of the International Olympic Committee looked out upon mountain-ringed Lake Leman and mulled over the news. When a river flows through a landscape, it reshapes the terrain, and a river of gold is no exception. The multimillion-dollar surplus from the Los Angeles Games would not only change the financial landscape of the IOC but would transform the map of the whole Olympic universe. Debates would rage over the disbursement of the funds, and financial issues would make—and break—the career of at least one ambitious sportsman. New policies on all sorts of issues would thenceforth reflect a heightened apprehension of the workings of the marketplace, the economics of television, the rhythms of the financial calendar.

When not studying balance sheets, the IOC was, to be sure, grappling with other matters: The evergreen issue of amateurism was surfacing once again, although "amateur" athletes' willingness to take pay for play had for some time been dwindling as a deadly sin. And, once more, the truculent politics of the Cold War were impinging on

the theoretically apolitical sphere of sport. The old Olympic ideal of friendly and peaceable competition risked sabotage by yet another boycott, triggered by the controversial choice of Seoul to host the 1988 Games.

But in the aftermath of Los Angeles, the top item on the Olympic agenda was, without doubt, money. Terms for the apportioning of profits had been settled years before the Games, at a time when the prospect of a significant surplus seemed unlikely. The 1979 contract between the IOC and LAOOC had stipulated that if the Games lost money, the United States Olympic Committee would make good any shortfall. If the Games made money, however, 60 percent of the profits would go to the USOC, 40 percent to the LAOOC for the development of athletics in Southern California. After the Games, the arrangement was amended: 40 percent to the USOC, 40 percent to the LAOOC, and 20 percent to America's national sports governing bodies, the groups overseeing each individual amateur sport.

As reports of a hefty surplus mounted, armies of petitioners lined up at the doors of both the

At the foundation's Paul Ziffren Sports Research Center, sports historians and scholars have a state of the art research facility at their disposal.

LAOOC and the USOC with their hands out. The Southern California Rapid Transit District, for instance, served notice that it would appreciate a $5 million reimbursement for extra bus service laid on during the Games. (The bus company would get nothing.) Moreover, a number of LAOOC employees grumped about the meager post-Games bonuses they had received for their pains—nothing like the $475,000 that Ueberroth was getting or the $350,000 that was going to Usher. (The workers would grump in vain.)

Meanwhile, the people who actually controlled the cash were making their own plans for spending it. There wasn't much argument when some 40 percent of the host city's surplus—nearly $90 million—went to create the Amateur Athletic Foundation. Based in Los Angeles, the AAF would use its Olympic legacy to create and maintain a world-class resource center and library, as well as an extensive program of community athletics. If the AAF was popular, though, much less enthusiasm was shown for the LAOOC's decision to award $2 million to a Los Angeles arts festival that, according to critics, had only a slender link to sports.

Far more controversial, however, was a suggestion from Ueberroth and Usher that $7 million from the Games' earnings should go to the Association of National Olympic Committees (ANOC) to reimburse foreign national Olympic committees for what they had paid to house their teams in the Olympic Village. The two Angelenos had approached IOC president Juan Antonio Samaranch with the idea. Naturally enough, Samaranch, caretaker of the welfare of all the world's Olympic committees, was delighted at the prospect. But Ueberroth's own LAOOC board of directors—as well as the USOC, which had veto power over all disbursements—were adamantly opposed. Critics in both camps argued that American corporations were responsible for the Games' profits, and those profits should stay in America. Moreover, no other nation had ever offered to subsidize U.S. Olympians who played on foreign soil, nor had the worldwide Olympic community ever thought of reimbursing their American brethren for the $11 million losses incurred by the 1980 Winter Games at Lake Placid. Anyway, four-fifths of the financial support for the Olympic movement already came from the United States. Finally, some critics suggested that self-interest lay behind Ueberroth's generosity: He wanted a seat on the IOC and was trying to curry favor with Samaranch.

With the money furor still unresolved, the USOC faced another crisis. At the beginning of 1985 it had elected a new president, John B. Kelly Jr., a second-generation Olympic oarsman, winner of a bronze medal at Melbourne 1956, and brother of glamorous Princess Grace of Monaco. Barely three weeks into his term, Kelly suffered a fatal heart attack while jogging along a Philadelphia street. The USOC's new vice president, Robert Helmick, found himself elevated to the presidency. Helmick was a lawyer from Des Moines, Iowa, who had once played water polo for an Iowa club. His involvement in the sport—as a player and as 1972 Olympic team manager—led eventually to the presidency of Fédération Internationale de Natation Amateur (FINA), the worldwide governing body for aquatic sports. In 1978 he became president of the Amateur Athletic Union but effectively presided over its eclipse in helping Congress draft the Amateur Sports Act. This landmark law took control of the nation's amateur athletics

away from the AAU and put the power firmly into the hands of the USOC.

Tall, white-haired, and elegantly handsome, Helmick was a man of imposing presence and luxurious tastes. He was also something of a shock to America's Olympic establishment. Unlike previous incumbents, he had no intention of being a figurehead who let the USOC's executive director run the show. Helmick wasted no time in announcing that he and he alone would henceforth sign all key television and sponsorship deals. To the bemusement of the USOC staff at their headquarters in Colorado Springs, he set up his own USOC office in Des Moines, and from Iowa came a new and virtuous agenda: Helmick declared himself in favor of cutting needless bureaucracy, upping the Olympic participation of women and minorities, and helping athletes financially, both through direct subsidies and by relaxing the rules for amateur status. He also paid a prompt visit to Samaranch in Lausanne to discuss the problematic Los Angeles surplus and whether any of it would go to the ANOC.

Before this interesting conversation could bear fruit, a seat fell vacant on the IOC. The senior U.S. member, Douglas Roby, announced his retirement. The choice of a successor rested entirely with Samaranch and the IOC, but the absence of a conventional election didn't stop interested parties from advancing their own candidacies. The stellar field included former U.S. Treasury Secretary William Simon and, of course, Ueberroth. But Ueberroth had made foes as well as friends in the Olympic movement: His newly published memoirs were highly unflattering to certain IOC members. And in any case, the USOC had its own favorite candidate—its long-serving executive director, F. Don Miller.

To many minds, Miller was perfect for the job. An innovative and farsighted manager, he had a genius for assessing problems and solving them. He had taken on the USOC's top administrative job in 1973 and had quickly spotted the organization's desperate need for ongoing financial stability. In response, he promoted the enlistment of sponsors and the licensing of Olympic paraphernalia, doing on a small scale what Ueberroth would later do on a vast scale to make the Los Angeles Games such a fiscal success. Moreover, Miller was much respected as a man relatively free of self-interest and truly devoted to sport.

But Miller and other hopefuls were soon disappointed. At its 1985 Session in Berlin, the IOC announced that Roby's replacement would be Robert Helmick. There were mutinous murmurings. How could the president of the world's richest National Olympic Committee (NOC), the one with the largest financial stake in the Olympic movement, function as a disinterested member of the international governing body— especially in the middle of a raging debate between the USOC and the ANOC? Had Helmick cut some kind of deal with Samaranch, promising USOC money for its foreign counterparts in return for the IOC seat?

Complete answers to those questions would never quite take on solid form, but there were clues: The ANOC would never see a penny of the Los Angeles profits, a fact indicating that Helmick did not use the money as a bargaining chip. (He could not have offered funds unilaterally in any case; the USOC board would have to give its blessing to any grant. And, as Ueberroth's abortive money offer testified, such a benediction was highly unlikely.)

It did seem, however, that Helmick had a distinctly international view of sport. During his visit with Samaranch, he had quietly promised his best efforts toward smoothing relations between the IOC and the USOC. Those relations had been strained for years, with the international body, primarily and traditionally a European institution, regarding the Americans as too independent, too parochial, too uppity. Helmick also pledged that he would try to involve more

Americans in the various international organizations concerned with governing sport.

Nine months after Helmick took his IOC seat, those promises began to take on substance: The IOC announced that the USOC was providing $4.2 million of the profits from the Los Angeles Games to set up a so-called Friendship Fund. Among other things, the fund would be used to underwrite sports competitions between U.S. teams and foreign ones. Any nation could petition for a match, and if the USOC thought American athletes would benefit from the contest, it would be scheduled. Several events were held, among them cycling competitions with Italy and with Switzerland and a track meet with Uganda.

In addition, the fund provided grants to improve

During the XXIII Olympiad, Robert Helmick, posing here in front of a group of national flags, rose to the presidency of the USOC and became an IOC member. One of his goals as USOC president was to foster a more international mindset within the American sports community.

MADAME AND THE IOC

For almost 20 years, Monique Berlioux was the most powerful woman in international amateur sports. Her start toward that lofty perch was pure serendipity. In March 1967, she approached the International Olympic Committee about producing a film on Olympic history. The committee didn't care for the project, but it liked her: She became the IOC's press secretary. So much for luck; then there was the matter of talent. Berlioux's toughness and managerial skills took her within two years to the IOC's top administrative post, and as executive director she would steer the vast bureaucracy through currents of unprecedented expansion.

The daughter of two swimming coaches, Berlioux had spent much of her early life in Paris pools, developing into one of the best backstrokers in France. She made the French Olympic team for London 1948, but any chance for a medal vanished after an emergency appendectomy three weeks before the Games. She retired from amateur swimming in the early 1950s and began a career as a journalist, writing two books on the Games.

As the IOC's chief administrator, Berlioux negotiated TV contracts, acted as liaison between the IOC and national Olympic committees, and edited the *Olympic Review*, the IOC magazine. Over the years she worked with three IOC presidents. The first two, Avery Brundage and Lord Killanin, were happy to give her wide latitude in decision making, and thus extensive power. That changed when Juan Antonio Samaranch took up residence at the IOC's Lausanne headquarters in 1981. The

transition was smooth initially, but by 1985 a strained atmosphere between the president and his executive director led to Berlioux's dismissal, an ungracious end to her years of service. Even so, her contribution to the Olympic movement—and to feminism—is undeniable: In an era when women had virtually no voice in international sport, she held her place among the giants.

training and coaching in foreign countries, and sometimes it supplied outright gifts, especially to sports programs in developing nations: sports gear for Belize and Bolivia and Guyana, for Chad and Gambia and Ghana. The fund would eventually metamorphose into three separate bureaucracies that continued its various functions.

Despite its far-flung good works, the Friendship Fund aroused controversy. In 1988 allegations surfaced in the press about the extremely lavish hospitality financed by the fund for IOC members visiting a USOC annual meeting in Washington, D.C., at Helmick's personal invitation. It

may not have been mere coincidence that the newspaper that broke the story was the *Gazette Telegraph*, based, like the USOC itself, in Colorado Springs. "The Friendship Fund," it reported, "has been used as a 'pork barrel' by a handful of Olympic officials to win prestigious positions in international sports organizations." The implication was clear enough: The fund was part of a power grab; Helmick, the paper suggested, was using the money to cement his own friendships with influential IOC colleagues.

Helmick's supporters countered with the argument that the Friendship Fund's whole purpose

was to strengthen U.S. ties to the international sport community and that hospitality to visitors was a legitimate part of that effort. As for Helmick himself, he seemed immune to criticism. In 1989, only four years after joining the IOC, he gained a seat on its 11-member Executive Board. Few newcomers had enjoyed such a speedy rise. But he didn't neglect his interests back at the USOC. His presidential term was drawing to an end, and according to the committee's constitution, the incumbent could not seek reelection. Helmick pointed out, however, that his only election had been to the vice presidency; his elevation had come as a result of John Kelly's untimely death. Now he sought and gained the chance to run for president in his own right.

Some students of Olympic politics surmised that the erstwhile water-polo player from Des Moines was swimming resolutely toward the position of heir apparent to Samaranch himself. But Helmick's ascent to the Olympic summit was suddenly aborted. In 1991 the newspaper *USA Today* printed allegations about his personal business dealings. He had, said the article, abused his power within the Olympic movement by selling his services as a private consultant to certain companies and organizations seeking to do Olympic-related business. Accusations of dubious dealings began to flow in from many directions. Stoutly denying that he had done anything unethical—or even unusual, for one in his position—Helmick nevertheless yielded to pressure and resigned as USOC president in September 1991.

The USOC had to act, either to clear Helmick's name or expose any misconduct. Two months after his resignation, the committee published the findings of an inquiry chaired by Arnold Burns, former deputy U.S. attorney general, concluding that Helmick had "repeatedly violated conflict of interest provisions of the USOC and created a perception that he was trafficking on his Olympic positions for the

benefit of private clients." The USOC released the report to the press but never officially accepted it. This was probably because the report's position—that no USOC member should be part of any concern doing business with the USOC—would have compromised any number of members, not just Helmick.

Nevertheless, the damage had been done. At the beginning of December, Helmick flew to Lausanne for a meeting of the Executive Board and officially terminated his links with the IOC. He did not, however, sever all ties to the sports world. Returning to the full-time practice of law, Helmick remained a member, albeit inactive, of the USOC's board of directors, and he became a founding director of the Greater Des Moines Sports Authority, which, among other things, oversees local Junior Olympics activities.

As for the Los Angeles 1984 profits that had come to figure so crucially in the careers of Helmick and others, most of the money was put to good use. The Amateur Athletic Foundation, established with the host city's share of the surplus, would prove invaluable, both to aspiring athletes and to sports historians and researchers. All the USOC's share, about $111 million, would go toward establishing the U.S. Olympic Foundation, whose purpose was to fund the USOC in perpetuity.

Helmick had certainly counted as a major player in the international arena of sport, but the man who made the most indelible mark on the Olympic movement during the 1980s wasn't even a member of the IOC. Horst Dassler, via the goods he manufactured, was present in spirit if not in flesh, wherever sport was played. His footwear skimmed the finish line at every track meet on the planet, glided on silver blades across the ice, pounded a billion miles of city pavement, soccer field, and gymnasium floor. Sweatshirts, jackets, and sports bags, on athletic champions and ordinary

Arm in arm during good times, young Adolf Dassler *(left)* and brother Rudolf look like the prosperous cobbler's sons they were. Adolf followed his father's trade by founding Adidas in 1920. Rudolf joined Adidas four years later, but he would eventually split with his brother and go on to establish the competing firm of Puma.

citizens alike, bore the triple stripes and trefoil logo of Adidas. In fact, the Dassler clan's products had overflowed sport and spilled into fashion, creating athletic chic for all the world.

The history of the Adidas empire resembled an old European folktale such as might have been collected by the Brothers Grimm or set to music by Richard Wagner. Its ingredients included a medieval Bavarian townscape, a journey to great wealth from the humblest beginnings, a lifelong rivalry between two ambitious siblings, and a family feud that lasted beyond the grave.

The saga began in the 1920s. Its original antagonists were two young German cobblers named Adolf and Rudolf Dassler, sons of a shoemaker and a laundress in the small factory town of Herzogenaurach. Together the brothers built up a shoemaking business, beginning with house slippers, then turning their attention to a new growth area—athletics shoes. By 1936, when their homeland hosted the Olympic Games, the Dasslers had become leaders in their field: Jesse Owens wore their spikes when he won his four gold medals.

But after Germany's defeat in World War II, the brothers quarreled. Rudolf, presumably because of connections with the Nazi Party, had been imprisoned by the American occupation forces; brother Adolf, although also a party member, stayed free. After a year in custody, Rudolf emerged with a burning grudge, convinced that Adolf hadn't tried hard enough to secure his release. With no hope of salvaging the partnership, the brothers went their separate ways. Each presided over his own sports-shoe factory, and the two factories were on opposite sides of the little river Aurach, which divided the town of Herzogenaurach. Rudolf christened his firm Puma after the fleet jungle cat; Adolf, whose nickname was Adi, named his company after himself, contracting Adi Dassler into Adidas.

From that moment on, the only discourse between the brothers was an endless volley of

lawsuits, restraining orders, disputes over advertising claims, and allegations of industrial espionage. Spurred on by their bosses, each design team strove to outwit its rival, firing fusillades of brilliant technical innovations.

But Adolf and Rudolf reserved their heaviest artillery for the battle to gain the hearts, minds, and custom of champions, especially when television changed the face of sport. No shoemaker could wish for a better shop window than the small screen lighting up the planet's living rooms; no advertiser could invent a more persuasive image than the sight of his product on a winner's foot as it crossed the finish line. Blandishments to both professionals and amateurs ranged from gifts of free equipment to under-the-table payoffs in cash. Savvy athletes began to wheel and deal like commodities brokers, jockeying between Adidas and Puma in search of the sweetest offer.

The showdown came at Mexico City 1968. By

With a clutch of Adidas soccer shoes in hand, Adolf Dassler stands in front of the German Soccer Federation's team bus before leaving for the World Cup matches in 1954. Dassler gave the team cleats with interchangeable studs, his new invention, and the Germans won the tournament.

The Adidas-France factory in Dettwiller was Horst Dassler's own little fief-dom within his father's empire. Horst established the branch in 1959. Within 10 years, it could outproduce its parent company. Dassler's first coup for Adidas came at Melbourne 1956 when he gave free shoes to gold-medal prospects.

that time, a second generation had joined the fray: Adi's boy Horst and Rudolf's eldest son, Armin. Adidas had struck its first blow three years before the Games by granting franchise rights to market Adidas shoes to a Mexican shoe company called Canada. In exchange, Mexican authorities granted Adidas the exclusive sports-shoe concession for the Olympic village, plus the right to import a consignment of its European-made products without paying the normal duty.

Outraged at this favoritism, Puma appealed in vain to the Mexican government. Next, Rudolf's firm tried to get a piece of the action by shipping its goods to Mexico under an ambiguous label

that could easily have been mistaken for Adidas's own. A sharp-eyed customs official caught on to this ruse. Despite Puma's denials of any attempt to deceive, the company's sales representative endured a brief but anxious stay in a government detention center.

With the Games under way, the action shifted to the Olympic Village. Rumors circulated about the sums that the two sports-shoe giants were prepared to offer. The number of zeros varied depending on the storyteller, but the amounts were certainly large enough to help athletes overcome any reservations about breaking rules or jeopardizing their amateur status.

The behind-the-scenes auction soon became an open secret. According to some estimates, as many as 200 competitors accepted payoffs. At least one athlete was, allegedly, naive enough to walk into the Olympic Village bank brandishing a check, made out in his name and drawn on Puma's account, for several thousand dollars. A few months after the Games ended, *Sports Illustrated* broke the story that would forevermore be known as the Shoe Wars.

Inevitably, the conflict cooled over the years, although the two companies still thirsted to share the winners' triumphs. After Los Angeles 1984, Adidas's own corporate literature would proudly announce that 124 of the 140 participating national teams had used Adidas products, and 259 medals had gone to athletes wearing Adidas gear.

On taking over Adidas after his father's death in 1978, Horst Dassler had grown ever more intent on forging profitable links between commerce and sport. Instead of simply signing up individual athletes, Horst concentrated on building relationships with national and international sports federations. Thanks to the share of television money flowing into their coffers, these bodies had waxed rich and powerful. And Horst Dassler spoke their language, literally and otherwise. He was fluent in several tongues, sociable, and an enthusiastic athlete himself. He had played hockey in his youth, thrown the javelin, run track. Off the field, he was a champion at networking, information gathering, assimilating, strategizing. "Wherever the action is," he declared, "we need to be there."

A lot of the action took place inside the corridors of Olympic power. In 1980, in an article in the IOC's own *Olympic Review*, Dassler had made his pitch: "Sport needs industry if it is to continue to grow," he averred. "Sport gives the opportunity for an exalted 'image' for industry's publicity, and so to work together would be mutually beneficial." And who better to broker this marriage made in heaven than Dassler himself? While still running Adidas, he had extended his interests into the lucrative field of sports marketing, negotiating new relationships between major advertisers and prime international athletic events.

At their 1983 Session in New Delhi, IOC members agreed on the need to free the Olympic Games from the golden shackles of America's television networks, whose purchase of broadcast rights had become the IOC's primary source of revenue. Getting free meant finding other motherlodes to mine, and that was where Horst Dassler and the IOC would come together on an official footing. Dassler had lobbied Juan Antonio Samaranch long and hard about exploiting the Olympics' endless commercial possibilities, and Peter Ueberroth's efforts in Los Angeles had underlined the point. If the LAOOC could court commercial sponsors to underwrite the Games, so could the IOC—and on a long-term basis and global scale. To explore these opportunities, Samaranch inaugurated the New Sources of Finance Commission, to be chaired by Horst Dassler.

A few months before the New Delhi Session, Dassler had set up a specialized sports-marketing company called International Sport Leisure, or ISL. The firm's first major contract was with the Fédération Internationale de Football Association (FIFA) to sell key events on the world soccer calendar, including the 1984 European championships in Paris and the 1986 World Cup in Mexico City. To create and carry out the new global marketing strategy for the Olympic Games, Samaranch looked no further than ISL. (And, doubtless, IOC leaders of an earlier generation writhed in their graves: Longtime IOC president Avery Brundage and his like-minded colleagues had regarded the Dasslers, with their relentless under-the-table payoffs, as mephistophelian corrupters of Olympism's finest ideals. Now, it seemed, the wiliest fox of all had been picked to guard the henhouse.)

But before Dassler could sell any Olympic

IOC president Juan Antonio Samaranch *(left)* awards Horst Dassler the Olympic Order, the IOC's highest honor, in 1984. Once accused of corrupting Olympic athletes with bribes, Dassler changed from rogue to savior in the 1980s by teaching the Olympic movement, now openly market-minded, how to sell itself.

sponsorships to corporate clients, he had to sell his approach to the rest of the Olympic family. Under the old system, each individual national Olympic committee had controlled all the Olympic marketing rights within its own borders; Dassler had to convince the NOCs to cede most of these rights to ISL, which would then market them worldwide on the IOC's behalf.

Dassler secured the help of Mexico's Mario Vazquez Raña, head of the ANOC, who persuaded the Latin American NOCs to come on board. Richer nations—the United States, Great Britain, Germany, France, Japan, Australia—took more urging, not to mention liberal cash incentives. These NOCs were not about to sign away their very lucrative marketing rights just for love of the Olympic ideal or for the sake of its guardians in Lausanne. First ISL had to promise each NOC more money than it could ever have hoped to raise from sponsors on its own. Fortunately, Dassler had ample resources for buying goodwill, especially once the massive Japanese advertising agency Dentsu had bought 49 percent of ISL.

In 1985, after two years of political and financial negotiations, Samaranch and Dassler announced the birth of TOP—The Olympic Program—for Calgary 1988 and Seoul 1988. Dassler courted the cream of the global marketplace, industrialists who understood the commercial logic of investing their wares with Olympic glamor and glory. Not everyone danced to his tune. The Campbell Soup Company, for instance, had paid the USOC $500,000 to sponsor the 1984 Olympic Winter Games at Sarajevo but drew the line at ISL's suggested $7.2-million price tag for Calgary; American Express, one of Peter Ueberroth's sponsors for Los Angeles, sent ISL packing for the same reason. In the end, nine companies entered the program. Coca-Cola, Kodak, VISA, Federal Express, Brother, National Panasonic, Philips, 3M, and Time, Incorporated collectively handed over more than $100 million for the privilege of using the Olympic rings worldwide on their products and packaging and in their advertisements.

Dassler lived to sell two of the Games: Calgary 1988 and Seoul 1988. But in April 1987 he

confronted an adversary impervious to a deal: Horst Dassler died of cancer at the age of 51. Nevertheless, even as Juan Antonio Samaranch led the mourning for "a great friend of the Olympic idea," a dozen multinational sponsors were already lined up for TOP II, the sponsorship program for Albertville 1992 and Barcelona 1992.

The days when Avery Brundage had struggled so fiercely to protect the Olympic rings from any taint of commerce were long gone. In the reign of Juan Antonio Samaranch, the IOC would struggle just as fiercely to ally sport and Mammon. Advocates of the new pragmatic, market-oriented approach pointed to the Olympic Solidarity Commission as proof that filthy lucre could be put to noble uses.

In 1961, Count Jean de Beaumont, a French IOC member, had set up an international committee to give financial aid to poorer NOCs and to help train athletes, coaches, and sports administrators worldwide. For nearly two decades the enterprise scraped along on a lot of good will and very little cash. Things changed radically in 1979, when Peter Ueberroth sold the television rights for Los Angeles 1984 to ABC. When the IOC got its $30-million share of the proceeds, the aid committee found itself rolling in more money than the Count de Beaumont could ever have dreamed of.

Relaunched in 1982 under the new name of the Olympic Solidarity Commission, the committee began translating ideals into action, with projects helping everyone from soccer players in Belize to fledgling archers in the Solomon Islands. Specialists in sports medicine, coaching, and administration carried their expertise to all points of the compass. NOCs in poorer countries got much-needed financial aid to buy equipment and send athletes to the Games. Because the efficient Ueberroth machine had passed on the television millions so many years in advance, Los Angeles itself reaped a benefit: Third World athletes who

On the grounds of the Amateur Athletic Foundation headquarters, Anita DeFrantz, one of two American IOC members, stands next to the Olympic Flame Helix, a memorial symbolizing the continuing Olympic spirit of Los Angeles 1984. DeFrantz, a bronze-medal rower at Montreal 1976, has served as AAF president since 1987.

POWER PLAY

While women played expanded roles on Olympism's athletic stage during the 1980s, they were also filtering in behind the scenes—where the real power lay. The International Olympic Committee, a men's club for almost nine decades, finally integrated its membership in 1981 with the induction of two women, Flor Isava-Fonseca and Pirjo Häggman. Isava-Fonseca, Venezuela's minister of sport, had obvious credentials; so did Finland's Häggman, a two-time Olympian.

The men-only barrier was down, and subsequent progress was slow but steady. Mary Glen-Haig of Great Britain became an IOC member in 1983, Princess Nora of Liechtenstein in 1984, Anita DeFrantz of the United States in 1986, Princess Anne of Great Britain in 1988, Carol Anne Letheran of Canada in 1990 and gymnastics great Vera Čáslaská of Czechoslovakia in 1995.

Like their male colleagues, the women IOC members have varied in the quality and quantity of their contributions to the Olympic movement. The two most active female members have been Isava-Fonseca and DeFrantz, who ascended to the Executive Board in 1990 and 1992 respectively. Their elevation to Olympism's top decision-making body—as much a milestone as the first women's Olympic marathon—marked real progress toward parity for women in international sports.

A poster designed by Swiss artist Hans Erni for the 1986 IOC Session in Lausanne combines ancient and contemporary elements. Its central figures are reminiscent of the Attic black-figure art of pre-Classical Greece.

be held midway through each Olympiad. In other words, there would be Olympic Games of one sort or the other every two years.

To ease the new arrangement into place, the 1992 Olympic Winter Games at Albertville would be followed two years later by those at Lillehammer, returning to the usual four-year interval before Nagano 1998. The change would prove as helpful to sponsors as to broadcasters, giving advertisers more opportunity and time to promote their Olympic connections.

In a climate so drenched with money, old distinctions between amateur athletes and professionals—already crumbling— were examined yet again. The minutes of the 1987 IOC Session in Istanbul recorded "one of the biggest debates ever," with 33 members clamoring to speak on the implications of tennis's return to the Games on an experimental basis. Tennis had left the Olympics after Paris 1924, the first sport to bow out because its leaders felt themselves to be in hopeless conflict with the IOC's strict view of amateurism. Now tennis was ready to return— world-class tennis with world-class athletes, and that meant professional athletes.

"Opinions," said the minutes, "were very divided—to say the least." Samaranch, with the shrewdness of a seasoned negotiator, placed the item last on the agenda of a morning session that would have no coffee break. Hunger, he reasoned, would help concentrate his colleagues' minds and speed up the discussion.

Stomachs might have rumbled, but so did the debate—for two solid hours. U.S. member Anita DeFrantz reminded her colleagues that any tennis player who wished to achieve his or her full potential had no alternative but to turn pro. Traditionalists argued that such careerism violated the most sacred tenets of Olympism. Romania's long-serving Alexandru Siperco countered by invoking the name of Pierre de Coubertin, declaring that the father of the modern Games had never intended such rigidity.

might not otherwise have been able to compete at the Games had their traveling expenses paid by Olympic Solidarity.

The glut of money would even change the Olympic calendar. Rich as the television networks might be, even they were beginning to complain that the cost of bidding in a single year for two sets of broadcast rights—one for the Summer Games and one for the Winter— imposed too big a fiscal burden. It was getting harder for the networks to recoup enough money from advertisers to turn an adequate profit on the ever-burgeoning outlays. Not wishing to kill the goose that was laying the golden eggs, the IOC voted at its 1986 Session in Lausanne to stagger the timing of the two festivals. Instead of taking place in the same year as the Summer Games, the Winter Games would thenceforth

Athletes in today's world, said Siperco, should be free to make a living from their sports. In the end, the IOC voted to welcome tennis home.

The bastion had been breached, and through the gap would soon pour career athletes from other sports. Most of the old, frayed restrictions against professionals, still in place at Los Angeles 1984, were dropped. Of course, inconsistencies remained among the individual sport federations as to what athletes were eligible to compete in the Olympics. Yet by 1992, even those most professional of all professionals, the well-paid stars of the National Basketball Association, became eligible for membership in Samaranch's new Olympic family.

The final resolution of the amateurism issue had been almost a century in coming, and nobody had expected it to arrive without fireworks. These were pale, however, compared with the political pyrotechnics detonated by the choice of Seoul as 1988 host city. The two Koreas, South and North, glowered at each other across the 38th parallel in seemingly endless enmity. North Korea first threatened to absent itself altogether if Seoul were chosen, then suddenly changed course and suggested that both Koreas host the Games. The two old enemies united as happy cohosts hardly seemed viable.

But if South Korea alone won the Olympic plum, might not that choice set off another Eastern bloc boycott? Montreal 1976, Moscow 1980, and Los Angeles 1984 had all survived major defections, but those Games had been diminished. No one wanted any more boycotts—not the IOC, not the sponsors now massively underwriting the Games, not the athletes, not the global audience who expected to watch all the world's best athletes compete against one another.

Samaranch resolved that boycotts would end. Between 1985 and 1988 he spent much of his time airborne, crisscrossing the continents in endless shuttle diplomacy. All options were considered. For a time, it looked as if archery, table tennis, some soccer and cycling, as well as women's volleyball—a sport with a large Eastern bloc following—might take place in North Korea. But by offering so much of what they had been asking for, Samaranch called the North Koreans' bluff—and won. North Korea dropped its aspirations to cohost and decided to sit out the Games. Two sympathetic Communist countries, Albania and Cuba, joined in the boycott. Only Cuba would be missed. And, in the end, Seoul would prove another brilliant financial success, bolstering the proposition that the Olympic Games were a party too good for any nation to willingly forego.

THE CANADIAN HERITAGE

From Cretaceous beasts to modern Mounties, Canada through the Ages was the theme for the Opening Ceremony of the 15th Olympic Winter Games. The Calgary Stampede band started the musical program by charging onto the infield of McMahon Stadium in wagons, a maneuver intended to simulate a pioneer land rush. An earlier era was represented by members of five Native American tribes from Alberta, who arrived on horseback (above). Even earlier times—a couple of hundred million years earlier—were suggested by the dinosaur-shaped balloons that lofted from the stadium. Unfortunately, winds gusting up to 40 miles per hour wreaked havoc with the faux lizards. Flashing forward, the salute ended with a formation of red-jacketed Royal Canadian Mounted Police cantering onto the field to begin the flag-raising ceremony.

As always, the traditional program began with the Parade of Nations. Spectators cheered marchers from 57 nations, a record number for a Winter Games. Athletes were welcomed by Frank King, president of Calgary's Olympic organizing committee, and by IOC president Juan Antonio Samaranch. Jean Sauvé, Canada's governor general, officially opened the Games, and Pierre Harvey, a Canadian cross-country skier, took the athlete's oath. As the Olympic banner rose on its staff, a squadron of planes decorated the sky with the Olympic rings.

The formalities over, the cultural celebration resumed, featuring western dancers strutting a fancy two-step on the infield, followed by a production number saluting Canada's French and English settlers.

ACES AND ALSO-RANS

For the jubilant spectators jammed 10-deep alongside the bobsled track, it was the moment when carnival came to Calgary. Crowds this big seldom assembled for the finals of the four-man bobs—and certainly not to see just one team, and certainly not to see a team as mediocre as the main attraction in this event. Nevertheless, this particular four-man crew had bemused officials and delighted the paying customers from the first moment it checked into Calgary's Olympic Village. Capturing the limelight instantly, basking in it, dancing in the discos, this crew had shamelessly peddled fund-raising T-shirts and the tapes of their own official anthem: "We be trainin', gainin', strainin', and painin', but we ain't complainin'."

If the sprightly tune sounded suspiciously like reggae, that's because it was. And if its singers seemed an utter anomaly among the chiseled, chilly, intent men who dominated international bobsledding, that's because they were. Geography alone marked them as odd in their sport because they came not from Germany or Austria, not from the French or Swiss or Italian Alps, not from any land of icy peaks and frosty climate—but from Jamaica: sun-splashed, palm-studded, balmy Jamaica, where sleds are as useful as toothpicks are to ducks, and snowflakes as rare as red diamonds.

The piquant combination of novelty, chutzpah, and grit had made the Jamaican sledders instant cult heroes at Calgary. Of course, no one expected them to win; it was enough that they were ludicrously and joyously there.

In the first of the four runs allotted to the four-man bobs, the new celebrities finished 24th among 26 entries and looked amateurish. No surprise. They were, after all, amateurs—increasingly rare creatures among modern Olympians. Their second run was even worse: They dropped one notch, to next to last.

Jamaican four-man bobsled team, Calgary 1988

The Jamaicans finish their third run in an unintentionally unorthodox way, fueling criticism that they were making a mockery of elite sport.

Now the islanders hoped for better as they set out on their third try. But as their green and yellow sled launched itself down the incline and zoomed into the first turn, their maverick bid for Olympic glory turned into the roller-coaster ride from hell. Cheers and laughter froze in a thousand throats as the sled flew out of control at a speed approaching 80 miles per hour.

Hammering unchecked down the sharp bends of the ice-slick chute, the metal pod slammed from wall to wall like a pinball, skittering wildly. Then it flipped over on its side, thrusting its riders' heads within inches of the icy surface, lacerating the track in a downward skid that seemed to last forever. When the battered juggernaut finally came to a halt, its occupants—dazed, but miraculously still intact—eased themselves out of the wreckage. Gathering their pride, they rose up and strode off the course like wounded warriors, waving to the cameras and shaking hands with admirers.

As the Jamaicans made their gelid exit, the controversy that had simmered throughout the 15th

Olympic Winter Games came to a boil. For these sunny island bobsledders were not the only oddities at Calgary. The same event that had attracted Jamaica had also lured entrants from the Virgin Islands and Mexico—as well as from Monaco, in the person of His Royal Highness Prince Albert, heir to a throne but a novice on the track. The eternally snowless island of Fiji in the South Pacific produced a contestant for the Nordic skiing events. And the perilous ski jump showcased the antics of a British daredevil who styled himself Eddie the Eagle, but whose aerodynamic skills seemed better suited to a henhouse than to the mountain aerie of that bird of prey.

In the view of some members of the winter sports establishment, such eccentrics not only undermined the dignity and debased the standards of the Games but also posed a physical threat to onlookers and participants. Mishandled equipment could ruin a track; sleds, skis, or bodies flying out of control might wreak unthinkable mayhem. (Indeed, even for the most competent athletes, winter sports venues are dangerous

A design inspired by Native-American art adorns the front of the Calgary 1988 winners' medals *(top left)*. Champions also received a diploma *(left)* to acknowledge their triumphs. Organizers minted 10,000 commemorative medals *(bottom)* as keepsakes for athletes and officials. A committee of volunteers created the stylized design of the Calgary skyline set against a background of the Rocky mountains for the front of it. The official snowflake logo of the Calgary Games was on the reverse of both the commemorative and winners' medals *(upper and lower right)*.

places: Calgary witnessed a gruesome fatal accident when a physician for the Austrian team collided with another skier on the slopes and fell to his death under a snow-grooming machine.)

But if the offbeat outsiders were dangerous, they nevertheless had an infectious charm—and they had friends as well as critics. Some Olympians pointed out that the oddball entries and lovable losers were probably the truest heirs to the philosophy of Pierre de Coubertin, founder of the modern Olympic movement, who believed that sport should be for everyone and that its highest aim was the joy of taking part— not a fistful of medals. "There's room for everyone," observed one Canadian Olympic veteran.

In Calgary's windswept, wide-open spaces, there surely seemed to be room for everyone, for the oddballs—and for the superstars: If these Games featured some engaging sideshows, their center stage was dominated by some titans of winter sports and some epic showdowns. It was

here that beautiful Katarina Witt of East Germany and America's Debi Thomas had their operatic skate-off, while male figure skaters from Canada and the United States jousted in the "Battle of the Brians." On the speed-skating oval, competitors moving at velocities almost faster than the eye could see sliced seven new world records out of the ice. Meanwhile, on the ski slopes, great feats were performed by both new and established champions: the mystical Swiss Pirmin Zurbriggen, Italy's swashbuckling Alberto Tomba, and a handful of female rivals from Europe's Alpine spine. The ski jump saw the triumphs of Finland's Matti Nykänen, whose three gold medals were rendered even shinier when his government awarded him a congratulatory $40,000.

For the West's athletic elite, success at Calgary spelled fame and fortune—the hallmarks of their Olympiad. Standing on the victors' podium, skiers and skaters used their gleaming

MASKS AND MADNESS

More than 2,000 Canadian artists from 18 different disciplines took part in the five-week-long Calgary Olympic Arts Festival, held in conjunction with the Games. Running from January 23 to February 28, the festival showcased literature, as well as visual and performing arts. Dance productions ranged from traditional presentations by the National Ballet of Canada to avant-garde offerings such as *Incognito* from the Desrosiers Dance Theater of Toronto. *Incognito* was an interpretation of a man's descent into madness.

Controversy surrounded *The Spirit Sings*, an exhibition of Native-American art and artifacts from the time of the Europeans' arrival in Canada. Protests by the Lubicon Indians, a tribe from northern Alberta, caused several museums to limit their contributions to the exhibition. Nevertheless, *The Spirit Sings* constituted the largest collection of Native-American art ever displayed, and it was the festival's most widely attended exhibit.

Olympic visitors didn't have to go to a gallery or museum to experience the arts festival. Some Olympic venues—as well as the lobbies, windows, and hallways of several Calgary skyscrapers—housed technological works reflecting hassles of the modern world. Most of the high-tech artwork was removed after the Games, but one exhibit found a permanent home. *Mask* was a collection of 30 oversize color photographs that adorned the entrance to the Saddledome, the venue for ice sports. It showed menacing examples of the protective face gear worn by professional ice hockey goalies between 1959 and 1985. The huge images were donated to the stadium after the Winter Games.

new medals to semaphore a message to their commercial sponsors and patrons: The price for endorsing products and displaying logos was about to rise.

For the Jamaican bobsledders, however, the most important payoff was probably survival with skulls intact. Even the team's most ardent supporters at Calgary must have wondered what had induced four men from pleasant climes to brave frigid snowfields in order to fling themselves nearly 5,000 feet down an icy chute. The short answer was simple: They wanted to.

The long answer began on a September day in 1987. George Fitch, a former U.S. diplomat based in Jamaica and later a businessman who traveled there often, was visiting with a friend on the island, enjoying a bottle of the excellent local rum and chatting about Jamaica's prospects in the coming Summer Olympics in Seoul. Jamaican athletes were no strangers to the Summer Games, and daydreaming, Fitch began to ponder how the islanders might redirect their talent into winter sports. Inspiration struck: Jamaica was producing some remarkably good sprinters, runners whose speed might afford an edge in pushing off the bobsled at the start of its run. Take some sprinters and make them sledders, and there you had it: a bobsled team.

The Jamaican Olympic Association didn't share Fitch's enthusiasm for this novel idea, and the IOC and the Fédération Internationale de Bobsleigh et de Tobogganing were equally cool. Even the island's athletes were skeptical. But Fitch was a persistent man, and he finally managed to gather a set of fighting-fit recruits: team captain and driver Dudley Stokes, who developed his fine hand-eye coordination as a helicopter pilot in the Jamaican army; brakeman Devon Harris, an army lieutenant; Michael White, another army man; and Chris Stokes, a college sprinter at Washington State University

and the only sprinter that Fitch managed to snare. An unofficial member of the party was Freddie Powell, a reggae-playing electrician who acted as general promoter and vendor of the team T-shirts that quickly became the top seller among the Games' souvenirs.

The Jamaicans' initiation into the mysteries of bobsledding was fast and furious: By the time Calgary rolled around, the best prepared among them had less than four months' training, and one member of the crew had arrived on the scene only a week before the Games began. Snow, for most of them, was familiar only from pictures on Christmas cards. In spite of these limitations, Jamaica's two-man team of Stokes and Harris made a tolerable showing at Calgary, finishing 30th out of 41 starters.

The rookies were not as naive or foolhardy as some of their critics imagined. The Jamaicans knew that they were raw beginners, but there was nothing whimsical about their dedication to the sport. After Calgary the islanders would continue their training and would compete again at Albertville 1992 and at Lillehammer two years later. At Lillehammer they would finish in an eminently respectable 14th place, ahead of the team from the United States. The Jamaicans were no fools when it came to marketing, either. After the 1988 Games they were, briefly, a hot ticket for commercials, and they were paid for the rights to the story that would ultimately become the film *Cool Runnings*, a highly fictionalized account that was nevertheless amusing—and a box-office hit.

In any case, some of the Jamaicans' travails at Calgary were shared even by the sport's front runners—the Swiss who won gold in the four-man event, the Soviets who triumphed in the two-man bobs, and the East German team that took the silver in both. The region's notorious Chinook, western cousin of the freakish wind known as the Föhn that plagued European skiers in the Alps, streamed in to lift the temperature

THE GAMES AT A GLANCE

	FEBRUARY 13	FEBRUARY 14	FEBRUARY 15	FEBRUARY 16	FEBRUARY 17	FEBRUARY 18	FEBRUARY 19	FEBRUARY 20	FEBRUARY 21	FEBRUARY 22	FEBRUARY 23	FEBRUARY 24	FEBRUARY 25	FEBRUARY 26	FEBRUARY 27	FEBRUARY 28
OPENING CEREMONY	■															
ALPINE SKIING			■	■	■		■	■	■	■		■	■	■	■	
BIATHLON									■			■		■		
BOBSLED									■	■					■	■
CROSS-COUNTRY SKIING		■	■		■		■		■			■			■	
FIGURE SKATING		■		■	■	■		■	■	■	■	■			■	■
HOCKEY	■	■	■	■	■	■	■	■	■	■	■	■	■	■		
LUGE		■	■	■		■	■									
NORDIC COMBINED												■	■			■
SKI JUMPING		■			■			■								
SPEED SKATING		■			■	■		■	■	■				■	■	■
CLOSING CEREMONY																■
DEMONSTRATION SPORTS																
CURLING		■	■	■	■		■	■								
FREESTYLE SKIING											■	■		■		
SHORT-TRACK SPEED SKATING										■	■	■	■			

almost instantly to an unseasonable springlike high. The bobsled run's state-of-the-art refrigeration system couldn't keep the course properly iced. The Chinook not only thawed the run but compounded the sabotage by blowing sand all over it.

Even if the organizers of the Calgary Olympics couldn't control the winds, they earned an accolade from IOC president Juan Antonio Samaranch: "These have been the best-organized Olympic Winter Games in history," he said. It was a formula phrase, a standard tribute offered by the IOC president to every host city that doesn't botch the job completely. But for a city that had, for three Olympiads in succession, failed in its bids for the Games, the words still sounded sweet.

When Calgary was finally named as the successful candidate for 1988, outsiders' reactions ranged from amusement to amazement. Standing in windswept isolation on the western edge of the Canadian prairies, with the rugged peaks of the Rocky Mountains rearing up some 50 miles away, the city—home of the world's biggest annual rodeo, the Calgary Stampede—had a reputation as the quintessential cow town. But year after year, while the cowboys struggled to stay aboard their bucking broncos, oil wells had sprung up among the cowpats, turning the prairie city into the prosperous home base for 800 of Canada's registered producers of oil and natural gas.

Riding on the crest of the 1970s oil boom, Calgary had mushroomed into a city of 640,000 people, with suburban sprawl creeping across the grasslands and glass-walled office towers stabbing at the skies. So futuristic was Calgary's architecture that the makers of the film *Superman II* chose it as the location for their fictional Metropolis.

Still, this burgeoning hub of industry liked to remember its pioneer roots. It named its urban thoroughfares after the old native trails that now lay buried under concrete. In its Wild West saloons, Stetson-wearing financial analysts, cowboy-booted computer experts, and buckskin-clad

Sharply contrasting old and new Calgary city halls both appear ready for the Winter Games.

advertising copywriters line-danced to a country-and-western beat. And, carrying cattle and chemicals alike, the mile-long freight trains still blew their lonesome whistles as they rumbled through town at night.

Since the beginning of the 1960s, Calgary's leaders had set their sights on lassoing the Winter Games. Rebuffed by the IOC in 1964, 1968, and 1972, most of the project's original promoters had long since lost heart when, in 1978, a few members of the Calgary Boosters' Club began contemplating another try.

Led by businessman Frank W. King, a small but enthusiastic band of boosters pondered why earlier bids had failed and faced the fact that Calgary, despite its northern setting and its proximity to prime ski areas, lacked first-rate facilities for winter sports. King and his colleagues decided to turn this weakness to their advantage: If Calgary got the Games, they said, the organizers would raise funds to build a stunning array of

world-class venues, establishing Calgary as a permanent center of sporting excellence—a lasting Olympic legacy for the benefit of the city, the province of Alberta, and all Canada. And this bequest would not consist merely of bricks and mortar but of a substantial development fund for training Canadian athletes.

The budget, initially drafted at brainstorming sessions around King's kitchen table, called for most of the funding to come from the sale of television rights and from corporate sponsorship. In support of this approach, King pointed to Los Angeles, where Peter Ueberroth was tearing ahead with his private-enterprise strategy for the 1984 Los Angeles Games. But King, unlike his California role model, also scripted a financial role for the public sector, with municipal, provincial, and federal contributions to get the ambitious construction program off the ground.

The boosters' first hurdle was a bid for the right to bid. Would-be host cities had to gain the

Canada Olympic Park

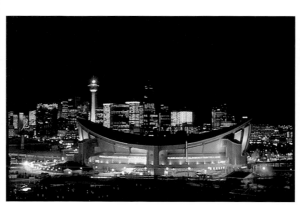

Olympic Saddledome

Nakiska

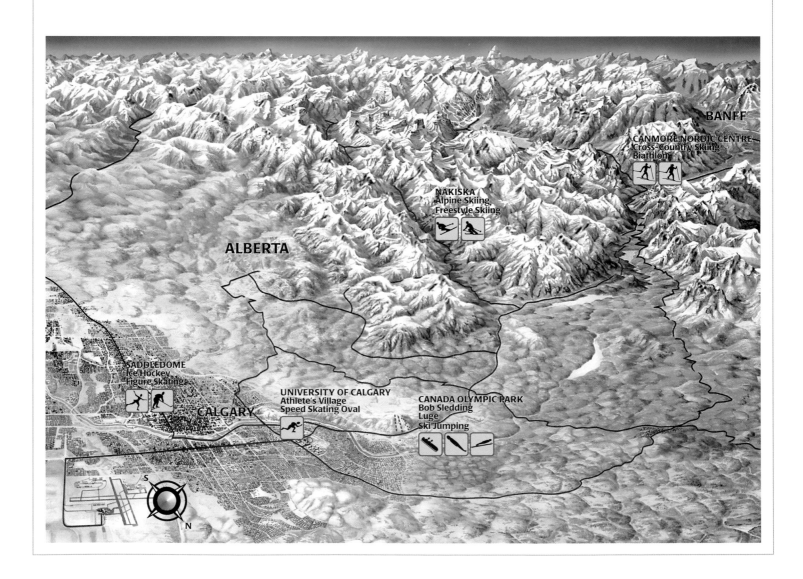

blessing of their own national Olympic committees before they could approach the IOC, and the Calgarians found themselves in a two-horse race against Vancouver. In autumn 1979 the Canadian Olympic Association, impressed with the concept of a long-term Olympic legacy, chose Calgary as its candidate. The second round brought King's team into the global arena, vying with Falun-Are in Sweden and with the Italian mountain resort of Cortina d'Ampezzo, host of the 1956 Winter Games.

The group launched into creative lobbying, ranging from gifts of white cowboy hats for IOC members to international fact-finding missions. Unlike some competitors, the Calgarians paid calls on warm-weather countries as well as the traditional winter-sports nations. This global approach may have helped swing the scales in Calgary's favor. At the IOC's Session in Baden-Baden in September 1981, the Canadians won the day.

The organizers, now known as Olympics Canada Olympiques, or OCO 88, had barely returned home and started building when disaster struck. Vicissitudes in the international oil market and massive taxes on energy consumption had sent the Canadian oil fields into economic free fall. Calgary businesses failed, and tens of thousands of workers found themselves unemployed.

Nevertheless, King and his associates pressed on. They sold broadcast rights to ABC for an unprecedented $309 million, more than double the price paid for the 1984 Winter Games at Sarajevo. In return for the huge outlay, OCO 88 kept faith with a 1987 IOC decision to extend the Games from the normal 12 days to 16, upping the number of potential advertising slots and thus giving ABC a better chance to capitalize on its investment. King also gathered an elite band of corporate supporters, among them Merrill Lynch, Kodak, IBM, Federal Express, and VISA. Even toymaker Mattel climbed on board with a special ice-skating Barbie doll.

With substantial resources thus in place, the construction program began. Out of a budget of U.S.$405 million came the new facilities King had promised: the dramatically shaped Saddledome—which some critics dismissed as a kitschy architectural nod to Calgary's cowboy heritage—for ice hockey and figure skating; the Canada Olympic Park, site for the ski jump, bobsled, and luge; the Nakiska Alpine ski complex, furnished with the latest snowmaking technology; the Canmore Nordic Centre for cross-country skiing; the Olympic Oval, North America's first fully enclosed speed-skating arena. In the heart of the city, the new Olympic Plaza supplied a stage for Olympic medal ceremonies, with a future role as a skating rink and downtown park. Its surface was paved with inscribed bricks commemorating the donations of individual Calgarians.

If Calgary's inhabitants felt they had a stake in the Games, so too did their fellow Canadians, as demonstrated by the stunning success of an Olympic torch relay that was the largest in the history of the Games. Holding the flame kindled from rays of the sun at Olympia, Greece, torchbearers set off on an 88-day run that would wind up covering some 11,000 miles of Canada's wintry terrain. The torch traveled farther north than ever before, crossing the Arctic Circle via dogsled, conveyed on foot and by helicopter, snowmobile convoys, wheelchair, and ferryboat.

The passionate enthusiasm for the relay seemed to ignite all Canada; people vied for a chance to run with the flame, entering lotteries for the privilege, paying for it, happily traveling thousands of miles at their own expense if no slot could be found for them near home. One successful bidder, who was killed in an accident shortly before the relay, virtually returned from the dead to take his turn: A friend carried his ashes along his allocated portion of the route. On February 13, Robyn Perry, a 12-year-old Calgary figure skater who represented Canadian youth, ran the final lap of the torch relay and

Robyn Perry ignites the Olympic cauldron. Moments later, the flame would rise 10 stories to become the centerpiece of a construction shaped like a giant tepee in homage to indigenous Native-American tribes. The Calgary torch imitates the shape of the Calgary Tower, a landmark building in the city. More than 6,500 Canadians carried the Olympic flame during its 88-day journey to McMahon Stadium.

touched the sacred flame to its cauldron in McMahon Stadium, site of both the opening and closing ceremonies.

Canada's enthusiasm for the Olympics won ample rewards: Building facilities and organizing events for the Games created some 14,000 person-years of employment and pumped an estimated U.S.$973 million into the national economy. More than 1,400 athletes flew in from 57 countries, and 180,000 visitors cheered from the sidelines. No Olympic Winter Games had ever been so inclusive and so diverse, even if some members of the IOC insisted that the ambiance had been, in the end, a little too welcoming to all comers. But spectators on site and a television audience in the millions begged to differ. Sport, as practiced by champions, was thrilling and uplifting. But a lovable loser was a great show.

In the very unofficial Olympic sport of amusing the public, Jamaica's bobsledders faced their stiffest competition from the nearsighted ski jumper nicknamed Eddie the Eagle. Eddie, or Michael Edwards, was a part-time plasterer by trade, hailing from the old English spa town of Cheltenham. His approach to the sport combined daredevil determination, an appetite for sheer terror, minimal experience, and awesome ineptitude.

"When I looked from the top of the jump," Eddie told reporters, reminiscing about his maiden voyage down a 70-meter hill, "I was so frightened that my bum shriveled up like a prune." It may have been a mercy that, on many jumps, he could barely see the horrific slope that he was traveling; his thick eyeglasses tended to fog up under the goggles.

The Fédération Internationale de Ski (FIS) sought to ban the bumptious Briton, fearing that such an unskilled novice might come to a gory end on the 90-meter jump. Undaunted, Eddie took his chances on both the 70- and 90-meter hills at Calgary. He achieved a triumphant last place on both, coming in 58th on the 70-meter and 55th on the 90-meter, scoring fewer than half the points achieved by any other jumper. The television cameras faithfully followed this glorious debacle, giving Eddie his brief but warming moment in the sun. When the Eagle

flew home from Calgary, he was greeted at London's Heathrow Airport by hundreds of fans, jostling cameramen and photographers, and a shoal of tabloid reporters waving checkbooks for the exclusive rights to his story.

While the loser's tale in the ski jump smacked of farce, the winner's was tinged with tragedy. Finland's Matti Nykänen, 24-year-old wonder of the ski-jumping world, was also the bad boy of the sport. A rebellious high-school dropout, Nykänen had spent his adolescence obsessively practicing jumps from a run in his hometown of Jyväskylä, sometimes making 60 leaps a week. Jyväskylä was also home to the coach employed by the Finnish Ski Federation, Matti Pulli. It was Pulli who discovered Nykänen as a 14-year-old and directed his training. The youth's dedication was an anomaly in an increasingly difficult personality. "With Matti," said Pulli, "you have to know where the genius stops and the lunatic starts."

The genius was indisputable. In 1982 the 18-year-old Nykänen made his mark on the international scene with the first of three World Cup titles and began accumulating a spectacular total of 1,479 World Cup points, 400 more than his nearest competitor. At Sarajevo 1984 he won Olympic gold in the 90-meter jump and silver in the 70-meter. But at the same time he also acquired a reputation as a troublemaker. He locked horns with coaches, bickered with teammates, drank himself into surly stupors, trashed a discotheque, was barred from competitions, and earned a two-month suspended jail sentence for stealing beer and cigarettes. Nevertheless, he remained the wayward darling of the Finnish press; his face on a magazine cover unfailingly sent circulation soaring.

When the devil wasn't in him, Nykänen—or, as his fans called him, Matti Nukes—was brilliant. No one on earth, it seemed, could understand the winds so well and travel so far on them.

These pins were created by the organizers and corporate participants of the Calgary 1988 Olympic Winter Games.

Judges, who grade jumpers on style as well as distance, found themselves compelled to forgive Nykänen's less than elegant takeoffs and landings.

At Calgary, Matti Nukes fulfilled the Olympic imperatives of Citius, altius, fortius: He was fastest, highest, strongest. In the 70-meter competition, to a chorus of 52,000 screaming spectators and a blue and white blizzard of Finnish flags, he began his run at a cautious 54 miles per hour, well below the Olympic average. Then he leaned forward and headed for outer space, sustaining his flight far longer than any mortal should have managed. In his second round, he repeated the miracle: The distances for the two jumps were identical: 294 feet (89.5 meters).

Analysts theorized about the soaring Finn's success. Some suggested that Nykänen's unorthodox style was not a flaw, but a product of his expert aerodynamic response to wind conditions: On lift-off, a flailing arm might not win points, but it could help build distance. Nykänen was, after all, a seasoned campaigner against the sort of fierce and capricious winds that challenged competitors in these Games: He had trained on Finland's Lahti hill, one of the few places in the world that, according to specialists, replicates Calgary's wind conditions.

Fellow jumpers sometimes remarked that Nykänen's body—his broad shoulders and light 132-pound frame—turned him when airborne into a human sail. U.S. ski jumper Mike Holland spoke only half in jest when he suggested to an interviewer that Nykänen was born with bird hormones. "Seriously," Holland continued, "he has just the right technique and featherlike physique. He floats through the air."

Nykänen's success off the 70-meter hill was stunningly repeated off the 90-meter and in the team events, giving Finland three gold medals. His admirers noted that the margin between the

Nukes' score on the 70-meter and that of Czech Pavel Ploc, his nearest rival, was much bigger than the gap between Ploc and the man who came 10th. "He is the best jumper in the past 100 years," exulted coach Pulli to the press, "the best ever in the world."

But the one challenger Matti Nukes couldn't outjump was his own troubled nature. After Calgary he continued what appeared to be a losing battle against alcoholism. He ran out of money and began selling his medals to raise cash. His personal life grew ever more chaotic.

Nykänen's downfall, mostly self-wrought, was made complete by a small but significant technical revolution in his sport. Back in 1985, a Swedish jumper named Jan Boklöv had been penalized for using a new kind of lift-off, placing his skis in a V shape instead of the orthodox parallel position. By 1989 aerodynamic tests had proved the worth of this innovation, and Boklöv used it that year to win the World Cup. The Vposition's virtues quickly commended themselves to the ski-jumping fraternity, and by Albertville 1992 every winner in individual competition was using the style. Not since the high jump's Fosbury Flop at Mexico City 1968 had a single move so changed the face of an Olympic sport. But despite dogged efforts, Nykänen could never master it. He failed to compete at Albertville (he had been drinking again and had walked out of his country's Olympic training camp), and he didn't even come close to qualifying for the Finnish team for Lillehammer 1994.

Matti Nykänen may have been the most driven Olympian at Calgary, but his was not the only powerful personality on the slopes. The men's Alpine contests on Mount Allan were dominated by two equally unforgettable but completely contrasting

stars: Switzerland's Pirmin Zurbriggen and the 21-year-old Italian firebrand, Alberto Tomba.

Zurbriggen arrived in Calgary with glittering credentials: the world junior championship at the age of 17; world downhill championship in 1985; overall 1986-1987 Alpine championship; four World Cup titles; and two world championships in 1987. He was entered in all five Olympic Alpine events, and experts believed he had more than a fighting chance to win them all. If he pulled off such a historic sweep, he would beat the achievement of his own longtime hero, the great Jean-Claude Killy, who had won three Alpine golds at Grenoble 1968.

Like Killy, the 25-year-old Zurbriggen was a high flier when it came to financial rewards for his sport, reaping $2 million for 1987 alone. But neither medals nor money had changed his nature: He was deeply religious and intensely private. Sports journalists never failed to remark on Zurbriggen's years as an altar boy, his numerous trips to Lourdes, his adoration of the pope, and his daily routine that included prayers, a strict six

hours' training, helping his mother with the dishes, and a 9:30 bedtime. "Being a champion doesn't mean I have to live the life of a rock star," was Zurbriggen's usual riposte.

Zurbriggen's first event in Calgary was the contest considered the jewel in the Alpine crown—the men's downhill. The course at Nakiska had been designed by veteran downhill champion Bernhard Russi, who had combined firsthand knowledge with technical expertise to challenge the downhill elite. His strategy was to create what he called a "flow of action," a rapid succession of changing terrains.

For the competitors, the experience would be like a ride inside a computer game, with a new obstacle rearing up every 10 seconds. The course began with a sharp descent and steep turns, then suddenly flattened out into a progression of jumps and rolls. It demanded strength, precision, and the ability to coordinate delicate movements at lightning speed. Arriving at Nakiska for a pre-race reconnaissance, Zurbriggen was jubilant. "It's like this course was designed for me," he

Pirmin Zurbriggen leaves snow in his wake on the slalom course. The Swiss superstar was a contender in every Alpine event.

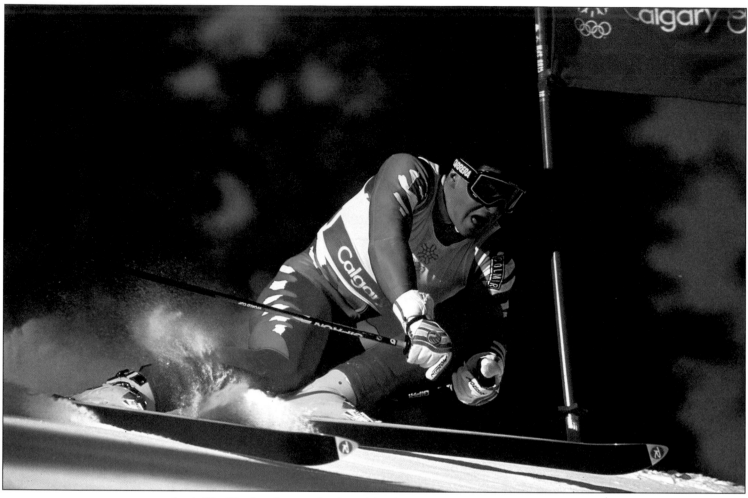

A perfect turn contributes to a golden run for Alberto Tomba. The flamboyant Italian shied away from the downhill to concentrate on the technical races. The strategy paid gold dividends in both slalom events.

exulted. "I will take plenty of risks. I like the wild parts of this downhill."

The steep pitches on the hill weren't the only wild elements at Nakiska. Screaming winds of 98 miles per hour forced a day's postponement of the race. When the contenders reconvened, the track was rendered even more difficult by a fresh overnight snowfall. In a close contest with his principal rival, compatriot Peter Müller, Zurbriggen skied with a brio that Killy himself would have envied, winning the gold medal by a nail-biting 0.51 of a second with a time of 1:59.63.

But the four other predicted gold medals eluded the Swiss mystic. The second ski event, the Alpine combined, was making its first Olympic appearance since 1948. This two-day competition entailed a downhill run and two slaloms. Zurbriggen maintained his primacy in the downhill and in the first of the two slaloms. But in the second slalom the tip of his right ski snagged one of the gate poles, throwing him onto his back. The gold went to Austria's Hubert Strolz.

The third contest, the super giant slalom, brought further disappointment for Zurbriggen. In this race, making its Olympic debut, skiers faced a steep, winding course that married the technical complexities of the slalom with the speed of the downhill. Flailed by the Chinook and inexperienced in the fiendish demands of this new ordeal, Zurbriggen and most of the other favorites slithered or stumbled off the course: Only 57 of the 94 entrants made it to the finish. The gold went to France's 23-year-old Franck Piccard, who had emerged from relative obscurity to take the bronze in the downhill.

The Super G, where so many dreams took a tumble, also marked the Olympic debut of the man who would cancel any hopes Zurbriggen might have nurtured for gold in the slalom and giant slalom. The new arrival's name was Alberto Tomba, known to his army of fans as Tomba La Bomba. If Pirmin Zurbriggen was every mother's dream, then Tomba was the protective papa's nightmare—a rich, charming, darkly handsome rapscallion who made men want to lock up their daughters.

Alberto was the son of the millionaire owner of an exclusive men's clothing store. The family lived luxuriously in a villa outside cosmopolitan Bologna, and the elder Tomba was a man who could afford to indulge his rambunctious son and often did. After all, Alberto had such an engaging zest for life. Unfortunately, the boy's high spirits—not to mention his big, finely coordinated body and his natural talent—had little guidance in the way of self-discipline. He was apt to break training by sneaking out for romantic rendezvous, quick to speak his mind, charmingly unencumbered by false modesty. He hung around the World Cup circuit for several years without winning a race.

Then, only three months before Calgary, Tomba won his first World Cup event—and promptly declared himself "the messiah of skiing." As though to prove it, he went on to win seven slaloms and giant slaloms within two and a half months, shooting from unknown to Olympic favorite. His father promised his 21-year-old rakehell son a Ferrari if Alberto could bring home a gold medal.

Sheer physical force was the key weapon in Tomba's arsenal. Of medium height and ruggedly built, he had a mightily muscled upper body that propelled him down the course. But brute strength alone could never make a slalom champion: He combined his might with a dancer's precision when negotiating the slalom gates. "Between the poles," remarked one of his coaches, Guido Siorpaes, "he seems a Nureyev."

In the giant slalom Tomba outskied both Zurbriggen and Strolz with a huge lead in the first run and a more modest margin in the second, achieving his first gold medal with a total time of 2:06.37. As fans rushed through the barriers to mob him, he exulted, "Oh, my God, I did it! I'm the strongest in the world." He predicted easy victory in the forthcoming slalom but was almost forced to eat his words: The race turned out to be the most closely contested slalom in the Olympic record books. Hampered by ruts in the course, Tomba finished the first run in third place. To make sure the gold didn't slip from his grasp on the second attempt, he shot through the gates like a catapult and zigzagged to a winning time of 1:39.47. West Germany's Frank Wörndl—who had beaten Tomba in the first round—was only 0.06 of a second behind. Two medals in hand, Alberto, typically impatient, didn't wait for his father's gift: He bought his own Ferrari—red, of course.

The winner's gold would inevitably be augmented by a shower of hard currency. Manufacturers vied with one another to persuade La Bomba to endorse their wares. The 16 million Italians who had watched their hero's double

Fans stretch to touch Alberto Tomba, whose expansive charm endeared him to spectators. Tomba's groupies followed his exploits for three Winter Games. He would give them reason to cheer at Albertville 1992, winning another gold and a silver, but by Lillehammer 1994 the magic would vanish.

West German Marina Kiehl takes flight during a moment of her winning downhill run. Her victory was the first for a West German woman since Rosi Mittermaier at Innsbruck 1976.

triumph on television christened him the Rambo of the Snows and began making plans for colossal welcoming celebrations for their new folk hero: an airlift to a massive tribute at his local soccer stadium near Bologna, a program of ski races dubbed the Tombiad. But Tomba still had unfinished business at Calgary, proclaiming that his new star status was just what he needed to improve his chances of impressing the alluring East German figure skater Katarina Witt.

While Tomba trumpeted his triumphs, female Alpine skiers were less flamboyantly engaged in their own struggles to control the slopes. Pundits had confidently tabbed the Swiss as the dominant power in the women's events. But unexpected challenges from their northern and eastern neighbors would upset any hopes of an easy sweep.

In the downhill, fierce winds—and equally fierce complaints about them—swirled over the course. Some participants felt that officials should never have allowed the event to take place under such difficult conditions. As tempestuous as the weather was the West German skier who would win the event, Marina Kiehl. Kiehl was something of a dark horse in the downhill; one pre-Games press briefing identified her as the likely star of the super giant slalom, but she had never won a downhill in her life. When the race began, however, she flailed her way to the gold in a time of 1:25.86.

As well as winning for its own sake, Kiehl had a hidden agenda. A decline in her pre-Olympic race results had made some West German officials contemplate dropping her from the Super G, her best race. The resulting wrath of this Alpine Fury caused the officials to offer a proposition: If she scored sixth or better in the downhill at Calgary, she could ski the Super G. Ironically, when Kiehl ran the super giant slalom, she finished a mortifying 13th.

The Super G winner was Austria's Sigrid Wolf, whose teammate Anita Wachter skied off with the gold in the Alpine combined. In both events, Austria's success resulted not only from its talented skiers but also from the methods of the Austrian women's team coach, Andreas Rauch. Aptly—in the homeland of that father of id and ego, Sigmund Freud—Rauch believed that psychology was a better training tool than extra push-ups. The coach initiated weekly group meetings where personal issues took priority, and he encouraged his skiers to see themselves as members of a mutually supportive team instead of a rivalry-ridden star system.

Sigrid Wolf said that Rauch's approach had helped her leap from moderate success to Olympic gold. "I was always thinking about the little things in racing: turns, bumps, compressions,"

Sigrid Wolf waves a bouquet after winning the Super G, one of two gold medals for the Austrian women's ski team.

Switzerland's Vreni Schneider holds her balance in her winning run of the giant slalom. Two days later she would win the slalom for a second gold medal.

she recalled. "Andreas told me to think of the sun and the sky and the clouds, and of the beautiful view from the course. That changed my mind, and my results, too."

With three of the five Alpine gold medals already gone, the Swiss could only hope to find balm for their bruised confidence in the two slalom events. The woman who supplied it, in both cases, was Vreni Schneider, a shoemaker's daughter from the small mountain town of Elm. The shy, unassuming Schneider had narrowly failed to make the Swiss Olympic team for Sarajevo. At Calgary the media at first ignored her, focusing instead on her higher-profile teammates, Maria Walliser and Michela Figini. Schneider's hunch-shouldered style looked clumsy on the slopes. But she was an artist at speeding through slalom gates, and in both slalom and giant slalom she deftly snatched gold medals as she did so. Boosted by her Calgary success, she would go on to an astonishing string of victories, winning 14 races in a row in the 1988-1989 season.

While Schneider zoomed to glory in the giant slalom, another racer, well behind her, was carrying the torch for Calgary's large squad of valiant outsiders. Seba Johnson, representing the U.S. Virgin Islands, was not only the sole female athlete from her tiny homeland and the first black Olympic

skier but, at 14, Calgary's youngest participant. Johnson finished the race in 28th place, no mean achievement in a contest where 35 of the 64 entrants never managed to complete the course at all.

Alpine skiers, by the nature of their sport, perform their pyrotechnics almost faster than the eye can see. Nordic skiers, on the other hand, operated throughout most of the history of their sport in an environment where skill and endurance were more important than speed. But the 1980s brought a revolution in cross-country ski techniques. Many skiers abandoned the classical method, with its diagonal stride and double poling, in favor of a set of much faster methods known collectively as skating. Skating allowed a variety of different strides and positions and often dispensed with one or both poles. At Sarajevo 1984 some athletes were disqualified for using skating techniques; by Calgary, the FIS had cobbled together a compromise that limited some events to the classical style, while others—the long-distance races and the relays—were freestyle.

The Nordic Centre at Canmore at the entrance to Banff National Park boasted cross-country trails combining tough climbs with sharply pitched descents. Competitors also had to grapple with varying surface textures: At

Dramatic skies illuminate a Rocky Mountain stream and rugged hills near the Canmore Nordic Centre. The city of Canmore, 50 miles west of Calgary, played host to biathletes and cross-country skiers.

Nordic skiers skate through a portion of the 4 x 10-kilometer relay at Calgary.

SKATING ON SKIS

Long frozen in Nordic tradition, cross-country skiing changed dramatically during the 1980s. In the time-honored classic cross-country technique, skiers propelled themselves forward with virtually no lateral motion, keeping each ski in a well-defined track. By the 1970s, however, a style known as "skating" was becoming a popular alternative. Skating skiers ignored the tracks in favor of pushing off the inside edge of each ski, mimicking the technique of speed skaters. The skating method had been around for decades, but athletes had reserved it mostly for hills or for occasions when a poor choice of ski wax slowed their progress and made extra momentum necessary.

Pauli Siitonen, a Finnish long-distance skier, was the first to regularly skate during races in the early 1970s. His success brought some disciples to skating, but the classical style remained the rule. So matters stood until

Bill Koch, an unheralded American skier, skated to a silver medal in the 30-kilometer race at Innsbruck 1976. Droves of imitators followed.

Skating was undeniably faster than the classical style, and variations soon appeared. Most important were the V-1, V-2, and diagonal techniques—all similar, their differences involving pole placement and stride angle. By 1985 most cross-country skiers were skating, in one form or another. But Scandinavian officials, who deemed skating a debasement of their sport, moved to outlaw it from competitions. The Fédération Internationale de Ski resolved the argument in 1986: Some races would be reserved for classical skiing; others would allow freedom of choice. At Calgary 1988, the decision meant that athletes in the two shorter races for men and women had to use the classical style; the longer races and the relays were open to all techniques.

some points the trail consisted of fine grains of real snow; elsewhere nature gave way to the pebbly synthetic version that had been applied just before the Games by manure spreaders from a nearby ranch. "I have never encountered such a difficult course," said the USSR's Aleksei Prokurorov, surprise winner of the 30-kilometer race.

But his team had come prepared by three weeks of high-altitude work in the Caucasus Mountains on a course similar to Canmore's. Along with gold and silver in the 30 kilometers, the Soviet men won both gold and bronze in the 15 kilometers. Their female comrades did even better, winning three gold medals, three silvers, and two bronzes across the spectrum of Nordic events, bested only in one race, the 5 kilometers, by Finland's Marjo Matikainen. Watching the Soviets win almost everything, one rival coach implied that the USSR cross-country skiers had resorted to blood doping, the infamous practice of reinjecting their own previously stored

A frenzied sprint to the front of the pack *(top)* marks the start of the 4 x 10-kilometer relay. Soviet Aleksei Prokurorov *(above)* contended for the lead during the race but fell in the latter stages to hand the event to Sweden. In the 30-kilometer race, the Russian stayed on his skis and won the gold medal.

Unaccustomed company during a portion of the 50-kilometer race prompts Gunde Svan (*left*) to maintain his pace. Svan was one of the world's greatest skiers. In a career spanning two Olympic Winter Games, he would win four gold medals, a silver, and a bronze.

blood in order to boost endurance during a race. The Soviet athletes denied it.

A dramatic high point at Canmore was the 50-kilometer race, Nordic skiing's answer to the marathon. Sweden's Gunde Anders Svan, winner of numerous World Cups and arguably the best skier of his generation, had suffered throughout his career from problems with high altitudes. But at Calgary it wasn't the height but the weather that bedeviled him: On the penultimate day of the Games, it was about to turn nasty. As Svan fought his way toward the finish, he could feel the winter storm that was roaring up just behind him. The pressure concentrated his energies sufficiently to drive him to a time of 2:04:30.9, more than 1 minute ahead of his closest competitor. The gold medal was his second of the Games; the first had been shared with his teammates in the 4 x 10-kilometer relay.

The Nordic combined—a ski-jump competition at Canada Olympic Park to be followed the next day by a 15-kilometer cross-country race at Canmore—fell victim to the capricious weather that had continually plagued the ski-jump venues. On

the day planned for the ski jumps, the Chinook blew up again, and officials decided there was no choice but to reschedule. Jumping and cross-country would both take place the next day—the last day of the Games. Besides taxing the athletes in competition, the solution also subjected them to an hour-long shuttle between the two locations. Much rubber was burned and adrenaline expended before Swiss skier Hippolyt Kempf won the individual event, and the West Germans claimed the gold in the team competition.

Medal winners in the Nordic events represented those nations traditionally dominant in cross-country, but these competitions also brought forth their own lovable losers. In the 50-kilometer race an inexperienced Mexican entrant, Roberto Alvarez, battling the snowstorms that front runner Svan had so narrowly avoided, came in 61st and last. He tarried so far behind that a search party was mustered before he turned up at the finish line a full 52 minutes after the second-to-last skier had come in.

Onlookers were also intrigued by the first-ever Nordic skier from the Pacific nation of Fiji. Rusiate Rogoyawa had, in fact, moved to Norway at

BROOMS, BALLET, AND BREAKNECK BATTLES

The world turns upside down for an in-flight aerial skier.

Sweden's Elisabeth Hogstrom aims her curling stone during the women's team competition.

Three sports vying for Olympic status—curling, freestyle skiing, and short-track speed skating—were on display at Calgary 1988. The demonstration events offered such a full slate that they almost constituted a separate Winter Games.

An icy amalgam of boccie and shuffleboard, curling, demonstrated at five Winter Games, has been slated for medal-event status at Nagano 1998. The sport involves four-member teams that play on a sheet of ice at least 146 feet long and 15 feet wide. One player slides a 44-pound stone toward a target while his teammates use brooms to sweep in front of the stone, smoothing the way for a longer, straighter glide. Teams alternate for 10 rounds, changing shooters each time, collecting points awarded for proximity to the target.

Freestyle skiing evolved from a 1960s American phenomenon called hot dog skiing. Freestyle has three disciplines: aerial, mogul, and ballet. In aerials, skiers launch themselves from a ramp, performing airborne twists and turns much like a diver's. Mogul skiing combines stunts performed along a run filled with bumps; contestants are judged for both time and style. Ballet skiers perform routines akin to those of figure skaters. Moguls would become an Olympic medal event at Albertville 1992, aerials at Lillehammer 1994.

Short-track speed skating, invented in the late 19th century, has Olympic bloodlines: Some of its rules were incorporated into the speed-skating events at Lake Placid 1932. In short track, skaters race in packs of four to six around a 122-yard-long oval of ice. The cramped and crowded quarters make for exciting races, with contact between skaters illegal but almost inevitable. Short-track speed skating would win Olympic status at Albertville 1992.

Striking a passionate pose, Katarina Witt is a sultry Carmen. The East German star's performance at Calgary made her the first woman since Sonja Henie to win consecutive figure-skating gold medals.

the age of 21, becoming the honorary son of a sports-minded family who encouraged him to ski. Undaunted by finishing 83rd out of 85 entrants in the 15 kilometers, Rogoyawa declared, "I think we should be given a chance to try our best. I can never become as good as the talents in Norway, but I can show that I can ski." Delivered at the end of the most commercial of Olympiads to date, it was a refreshing sentiment.

Of necessity, skiers practice their sport inside an armor of protective clothing, their faces screened by masks or goggles, their forms little more than shapes in motion to most viewers. Figure skaters are different. They perform with limbs and faces exposed to view, with every tiny movement, every nuance of emotion open to scrutiny by fans and judges. Their sport—the only one of the Winter Games in which the judging is overwhelmingly subjective—demands not only athletic skill but showmanship, style, personality, and passion.

Aficionados of this most theatrical of sports looked forward at Calgary to the confrontation between two leading ladies of the ice, Katarina Witt of East Germany and America's Debi Thomas. Their encounter would be immortalized in Olympic history as the Battle of the Carmens.

Katarina Witt at 22 had long been the superstar of international figure skating—gold medalist at Sarajevo 1984, six-time European champion, and world champion for 1984, 1985, and 1987. She was a charismatic figure, celebrated for her elegance and beauty on and off the ice. Had she come from the West, she would have enjoyed the luxury commensurate with her celebrity; as an East German she took her prizes in the form of a better-than-average apartment, a subsidized wardrobe of costumes, and a new East German-made Wartburg car acquired without the usual 10-year stint on a waiting list.

Despite her inescapable fame, Witt tried to stay true to her roots. "When I do well, coming from a socialist country like the G.D.R., other countries have grounds to respect us," she told reporters. "It is the working people who provide the basis for me to pursue skating at all."

Witt's American opponent was no pampered darling herself. Debi Thomas was one of the few black athletes in the snow-white sphere of winter sports and the first black ice-skater to win a world singles championship. (That victory had been over Katarina Witt in 1986, rupturing what would have otherwise been Witt's unbroken four-year winning streak.) Thomas was a premed student at Stanford University. Her lifelong passion for skating had entailed considerable financial sacrifice for her mother, a computer programmer and systems analyst in California's Silicon Valley. Thomas had not suffered a poverty-blighted ghetto childhood, but she was not immune from racism: She and her mother had once returned from a skating competition to find a cross burning on their front lawn.

Thomas was an athletic powerhouse, a master of rigorous triple jumps, an exponent of a vibrant, transatlantic energy that contrasted with the subtler Old World grace that Witt embodied. The American was impatient with those who treated the sport like the battle of the Barbie dolls, and her mother spoke with horror of the classic "rink mom" whose sharklike radar scanned for sponsors to boost her little ice princess's career. Without glitz or parental game playing, Thomas had achieved much: In addition to the world championship she had taken away from Witt, she had twice been U.S. champion.

Now, at Calgary's Saddledome, the long-running rivalry between the scrappy American and the glamorous German would reach its climax. There was other fine talent on hand: Japan's Midori Ito, America's Jill Trenary and Caryn Kadavy, and Canada's own Elizabeth Manley. In other circumstances, any one of them would have been a likely winner. But all eyes were on

The Debi Thomas version of Carmen goes into a spin. After Calgary, Thomas put away her skates to concentrate on premed studies at Stanford.

Witt and Thomas. Witt seemed to thrive on the attention; Thomas did not. "Every time I open the paper, they're trying to make this thing between me and Katarina," she complained. "It bugs me." But whether she liked it or not, the scene was already scripted. The world was expecting *High Noon* in tights.

And, whether she meant to or not, Thomas helped fuel the hype. In the days before the finals, a controversy erupted over Witt's scantily cut costumes. "Her costumes belong in an X-rated movie," Thomas opined. Witt, who doubtless knew how good she looked in those little high-in-the-thigh numbers, stayed smilingly above the fray.

In the end, costumes probably didn't matter much. In 1988 the figure-skating singles had three components: First came the compulsory exercises, or figures, consisting of loops and squiggles traced on the ice. This time-honored but boring enterprise would later be dropped, but at Calgary it accounted for 30 percent of a skater's total score. Thomas led Witt by a small margin after the figures. Then came the two-minute short program—worth 20 percent of the score—a routine that mandated specific jumps, spins, and steps. Witt skated first. She had opted

for a tribute to Broadway, wearing a chorine's plumes and rhinestones, tapping and twirling through a sequence of show tunes with a technical acuity that impressed the judges. Afterward, she lingered at rinkside to watch Thomas, clad in a spangled black body stocking, light up the ice with an explosive rock-and-roll routine. It had the whole audience clapping in rhythm, but the judges, who awarded separate sets of points for technical skill and for artistry, preferred Witt's silky style. The stage was thus set for a showdown two days later with the four-minute-long freestyle program, the source of half the competitors' total points.

The skating world waited breathlessly for a toe-to-toe confrontation; everyone who cared knew that both Witt and Thomas had created routines based on Georges Bizet's opera *Carmen*. To prepare for the role, Witt had given herself to intensive study of the opera and the inner life of its tragic heroine, a sultry, Spanish cigarette-factory worker who dies at the hands of a jilted lover. Thomas had concentrated on developing her own theatrical technique, working with ballet stars Mikhail Baryshnikov and George de la Pena. The two skaters' interpretations were very different: "Her Carmen dies, mine doesn't," said Thomas. Witt's was a doomed seductress, Thomas's a rebellious firebrand who would—in this particular version of the tale—live to love another day.

Witt, scarlet-clad, flashed and flirted as provocatively as the legendary cigarette girl herself, dazzling both crowd and judges as she sank sexily to the ice in her metaphorical dying gasp after a flawless performance. Thomas, who skated last in the competition, seemed totally unnerved: Her hope had been to pit her stronger style against Witt's greater artistry; but ironically, it would be her athletic superiority that deserted her. Her bold opener was intended to be a tour de force of triple toe loops taken back to back. On the second jump, when only one foot should have touched down on the ice, both landed. Rattled, Thomas made other lapses, knowing she had lost her chance for gold.

Although Witt was good enough to claim overall victory in the women's singles, hers was not the highest-scoring long program. Top marks there went to Canada's Elizabeth Manley, who had been virtually eclipsed by the media frenzy over Witt and Thomas. Manley's effervescent routine with its quintet of impeccable triples hoisted the crowd to its feet in approbation that was more than simple support for the home team's star. Even the impassive judges were impressed, with seven of the nine rating Manley's performance higher than Witt's and awarding the Canadian enough points for the silver medal. Thomas, brave in adversity, accepted the bronze. It was not the color she had hoped for, but it was historic nevertheless: the first medal awarded to a black athlete in an Olympic Winter Games.

While their female counterparts fought the Battle of the Carmens, two male figure skaters conducted the much-ballyhooed Battle of the Brians. Brian Orser of Canada and Californian Brian Boitano had, after years on the international circuit, become close friends as well as closely matched rivals. Orser had narrowly missed the Olympic gold medal at Sarajevo and had won the world championship in 1987, besting Boitano, the world champion the previous year. Both brilliant skaters, the Brians had different strengths: Orser, a consummate performer who knew how to work a crowd, was perhaps the more artistic of the two. Boitano, who at 5 foot 11 inches towered over most other male skaters, was the master technician, a cool, powerful engineer of ice-borne aerodynamics. "A technical robot" was his own self-deprecating phrase.

As in the Battle of the Carmens, the climax of the Brians' clash came after the short program. Boitano stood slightly ahead on points, but there was room for Orser to make up the difference if he could skate error-free. The Brians, like the

Carmens, had chosen similar dramatic themes for the freestyle: Both were dressed in 19th-century military regalia for routines with a martial feel. Boitano would skate in 19th place, Orser only minutes later as No. 21.

Boitano's program showcased his technical gifts, even though he knew this approach might cost him points for artistry. To compensate, he would try to expose his emotions in a way he had never done before. His choreographer, Sandra Bezic, emphasized that need with her last piece of advice just before he took the ice. "It's your moment," she told him. "Show them your soul!"

And so he did. The superb technique was there: eight perfect triple jumps, an airborne death drop, a backward-leaning spread eagle that wrenched a gasp of awe from the crowd. But as the program reached its conclusion, there was more: The skater seemed to have made a brief transit through Nirvana. "It felt like angels were lifting me and spinning me," he said through tears after leaving the ice.

Inevitably, Orser began his program with mixed

An inspired Brian Boitano of the U.S. comes to earth after one of the many perfect jumps in his long program. Boitano's pointedly emotional performance at Calgary proved that he could join passion to technical excellence.

Canada's Brian Orser dazzles with an airborne maneuver. His long program, though spectacular, was only good enough to assure him the silver medal.

emotions. He knew how good Boitano had been, but he also knew that the gold might still lie within his reach. His strong, flowing performance—also structured around eight triple jumps—was almost flawless. But almost was not quite enough: A slightly miscalculated landing in one jump, the conversion of a final triple into a double, a subtle sign of flagging energy, all conspired to shave vital fractions off his score. Four judges gave him a higher rating than Boitano—even in one case (from the Canadian judge) that rarity of figure skating, a perfect 6.0—but in the end, the Brian with the silver medal could not dispute the justice of his friend's claim to the gold.

Singles champions such as Witt and Boitano are individualists. But for skaters who compete in pairs and ice dancing, the self must give way partly to a partnership, where two bodies move across the ice as if governed by a single impulse. For the unschooled observer, there may seem little difference between pairs skating and ice dance: Both require grace, strength, and close synchrony. But

to the aficionado, the gulf between these disciplines is wide. Pairs skating is notable for its breathtaking lifts and throws and for the matched maneuvers performed by skaters who are not touching. In contrast, ice dancing—less muscular if perhaps more intricate—requires the partners to stay in close contact throughout all but a few moments of the routine, and the man must never lift his partner above his shoulders.

In both events, Soviet skaters, heirs to a venerable tradition of grand ballet on and off the ice, glided away with the gold. In the pairs final, 6-footer Sergei Grinkov and petite Ekaterina Gordeeva—who had to stand up very straight to achieve 5 feet in height—used this visually arresting disparity to great advantage in exuberant lifts and landings. Their ice-dancing compatriots, Andrei Bukin and Natalia Bestemianova, with an Olympic silver medal from 1984 and a trio of world championships to their credit, brought unprecedented unity to the normally argumentative judges' panel. Not surprisingly, the Soviet judge

The battling Brians, Orser *(left)* and Boitano *(center)*, join bronze medalist Viktor Petrenko of the Soviet Union on the winners' podium. Petrenko would ascend the top step four years later at Albertville.

Unorthodox angularity marks the style of the French ice-dancing brother and sister Isabelle and Paul Duchesnay. Crowds loved their avant-garde routine; judges were unmoved.

Sergei Grinkov tosses Ekaterina Gordeeva into the air—a comparatively effortless action, given her tiny size. Mismatched physically, the Soviet skaters skillfully used the anomaly to craft harmony in their pairs routines.

Andrei Bukin waves to an appreciative crowd after finishing his free-dance program with partner Natalia Bestemianova. Known as B & B in skating circles, the Soviet pair was the unanimous choice for first place.

gave them a perfect 6.0 for artistry—but so did the judges from Italy and France.

The judges were less captivated by the French brother-sister team of Isabelle and Paul Duchesnay. Clad in jungle costumes, the Duchesnays cavorted in their short program to a rhythmic African beat. The routine had been choreographed by British Olympic superstar Christopher Dean (he and Isabelle were briefly, tempestuously, married), and the crowd loved it. But it bombed with the judges, who grudgingly awarded them eighth place. Fans of the Duchesnays' postmodernist experiment claimed that the dance was simply too sophisticated for the conservative panel.

If figure skating is theater on ice, then speed skating is ballistics, a barrage of flesh-and-blood missiles hurling themselves at the finish line. There are no show tunes or spangles here: It's a nonsubtle sport for the very fast and the very tough. But even human bullets have hearts, and the Olympic Oval at Calgary would be the scene of traumas as well as triumphs as competitors' skate blades carved up seven world records and three Olympic marks, setting new standards in all 10 events.

Sweden's Sven Tomas Gustafson's triumphs in both the 5,000- and 10,000-meter races proved luck could change. After he won a gold medal and a silver at Sarajevo, Gustafson's life had been blighted by a leg injury, a serious illness, and the death of his father, all conspiring to sap his confidence and will to win. "I was a lost ex-athlete," he recalled. But by the time he reached Calgary, he had found himself. In a spectacular comeback, he set two world records: 6:44.63 in the 5,000 meters and, four days later, 13:48.2 in the 10,000.

Sadly, no such Hollywood ending greeted the efforts of U.S. skater Dan Jansen, who had been rated as one of his country's likeliest winners. On the day of the 500 meters, Jansen learned that a much-loved sister had just died of leukemia; her last message to him had been to skate the race anyway. He did, despite his grief, and fell before reaching the finish, then suffered a similar mishap during the 1,000-meter contest. Gold in the 500 meters went to East German star Uwe-Jens Mey, who clocked a world-record time of 36.45. Mey would win the event again at Albertville four years later.

In the women's speed events, however, the United States had something to celebrate. Sprint skater Bonnie Blair, 23, became the only American to win more than one medal at Calgary, bringing home the gold—plus a world record of 39.1 seconds—in the 500 meters and a bronze in the 1,000. Blair, runt of the litter in a large skating-mad family from Illinois, had learned to navigate on ice as soon as she could walk. As her skills developed, her local police department

The Netherlands' Yvonne van Gennip skates to victory in the 3,000-meter race. Van Gennip's great final lap times gave her a sweep of the distance events, frustrating the East Germans, who were favored in every race. America's Bonnie Blair (below), who turned in the fastest 500-meter time, added more insult by taking the sprint title.

started sponsoring her efforts. In 1987 she became more than just a local heroine, winning the gratitude of the international speed-skating sorority by proving that it was possible to beat the East Germans, who had long dominated women's speed skating. Blair's victory over them at the 1987 world championships had set a 500-meter world record of 39.43.

Calgary produced another threat to East German hegemony in the person of Dutch skater Yvonne van Gennip. Like Debi Thomas, van Gennip was an aspiring physician who had temporarily put aside her anatomy textbooks for the sake of her sport. A veteran of the Sarajevo Games, where she finished sixth in the 1,000 meters, van Gennip had little reason for optimism at Calgary. She had undergone an operation on an injured foot barely two months before the Games, lost irreplaceable weeks of workout time, and watched East German favorites Karin Kania and Andrea Ehrig scorch the ice in all their pre-Olympic events.

After arriving at the Olympic Village, van Gennip decided to calm her nerves by a visit to a nearby church. Sitting in the sanctuary, she felt a sudden sense of serenity and strength. Then she took to the ice and

America's Dan Jansen sprawls on the ice after catching an edge. The curse that hovered over him at Calgary would finally lift at Lillehammer 1994.

scooped up the gold in all three long-distance races, setting an Olympic record in the 1,500 meters and world records in the 3,000 and 5,000. No female Olympic speed skater had triumphed so thoroughly since Lydia Skoblikova of the USSR won a quartet of gold medals at Innsbruck 1964.

Of course, East Germany didn't go home empty-handed. In the biathlon, the grueling combination of cross-country skiing and rifle shooting, the G.D.R.'s Frank-Peter Roetsch won the 10- and 20-kilometer events. The sport itself had originated as a test of the skills required by border patrols in mountainous regions; fittingly, Roetsch himself was a member of an East German police force. He had won a silver medal at Sarajevo and been one of the brightest stars in the 1987 world championships before becoming the first biathlete to win gold in both individual events.

The luge was an even greater success story for the G.D.R. Some athletes regard this sport as the most dangerous of all winter events. The competitors, known as sliders, lie supine on the luge and descend the track feet first, using only legs and shoulders to guide their sleds. The East Germans had always been a power in the luge, and Calgary would be no exception. The men's team won both the singles and the two-man events, and the women took all three prizes in the singles race—the only luge contest open to their sex.

Even the treacherous luge had its lovable loser. A Los Angeles lawyer named Raymond Ocampo,

a U.S. citizen born in the Philippines, had to jump through bureaucratic hoops to establish his right to compete for his native land. The case passed back and forth among the IOC, the USOC, and Philippines authorities who, at the eleventh hour, threatened to rescind the accreditation that Ocampo had received nearly a year before the Games. But Ocampo finally won the day and slid triumphantly across the finish line, 35th in a field of 38.

Spirited fighters such as Ocampo might win the

Aiming for greatness, East Germany's Frank-Peter Roetsch fires at targets along the 10-kilometer biathlon course. Roetsch was not the best marksman of the day, but he was the fastest skier. His 10-kilometer triumph, along with his 20-kilometer victory three days earlier, made him the first athlete ever to win two individual biathlon events at a Winter Games.

A hard-checking Canadian momentarily slows Soviet Valery Kamesky during the medal round of the ice hockey tournament. The 1988 USSR team was said to be below par by Soviet standards, but it lost only one game in a successful defense of its Olympic title.

affection of the crowds, but the Soviet ice hockey team knew that if it left Calgary without a medal, it would be regarded as anything but lovable back home. For more than three decades, the Soviets had seemed to own a perch on the winners' podium. Apart from a bronze medal at Squaw Valley 1960 and a silver after an upset at U.S. hands at Lake Placid 1980, they had captured every gold medal since 1956. But prior to the Calgary Olympics, the USSR team had shown signs of age and fatigue, giving away the world championship to Sweden, then being crushed on home turf by Canada just two months before the Winter Games. In hockey circles it was whispered that if coach Viktor Tikhonov couldn't win at Calgary, he could say farewell to his job.

The hockey schedule was punishing, with 45 matches packed into the 16 days of the Games. The Soviets, in spite of the alleged doom hovering over them, exceeded almost everyone's expectations. The only threat to them came unexpectedly from the Finns, who rose from a first-round loss to the Swiss to beat the mighty Canadians and face down Sweden in a tie. But even as hype about Finland's prospects escalated, the team got trounced by Czechoslovakia. Nevertheless, when the Finns did finally meet the USSR, they managed to inflict the Soviet squad's

only defeat and thus earn the silver. It was the first ice hockey medal ever won by a Finnish Olympic team, and it provided yet another opportunity for the Calgary crowd to celebrate the valiant efforts of an underdog.

To bring its 16-day pageant to an end, Calgary staged a spectacle mingling ice and fire, a modern version of the festivals that once illuminated dark winters in the northern world. The closing ceremony was a rollicking affair, attended by 60,000 spectators, held in McMahon Stadium under a sky striped with fireworks. In keeping with Calgary's Wild West spirit, the festivities were as exuberant as the Games themselves had been.

There was, however, one quiet moment that preceded the fun: The great Olympic torch was extinguished, and as it died each spectator held up a glowing candle, symbolically keeping the flame alive. The gesture had a subtle subtext, coming as it did at the end of the Olympiad that had changed the Games forever. Los Angeles, then Calgary, marked the final breach in the crumbling wall that had stood between the Olympic sanctum and the commercialism of the modern world. Corruption had entered the temple, said the critics, but their voices were softer now, and soon they would be silent. At whatever cost, the Games would continue. The flame would not die.

The Olympic banner comes down during the closing ceremony in Calgary's McMahon Stadium. The flag's descent marked the end of what IOC president Juan Antonio Samaranch called "the best organized Winter Games in history."

∞∞APPENDIX

CALENDAR OF THE XXIII OLYMPIAD
JULY 28, 1984-SEPTEMBER 16, 1988

1984

JULY 28-AUGUST 12	**20TH SUMMER GAMES AT LOS ANGELES**
JULY 21-23, 30, & AUGUST 2, 4, 6, 11-13	144th IOC Executive Board Meeting at Los Angeles
JULY 25-26	**88th Session of the IOC at Los Angeles**
NOVEMBER 7-8	145th IOC Executive Board Meeting at Mexico City
NOVEMBER 9-23	IOC Executive Board with NOCs at Mexico City
NOVEMBER 30-DECEMBER 1	146th IOC Executive Board Meeting at Lausanne
DECEMBER 1-2	**89th Session of the IOC at Lausanne**

1985

FEBRUARY 16-24	12th University Winter Games at Bulluno
FEBRUARY 25-28	147th IOC Executive Board Meeting at Calgary
FEBRUARY 28	37th IOC Executive Board with W/IFs at Calgary
MARCH 24-29	3rd International Winter Special Olympics at Park City
APRIL 6-9	14th Carifta Games at Barbados
MAY 28	148th IOC Executive Board Meeting at Lausanne
MAY 29	38th IOC Executive Board with IFs at Lausanne
MAY 31- JUNE 1, 4, 6	149th IOC Executive Board Meeting at Berlin (GDR)
JUNE 4-6	**90th Session of the IOC at Berlin (GDR)**
JULY 4-7	2nd European Special Olympics at Dublin
JULY 9-20	15th Summer Games for the Deaf at Los Angeles
JULY 25-AUGUST 4	2nd World Games at London
AUGUST 24-SEPTEMBER 4	13th University Summer Games at Kobe
OCOTBER 15-18	150th IOC Executive Board Meeting at Lisbon
DECEMBER 5-6	151st IOC Executive Board Meeting at Lausanne

DECEMBER 8-17	13th South East Asian Games at Bangkok
DECEMBER 20-26	2nd South Asian Federation Games at Dhaka

1986

JANUARY 4-12	3rd Central American Games at Guatemala
FEBRUARY 10	39th IOC Executive Board with W/IFs at Lausanne
FEBRUARY 10-12	152nd IOC Executive Board Meeting at Lausanne
MARCH 1-8	1st Winter Asian Games at Sapporo
APRIL 22-24	153rd IOC Executive Board Meeting at Seoul
APRIL 26	24th IOC Executive Board with NOCs at Seoul
JUNE 24-JULY 5	15th Central American and Caribbean Games at Santiago de los Caballaeros
JULY 5-20	1st Goodwill Games at Moscow
JULY 24-AUGUST 2	13th Commonwealth Games at Edinburgh
SEPTEMBER 16-17, 19	154th IOC Executive Board Meeting at Seoul
SEPTEMBER 18	40th IOC Executive Board with IFs at Seoul
SEPTEMBER 20-OCTOBER 5	10th Asian Games at Seoul
OCTOBER 10-11	155th IOC Executive Board Meeting at Lausanne
OCTOBER 13-17	**91st Session of the IOC at Lausanne**
NOVEMBER 29 - DECEMBER 7	3rd South American Sport Games at Chile
DECEMBER 11-13	156th IOC Executive Board Meeting at Lausanne

1987

NOVEMBER 20-27	3rd South Asian Federation Games at Calcutta
FEBRUARY 7-14	11th World Winter Games for the Deaf at Oslo
FEBRUARY 11-12	157th IOC Executive Board Meeting at Lausanne
FEBRUARY 13	41st IOC Executive Board with W/IFs at Lausanne

FEBRUARY 21-28	13th University Winter Games at Stroske Pleso
APRIL 22-23	158th IOC Executive Board Meeting at Lausanne
APRIL 24	42nd IOC Executive Board with IFs at Lausanne
MAY 7-8	159th IOC Executive Board Meeting at Istambul
MAY 9-12	**92nd Session of the IOC at Istambul**
JULY 8-19	14th University Summer Games at Zagreb
JULY 8-22	1st Games of the French Speaking Countries at Casablanca
JULY 31-AUGUST 8	7th International Special Olympics at South Bend
AUGUST 1-12	4th African Games at Nairobi
AUGUST 8-23	10th Pan American Games at Indianapolis
SEPTEMBER 9-20	14th South East Asain Games at Jakarta
SEPTEMBER 10-25	10th Mediterranean Games at Latakia
SEPTEMBER 15-16	160th IOC Executive Board Meeting at Lausanne
SEPTEMBER 10-25	10th Mediterranean Games at Latakia

1988

JANUARY 17-24	4th Winter Paralympic Games at Innsbruck
FEBRUARY 6-7	162nd IOC Executive Board Meeting at Calgary
FEBRUARY 9-11	**93rd Session of the IOC at Calgary**
FEBRUARY 12	43rd IOC Executive Board with W/IFs at Calgary
FEBRUARY 13-28	**15TH WINTER GAMES AT CALGARY**
APRIL 24	44th IOC Executive Board with S/IFs at Lausanne
APRIL 27-28	163rd IOC Executive Board Meeting at Stockholm
JULY 24-26	164th IOC Executive Board Meeting at Lausanne

Saturday, July 28

AM	EVENT
4:30	Opening Ceremony . . . . L.A. Memorial Coliseum . . . .

Sunday, July 29

AM	EVENT
8:00	Equestrian . . . . Santa Anita Park . . three-day event (dressage test)
9:00	Swimming . . . . USC . women's 100-m freestyle, heats . women's 100-m freestyle, heats . . . . women's 400-m ind. medley, heats . . . . men's 200-m freestyle, heats
9:00	Basketball . . . . The Forum . men's, preliminaries (2 games)
9:00	Modern Pentathlon . . . . Coto De Caza , Orange County
9:00	Shooting . . . . Coal Canyon, Orange County . . . . free pistol . . . . sport pistol . . . . clay target-trap
9:00	Cycling. . . . . . . Mission Viejo . women's 79-km ind. road race
10:00	Volleyball . . . Long Beach Arena men's, preliminaries (2 matches)
11:00	Boxing . . . . L.A. Memorial Sports Arena . . . . preliminary bouts

PM	EVENT
1:00	Cycling . . . . Mission Viejo . . men's 190-km ind. road race
1:45	Field Hockey . . . . Field East L.A. College . . . . men's, preliminaries (3 games)
2:00	Weight Lifting . . . . Loyola Marymount University . . . . flyweight (up to 52 kg), preliminaries . . . .
2:30	Basketball . . . . The Forum . men's, preliminaries (2 games)
3:00	Gymnastics. . . . . Pauley Pavilion, UCLA . . . . men's compulsory exercises
4:00	Modern Pentathlon . . . . Coto de Caza . . . .
4:15	Swimming . . . . USC women's 100-m freestyle, finals men's 100-m breaststroke, finals . . . . women's 400-m ind. medley, finals . . . men's 200-m freestyle, finals
6:00	Boxing . . . . L.A. Memorial Sports Arena . . . . preliminary bouts
6:00	Weight Lifting, freestyle . . . . . . Loyola Marymount University . . . . flyweight (up to 52kg), preliminaries . . . .
6:30	Gymnastics. . . . . Pauley Pavilion, UCLA . . . . men's compulsory exercises
6:30	Volleyball . . . Long Beach Arena men's, preliminaries (2 matches)
7:00	Soccer. . . . . Rose Bowl . . . . . . first round (4 matches)
8:00	Basketball . . . . The Forum . men's, preliminaries (2 games)

Monday, July 30

AM	EVENT
7:30	Rowing. . . . . Lake Casitas . . . . women's, heats
8:00	Equestrian . . . . Santa Anita Park . . three-day event (dressage test)

AM	EVENT (col 2)
8:00	Modern Pentathlon . . . . Coto De Caza, Orange County .
8:30	Swimming . . . . USC . . . men's 100-m butterfly, heats women's 200-m freestyle, heats men's 400-m ind. medley, heats men's 4 x 200-m freestyle relay, heats . . . .
9:00	Basketball . . . . The Forum women's, round robin (1 game) . . men's, preliminaries (1 game)
9:00	Shooting . . . . Coal Canyon . . small-bore rifle English match . . . . clay target-trap . . . . running game target
10:00	Cycling . . . . CSU Dominguez Hills . . . . ind. pursuit, qualifications . . . . 1-km time trial, final
10:00	Gymnastics. . . . . Pauley Pavilion, UCLA . . . . women's compulsory exercises
10:00	Volleyball . . . Long Beach Arena . . . . . . women's, preliminaries (2 matches). . . . .
11:00	Boxing . . . . A. Memorial Sports Arena . . . . preliminary bouts
12:00	Wrestling . . . . Anaheim Convention Center. . . . Greco-Roman, (48, 62, 90 kg), preliminary bouts . . . .

PM	EVENT
1:45	Field Hockey . . . . Field East L.A. College . . . . men's, preliminaries (3 games)
2:00	Weight Lifting . . . . Loyola Marymount University . . . . . bantamweight (up to 56 kg), preliminaries. . . . .
2:30	Basketball . . . . The Forum women's, round robin (2 games)
4:00	Soccer. . . . . Rose Bowl . . . . . preliminaries (2 games)
4:15	Swimming . . . . USC . . . men's 100-m butterfly, finals women's 200-m freestyle, finals men's 400-m ind. medley, finals . . women's 200-m breaststroke, finals . . . . men's 4 x 200-m freestyle relay, finals . . . .
5:30	Gymnastics. . . . . Pauley Pavilion, UCLA . . . . women's compulsory exercises
6:00	Boxing . . . . L.A. Memorial Sports Arena . . . . preliminary bouts
6:00	Weight Lifting . . . . Loyola Marymount University . . . . . bantamweight (up to 56 kg), preliminaries. . . . .
6:00	Wrestling . . . . Anaheim Convention Center. . . . Greco-Roman (48, 62, 90 kg), preliminary bouts . . . .
6:30	Volleyball . . . Long Beach Arena . . . . . . women's, preliminaries (2 matches). . . . .
7:00	Soccer. . . . . Rose Bowl . . . . . . first round (4 matches)
8:00	Basketball . . . . The Forum women's, round robin (1 game)

Tuesday, July 31

AM	EVENT
7:30	Rowing. . . . . Lake Casitas . . . . men's, heats
8:30	Field Hockey . East L.A. College . men's, preliminaries (3 games)

AM	EVENT (col 3)
8:30	Swimming . . . . USC women's 400-m freestyle, heats . . . men's 100-m freestyle, heats . . . women's 100-m backstroke, heats . . . . men's 200-m backstroke, heats . . women's 4 x 100-m freestyle relay, heats . . . .
9:00	Basketball . . . . The Forum women's, round robin (1 game)
9:00	Shooting . . . . Coal Canyon . . . . clay target-trap . . . . running game target . . . . women's air rifle
9:30	Gymnastics. . . . . Pauley Pavilion, UCLA . . . . men's optional exercises
10:00	Cycling . . . . CSU, Dominguez Hills. . . . . ind. pursuit, quarterfinals . . . . sprint series . . . . points race, qualification
10:00	Volleyball . . . Long Beach Arena men's, preliminaries (2 matches)
11:00	Boxing . . . . L.A. Memorial Sports Arena . . . . preliminary bouts
11:00	Team Handball . . . . CSU, Fullerton . . . . men's, preliminaries (3 games)

PM	EVENT
12:00	Wrestling . . . . Anaheim Convention Center. . . . . Greco-Roman (48, 52, 62, 74, 90, over 100 kg)
1:30	Yachting . . . Long Beach Marina . . . . . . all classes, first race
2:00	Modern Pentathlon . . . . Coto De Caza, Orange County .
2:00	Weight Lifting . . . . Loyola Marymount University . . . . . featherweight (up to 60 kg), preliminaries. . . . .
2:30	Basketball . . . . The Forum women's, round robin (1 game) . . men's, preliminaries (1 game)
2:30	Field Hockey . . . . Field East L.A. College . . . . women's, round robin (1 game)
3:00	Gymnastics. . . . . Pauley Pavilion, UCLA . . . . men's optional exercises
4:00	Baseball . . . . . Dodger Stadium . . . . first round (2 games)
4:15	Swimming . . . . USC women's 400-m freestyle, finals . . . men's 100-m freestyle, finals women's 100-m backstroke, finals . men's 200-m backstroke, finals . . women's 4 x 100-m freestyle relay, finals . . . .
6:00	Boxing, ... L.A. Memorial Sports Arena . . . . preliminary bouts
6:00	Weight Lifting . . . . Loyola Marymount University . . . . . featherweight (up to 60 kg) preliminaries. . . . .
6:00	Wrestling . . . . Anaheim Convention Center. . . . Greco-Roman (48, 52, 62, 74, 90, over 100 kg), preliminaries .
6:30	Gymnastics. . . . . Pauley Pavilion, UCLA . . . . men's optional exercises, team finals . . . .
6:30	Team Handball. . CSU, Fullerton . men's, preliminaries (3 games)
6:30	Volleyball . . . Long Beach Arena men's, preliminaries (2 matches)
7:00	Soccer. . . . . Rose Bowl

AM	EVENT (col 4)
	. . . . . . first round (4 matches)
8:00	Basketball . . . . The Forum women's, round robin (1 game) . . men's, preliminaries (1 game)

Wednesday, August 1

AM	EVENT
7:30	Rowing. . . . . Lake Casitas . . . . men's repechage . . . . women's repechage
8:00	Field Hockey . . . . East L.A. College . . . . men's, preliminaries (1 game)
8:30	Water Polo . . . . Peppperdine University . . . . preliminaries (2 games)
9:00	Basketball . . . . The Forum . men's, preliminaries (2 games)
9:00	Fencing . . . . L.B. Convention Center . . . . foil, men's ind., preliminaries
9:00	Modern Pentathlon . . . . Coto De Caza, Orange County .
9:00	Shooting . . . . Coal Canyon . . . small-bore rifle, 3 positions . . . . men's rapid-fire pistol
10:00	Cycling . . . . CSU, Dominguez Hills. . . . . ind. pursuit, semifinals & finals . . . . sprint, quarterfinals . . . . points race, qualification
10:00	Equestrian . . . . Santa Anita Park three-day event (endurance test)
10:00	Gymnastics. . . . . Pauley Pavilion, UCLA . . . . women's optional exercises
10:00	Volleyball . . . Long Beach Arena women's, preliminaries (2 games)
10:00	Weight Lifting . . . . Loyola Marymount University . . . . . lightweight (up to 67.5 kg), preliminaries. . . . .
11:00	Boxing . . . . L.A. Memorial Sports Arena . . . . preliminary bouts

PM	EVENT
12:00	Wrestling . . . . Anaheim Convention Center. . . . . Greco-Roman (52, 57, 68, 74, 82,100, over 100 kg), preliminaries . . . . Greco-Roman (48, 62, 90 kg), finals. . . . .
1:30	Water PoloPepperdine University . . . . . preliminaries (2 games)
1:30	Yachting . . . Long Beach Marina . . . . second race
1:45	Field Hockey . . . . Field East L.A. College . . . . men's, preliminaries (2 games) women's, round robin (1 game)
2:00	Weight Lifting . . . . Loyola Marymount University . . . . lightweight (up to 67.5 kg), preliminaries. . . . . . .
2:30	Basketball . . . . The Forum . men's, preliminaries (2 games)
4:00	Baseball . . . . . Dodger Stadium . . . . first round (2 games)
4:00	Soccer. . . . . Rose Bowl . . . . . . first round (4 matches)
5:00	Modern Pentathlon . . . . Coto De Caza, Orange County .
5:30	Gymnastics. . . . . Pauley Pavillion, UCLA . . . . women's optional exercises, team finals . . . .
6:00	Boxing . . . . L.A. Memorial Sports Arena . . .

.... preliminary bouts
6:00 Weight Lifting ....
Loyola Marymount University . .
. . . lightweight (up to 67.5 kg),
preliminaries . . . .
6:00 Wrestling . . . .
Anaheim Convention Center. . .
. . . . Greco-Roman
(52, 57, 68, 74, 82, 100, over
100 kg), preliminaries . . . .
. . . . Greco-Roman
(48, 62, 90 kg), finals . .
6:30 Team Handball . . . .
CSU, Fullerton
women's, round robin (3 games)
6:30 Volleyball . . . Long Beach Arena
. . . . . women's, preliminaries
(2 matches)
7:00 Soccer. . . . . Rose Bowl
. . . . . . first round (4 matches)
7:30 Water Polo . . . .
Pepperdine University . . . .
. . . . . preliminaries (2 games)
8:00 Basketball . . . . The Forum
. men's, preliminaries (2 games)

Thursday, August 2

AM	EVENT

7:30 Rowing. . . . . Lake Casitas
. . . . men's, semifinals
. . . . women's, semifinals
8:30 Field Hockey . . . .
Field East L.A. College. . . . . . .
. men's, preliminaries (2 games)
8:30 Swimming . . . . USC
. . . men's 400-m freestyle, heats
. women's 100-m butterfly, heats
men's 200-m breaststroke, heats
. . women's 100-m breaststroke,
heats . . . .
men's 4 x 100-m freestyle relay,
heats . . . .
women's 800-m freestyle, heats
8:30 Water Polo . . . .
Pepperdine University . . . .
. . . . . preliminaries (2 games)
9:00 Basketball . . . . The Forum
women's, round robin (1 game)
. . men's, preliminaries (1 game)
9:00 Fencing . . . .
L.B. Convention Center . . . . . .
. . foil, men's ind., preliminaries
foil, women's ind., preliminaries
9:00 Shooting . . . . Coal Canyon
. . . . . women's small-bore rifle,
3 positions . . . .
. . . . rapid-fire pistol
. . . . clay target-skeet
10:00 Cycling . . . .
CSU, Dominguez Hills. . . . . . .
. . . . sprint, semifinals
. . . . team pursuit, qualification
& quarterfinals . . . .
10:00 Volleyball . . . Long Beach Arena
men's, preliminaries (2 matches)
10:00 Weight Lifting . . . .
Loyola Marymount University . .
. . . . middleweight
(up to 75 kg), preliminaries. . . .
11:00 Boxing. . . . . . L.A. Sports Arena
. . . . preliminary bouts
11:00 Team Handball . . . .
CSU, Fullerton . . . .
. men's, preliminaries (3 games)

PM	EVENT

12:00 Wrestling . . . .
Anaheim Convention Center. . .
. . . . Greco-Roman
(57, 68, 82, 100 kg), preliminaries
. . . . Greco-Roman

(52, 75, over 100 kg), finals . . .
1:30 Water Polo . . . .
Pepperdine University . . . .
. . . . . . preliminaries (2 games)
1:30 Yachting . . . Long Beach Marina
. . . . third race
2:00 Weight Lifting . . . .
Loyola Maymount University . .
. . . . middleweight
(up to 75 kg), preliminaries . . .
2:30 Basketball . . . . The Forum
women's, round robin (1 game)
. . men's, preliminaries (1 game)
2:30 Field Hockey . . . .
East L.A. College. . . . .
women's, round robin (1 game)
. . men's, preliminaries (1 game)
4:00 Baseball . . . . . Dodger Stadium
. . . . first round (2 games)
4:15 Swimming . . . . USC
. . . men's 400-m freestyle, finals
. women's 100-m butterfly, finals
men's 200-m breaststroke, finals
. . women's 100-m breaststroke,
finals . . . .
. . . . men's 4 x 100-m freestyle
relay, finals . . . .
5:30 Gymnastics. . . . .
Pauley Pavilion, UCLA . . . .
. . . . . men's all-around, finals
6:00 Boxing . . . .
L.A. Memorial Sports Arena . . .
. . . . preliminary bouts
6:00 Weight Lifting . . . .
Loyola Marymount University . .
. . . . middleweight
(up to 75 kg), preliminaries. . . .
6:00 Wrestling . . . .
Anaheim Convention Center. . .
. . . . Greco-Roman
(57, 68, 82, 100 kg), preliminaries
. . . . Greco-Roman
(52, 74, over 100 kg), finals . . .
6:30 Volleyball . . . Long Beach Arena
men's, preliminaries (2 matches)
7:00 Soccer. . . . . Rose Bowl
. . . . . . first round (4 matches)
7:30 Water Polo . . . .
Pepperdine University . . . .
. . . . . . preliminaries (2 games)
8:00 Basketball . . . . The Forum
women's, round robin (1 game)
8:00 Fencing . . . .
L.B. Convention Center . . . . . .
. . . . . . foil, men's ind., finals

Friday, August 3

AM	EVENT

8:00 Field Hockey . . . .
Field East L.A. College. . . . . . .
women's, round robin (1 game)
. . men's, preliminaries (1 game)
8:00 Rowing. . . . . Lake Casitas
. . . men's, finals (7-12 places)
. . women's, finals (7-12 places)
8:30 Swimming . . . . USC
. . . . women's 200-m
ind. medley, heats . . . .
. . men's 200-m butterfly, heats
. men's 100-m backstroke, heats
. women's 4 x 100-m medley
relay, heats . . . .
. men's 1,500-m freestyle, heats
8:30 Water Polo . . . .
Pepperdine University . . . .
. . . . . . preliminaries (2 games)
9:00 Basketball . . . . The Forum
women's, round robin (1 game)
. . men's, preliminaries (1 game)
9:00 Fencing . . . .

L.B. Convention Center . . . . . .
foil, women's ind., preliminaries
. . . . sabre, men's ind.,
9:00 Shooting . . . . Coal Canyon
. . . . men's air rifle
. . . . clay target-skeet
9:30 Athletics. . . . .
. . . . heptathlon
. . . (100-m hurdles, high jump)
men's triple jump, qualifications
men's 400-m hurdles, first round
. . . women's 400-m, first round
women's shot put, qualifications
. . . . men's 100-m, first &
second rounds . . . .
10:00 Cycling . . . .
CSU, Dominguez Hills. . . . . . .
. . . . team pursuit,
semifinals & final . . . .
. . . . sprint, finals
. . . . points race, final
10:00 Volleyball . . . Long Beach Arena
. . . . . . women's, preliminaries
(2 matches)
11:00 Boxing . . . .
L.A. Memorial Sports Arena . . .
. . . . preliminary bouts
11:30 Equestrian . . . . Santa Anita Park
. . three-day event (jumping test)

PM	EVENT

12:00 Wrestling . . . .
Anaheim Convention Center. . .
. . . . Greco-Roman
(57, 68, 82, 100 kg), preliminaries
1:00 Baseball, ... Dodger Stadium
. . . . first round (2 games)
1:30 Water Polo . . . .
Pepperdine University . . . .
. . . . . . preliminaries (2 games)
1:30 Yachting . . . Long Beach Marina
. . . . fourth race
1:45 Field Hockey . . . .
Field East L.A. College. . . . . . .
. men's, preliminaries (2 games)
women's, round robin (1 game)
2:30 Basketball . . . . The Forum
women's, round robin (1 game)
. . men's, preliminaries (1 game)
4:00 Athletics . . . . L.A. Coliseum
. . . women's 800-m, first round
. . heptathlon (shot put, 200-m)
. . . men's 800-m, first round
. . . . . men's 20-km walk, final
. . . . . women's shot put, final
. . men's 10,000-m, first round
5:00 Swimming . . . . USC
men's 200-m ind. medley, finals
. . men's 200-m butterfly, finals
women's 800-m freestyle, finals
. men's 100-m backstroke, finals
. . women's 4 x 100-m medley
relay, finals . . . .
5:30 Gymnastics. . . . .
Pauley Pavilion, UCLA . . . .
. . . . . women's all-around, finals
6:00 Boxing . . . .
L.A. Memorial Sports Arena . . .
. . . . preliminary bouts
6:00 Wrestling . . . .
Anaheim Convention Center. . .
. . . . Greco-Roman
(57, 68, 82, 100 kg), finals . . . .
6:30 Team Handball . . . .
CSU, Fullerton . . . .
women's, round robin (3 games)
6:30 Volleyball . . . Long Beach Arena
. . . . . . women's, preliminaries
(2 matches)
7:00 Soccer. . . . . Rose Bowl
. . . . . . first round (4 matches)
7:30 Water Polo . . . .

Pepperdine University . . . .
. . . . . preliminaries (2 games)
8:00 Basketball . . . . The Forum
women's, round robin (1 game)
. . men's, preliminaries (1 game)
8:00 Fencing . . . .
L.B. Convention Center . . . . . .
. . . . . foil, women's ind., finals

Saturday, August 4

AM	EVENT

8:00 Rowing. . . . . Lake Casitas
. . . women's, finals (1-6 places)
8:30 Field Hockey . . . .
Field East L.A. College. . . . . . .
. men's, preliminaries (2 games)
8:30 Swimming . . . . USC
men's 200-m ind. medley, heats
women's, 200-m butterfly, heats
women's 200-m backstroke, heats
. . . . men's, 4 x 100-m medley
relay, heats . . . .
9:00 Basketball . . . . The Forum
. men's, preliminaries (2 games)
9:00 Fencing . . . .
L.B. Convention Center . . . . . .
. foil, men's team, preliminaries
. sabre, men's ind., preliminaries
9:00 Shooting . . . . Coal Canyon
. . . . clay target-skeet
9:30 Athletics . . . . L.A. Coliseum
. . . . heptathlon (long jump)
. . . . . men's 400-m, first round
. women's 400-m, second round
men's javelin throw, qualifications
. . . women's 100-m, first round
10:00 Baseball, ... Dodger Stadium
. . . . first round (2 games)
10:00 Volleyball . . . Long Beach Arena
men's, preliminaries (2 matches)
10:00 Weight Lifting . . . .
Loyola Marymount University . .
. . . . light heavyweight
(up to 82.5 kg), preliminaries . .
11:00 Boxing . . . .
L.A. Memorial Sports Arena . . .
. . . . preliminary bouts
11:00 Team Handball . . . .
CSU, Fullerton . . . .
. men's, preliminaries (3 games)

PM	EVENT

2:00 Equestrian . . . . Santa Anita Park
. . jumping training competition
2:00 Weight Lifting . . . .
Loyola Marymount University . .
. . . . light heavyweight
(up to 82.5 kg), preliminaries . .
2:30 Basketball . . . . The Forum
. men's, preliminaries (2 games)
2:30 Field Hockey . . . .
Field East L.A. College. . . . . . .
. . men's, preliminaries (1 game)
women's, round robin (1 game)
4:00 Athletics . . . . L.A. Coliseum
. women's 100-m, second round
. . . . heptathlon (javelin throw,
800-m, final events). . . . .
. . . . . . men's 100-m, semifinal
. . . women's 800-m, semifinal
. . men's 800-m, second round
. . . men's triple jump, semifinal
. men's 400-m hurdles, semifinal
. . . . men's 100-m, final
4:00 Judo . . . . CSU, Los Angeles
. . . . extra lightweight
5:00 Swimming . . . . USC
men's 200-m ind. medley, finals
. women's 200-m butterfly, finals
. men's 1,500-m freestyle, finals
women's 200-m backstroke, finals

5:30	..... men's 4 x 100-m medley relay, finals .... Gymnastics.......... Pauley Pavilion, UCLA .... men's apparatus, finals
6:00	Boxing. L.A. Memorial Sports Arena ... . preliminary bouts
6:00	Weight Lifting .... Loyola Marymount University .. .. light heavyweight (up to 82.5 kg), preliminaries ..
6:30	Team Handball CSU, Fullerton .... men's, preliminaries (3 games)
6:30	Volleyball... Long Beach Arena men's, preliminaries (2 games)
8:00	Basketball .... The Forum . men's, preliminaries (2 games)
8:00	Fencing .... L.B. Convention Center .... sabre, men's ind., finals

Sunday, August 5

AM	EVENT
8:00	Athletics....... L.A. Coliseum .... women's marathon .... women's javelin throw, qualifications .... women's 400-m hurdles, first round. .... men's 110-m hurdles, first round .... men's hammer throw, qualifications ....
8:00	Field Hockey .... Field East L.A. College....... ... men's, preliminary (1 game) women's, round robin (1 game)
9:00	Basketball .... The Forum women's, round robin (2 games)
9:00	Cycling .... CSU, Dominguez Hills. ...... 100-km road race, team time trial
9:00	Fencing .... L.B. Convention Center .... foil, men's team, preliminaries foil, women's team, preliminaries
10:00	Diving .... USC ...... women's springboard, preliminaries. ....
10:00	Volleyball... Long Beach Arena women's, semifinals (2 matches)
10:00	Weight Lifting .... Loyola Marymount University.. .... middle heavyweight (up to 90 kg), preliminaries. ....
11:00	Boxing .... L.A. Memorial Sports Arena ... . preliminary bouts

PM	EVENTS
1:00	Baseball ..... Dodger Stadium .... first round (2 games)
1:45	Field Hockey .... Field East L.A. College....... . men's, preliminaries (2 games) women's, round robin (1 game)
2:00	Weight Lifting .... Loyola Marymount University.. .... middle heavyweight (up to 90 kg), preliminaries. ....
2:30	Basketball .... The Forum .... men's, semifinals (1 game)
3:00	Diving .... USC ...... women's springboard, preliminaries. ....
3:00	Soccer........... Rose Bowl ...... quarterfinals (1 match)
4:00	Athletics....... L.A. Coliseum ... women's 100-m, semifinals & final ....

	. men's long jump, qualifications .... men's 110-m hurdles, second round .... men's 400-m, second round .... women's 400-m, semifinal ..... men's Javelin throw, final ...... men's 800-m, semifinal ... men's 400-m hurdles, final
4:00	Judo .... CSU, Los Angeles .... half lightweight
5:30	Gymnastics.......... Pauley Pavilion, UCLA .... women's apparatus, finals
6:00	Boxing .... L.A. Memorial Sports Arena ... . preliminary bouts
6:00	Weight Lifting .... Loyola Marymount University.. .... middle heavyweight (up to 90 kg), preliminaries. ....
6:30	Basketball .... The Forum women's, round robin (1 game) .... men's, semifinals (1 game)
6:30	Team Handball .... CSU, Fullerton .... women's, round robin (3 games)
6:30	Volleyball... Long Beach Arena women's, semifinals (2 matches)
7:00	Soccer........... Rose Bowl ...... quarterfinals (1 match)
8:00	Fencing .... L.B. Convention Center .... foil, men's team , finals

Monday, August 6

AM	EVENT
7:30	Canoeing ...... Lake Casitas .... men's 500-m, heats .... women's 500-m, heats
8:30	Field Hockey .... Field East L.A. College .... men's, preliminaries (2 games)
8:30	Water Polo .... Pepperdine University .... final round (2 games)
9:00	Tennis .... UCLA .... preliminaries (16 matches)
9:30	Athletics....... L.A. Coliseum .... pole vault, qualifications ... men's 200-m, first & second rounds .... women's 3,000-m, first round
10:00	Basketball .... The Forum . men's, quarterfinals (2 games)
10:00	Synchronized Swimming .. USC ..... duet routines, preliminary
11:00	Boxing .... L.A. Memorial Sports Arena ... . preliminary bouts
11:00	Team Handball .... CSU, Fullerton .... men's, preliminaries (3 games)

PM	EVENT
1:00	Baseball ..... Dodger Stadium .... semifinals (2 games)
1:30	Water Polo .... Pepperdine University .... final round (2 games)
1:30	Yachting ... Long Beach Marina .... fifth race
2:00	Weight Lifting .... Loyola Marymount University.. .... first heavyweight (up to 100 kg), preliminaries. ..
2:30	Field Hockey .... Field East L.A. College......... .. men's, preliminaries (1 game) women's, round robin (1 game)
4:00	Athletics....... L.A. Coliseum ...... men's 110-m hurdles,

---

	semifinal & final .... men's hammer throw, final .... women's 400-m hurdles, semifinal .... men's 400-m, final ...... women's 400-m, final ...... women's 800-m, final ..... men's long jump, final ..... men's 800-m, final ... women's javelin throw, final ... men's 3,000-m steeplechase ...... men's 10,000-m, final
4:00	Judo .... CSU,L.A. .... lightweight
4:30	Diving .... USC ... women's springboard, finals
5:00	Basketball .... The Forum . men's, quarterfinals (2 games)
5:00	Soccer........... Rose Bowl .... quarterfinals (1 match)
6:00	Boxing ..... L.A. Sports Arena .... preliminary bouts
6:00	Weight Lifting .... Loyola Marymount University.. .... first heavyweight (up to 100 kg), preliminaries. ..
6:30	Team Handball .... CSU, Fullerton .... men's, preliminaries (3 games)
6:30	Volleyball... Long Beach Arena men's, preliminaries (2 matches)
7:00	Soccer........... Rose Bowl ...... quarterfinals (1 match)
7:30	Water Polo .... Pepperdine University .... final round (2 games)

Tuesday, August 7

AM	EVENT
7:30	Canoeing ...... Lake Casitas .... men's 1,000-m, heats and repechage .... women's 500-m, heats and repechage ....
8:00	Field Hockey .... Field East L.A. College......... . men's, preliminaries (1 game) women's, round robin (1 game)
8:30	Water Polo .... Pepperdine University .... final round (2 games)
9:00	Fencing .... L.B. Convention Center ...... foil, women's team, preliminaries . épée, men's ind., preliminaries
9:00	Tennis .... UCLA .... preliminaries (16 matches)
10:00	Diving .... UCLA men's springboard, preliminaries
10:00	Equestrian .... Santa Anita Park .... team jumping competition
10:00	Volleyball... Long Beach Arena .... women's, finals (2 matches; 5-8 places) ......
11:00	Boxing ..... L.A. Sports Arena .... quarterfinal bouts
12:00	Wrestling .... Anaheim Convention Center. .. .. freestyle (48, 62, 90 kg), preliminaries ..

PM	EVENT
1:30	Water Polo .... Pepperdine University .... final round (2 games)
1:30	Yachting ... Long Beach Marina .... sixth race
1:45	Field Hockey .... Field East L.A. College......... women's, round robin (1 game) . men's, preliminaries (2 games)

2:00	Weight Lifting .... Loyola Marymount University . . .. second heavyweight (up to 110 kg), preliminaries. ..
4:00	Baseball ..... Dodger Stadium .... finals (2 games)
4:00	Diving .... USC men's springboard, preliminaries
4:00	Judo .... CSU, L.A. .... half middleweight
4:00	Volleyball ... Long Beach Arena .... women's, finals (1 match; 3-4 places)
5:00	Basketball .... The Forum .... women's, finals (2 games; 1-4 places)........
6:00	Boxing .... L.A. Memorial Sports Arena ... . quarterfinal bouts
6:00	Weight Lifting .... second heavyweight (up to 110 kg), preliminaries. ..
6:00	Wrestling .... Anaheim Convention Center. .. .. freestyle (48, 62, 90 kg), preliminaries. ..
6:30	Team Handball .... CSU, Fullerton .... women's, round robin (3 games)
7:30	Water Polo .... Pepperdine University .... final round (2 games)
8:00	Fencing .... L.B. Convention Center .... foil, women's team, finals
8:30	Volleyball... Long Beach Arena .... women's, finals (1 match)

Wednesday, August 8

AM	EVENT
7:30	Canoeing ...... Lake Casitas ..... men's 500-m, semifinals
9:00	Basketball .... The Forum ... men's, semifinals (2 games)
9:00	Fencing .... L.B. Convention Center ...... sabre, men's team, preliminaries . épée, men's ind., preliminaries
9:00	Tennis .... UCLA .... preliminaries (16 matches)
9:00	Volleyball... Long Beach Arena .. men's, semifinals (2 matches) .... men's, final round (1 match; 9-10 places)
9:30	Athletics....... L.A. Coliseum .... men's decathlon (100-m, long jump, shot put) .. ... men's discus, qualifications ...... women's 200-m, first & second rounds .... women's 1,500-m, first round
10:00	Archery ...... El Dorado Park .... women's 70-m .... men's 90-m
10:00	Synchronized Swimming .. USC .... duet routines, final
11:00	Boxing .... L.A. Memorial Sports Arena ... . quarterfinal bouts
11:00	Team Handball .... CSU, Fullerton .... men's, preliminaries (3 games)

PM	EVENT
12:00	Wrestling .... Anaheim Convention Center. .. .. freestyle (48, 52, 62, 74, 90, over 100 kg), preliminaries
1:30	Yachting ... Long Beach Marina .... seventh race
2:00	Equestrian .... Santa Anita Park

2:00 Weight Lifting . . . .
Loyola Marymount University . .
super heavyweight, preliminaries
2:30 Archery . . . . . El Dorado Park
. . . . women's 60-m
. . . . men's 70-m
3:00 Basketball . . . . The Forum
. . . men's, semifinals (1 game)
4:00 Athletics . . . . . . L.A. Coliseum
. men's 200-m, semifinal & final
. . . . . . men's decathlon
(high jump, 400-m) . . . .
. . . . . . men's pole vault, final
. . women's 400-m hurdles, final
. . . men's 400-m, final
. . . men's 5,000-m, first round
women's long jump, qualifications
. . . women's 3,000-m, semifinal
. . men's 3,000-m steeplechase,
semifinal . . . .
4:00 Judo . . . . CSU, L.A.
. . . . middleweight
4:30 Diving . . . . USC
. . . . men's springboard, finals
6:00 Boxing . . . .
L.A. Memorial Sports Arena . . .
. . . . quarterfinal bouts
6:00 Soccer . . . . Rose Bowl
. . . . semifinals (1 game)
6:00 Weight Lifting . . . .
Loyola Marymount University . .
super heavyweight, preliminaries
6:00 Wrestling . . . .
Anaheim Convention Center . . .
. . . . . freestyle (48, 52, 62, 74,
90, over 100 kg), preliminaries
6:30 Team Handball . . . . . Cal. Poly.
. men's, preliminaries (3 games)
6:30 Volleyball . . . Long Beach Arena
. . men's, semifinals (2 matches)
7:00 Basketball . . . . The Forum
. . . men's, semifinals (1 game)
7:00 Field Hockey . . . .
Field East L.A. College . . . . . .
. . . men's, semifinals (2 games)
8:00 Fencing . L.B. Convention Center
. . . . . . épée, men's ind., finals
8:30 Soccer . . . . Rose Bowl
. . . . semifinals (1 game)

Thursday, August 9

AM   EVENT
7:30 Canoeing . . . . . . Lake Casitas
. . . . men's 1,000-m, semifinals
. . . women's 500-m, semifinals
8:00 Field Hockey . . . .
Field East L.A. College . . . . . .
. . men's, semifinals (2 games)
8:30 Water Polo . . . .
Pepperdine University . . . .
. . . . final round (2 games)
9:00 Tennis . . . . UCLA
. . . . . quarterfinals (8 matches)
9:30 Athletics . . . . . . L.A. Coliseum
. . . . . . decathlon (discus throw,
110-m hurdles, pole vault) . . . .
. . . . women's 100-m hurdles,
first round . . . .
. . . . women's high
jump, qualifications . . . .
women's 200-m, semifinal & final
. . . . decathlon (javelin throw,
1500-m, final event) . . . .
. . . . men's 1,500-m, first round
. . . women's 1,500-m, semifinal
10:00 Archery . . . . . El Dorado Park
. . . . women's 50-m
10:00 Basketball . . . . The Forum
. . . . men's, final round

(2 games, 9-12 places) . . . . . .
10:00 Diving . . . . USC
women's platform, preliminaries
11:00 Boxing . . . .
L.A. Memorial Sports Arena . . .
. . . . semifinal bouts

PM   EVENT
12:00 Fencing . L.B. Convention Center
sabre, men's team, preliminaries
12:00 Wrestling . . . .
Anaheim Convention Center . . .
. . freestyle (52, 57, 68, 74, 82,
100, over 100 kg), preliminaries
. freestyle (48, 62, 90 kg), finals
1:15 Field Hockey . . . .
Field East L.A. College . . . . . .
women's, round robin (1 game)
. . . men's, semifinals (2 games)
1:30 Synchronized Swimming . . USC
. . . . duet routines, final
1:30 Water Polo . . . .
Pepperdine University . . . .
. . . . final round (2 games)
2:00 Equestrian . . . . Santa Anita Park
. . . team dressage competition
2:30 Archery . . . . . . El Dorado Park
. . . . women's 30-m
. . . . men's 30-m
4:00 Judo . . . . CSU, L.A.
. . . . half heavyweight
4:30 Diving . . . . USC
women's platform, preliminaries
6:00 Boxing . . . .
L.A. Memorial Sports Arena . . .
. . . . semifinal bouts
6:00 Gymnastics, rhythmic . . . .
Pauley Pavillion, UCLA . . . . . .
. . . . . women's, preliminaries
6:00 Wrestling . . . .
Anaheim Convention Center . . .
. . freestyle (52, 57, 68, 74, 82,
100, over 100 kg), preliminaries
. . . . (48, 62, 90 kg), finals
6:30 Team Handball . . . .
CSU, Fullerton . . . .
women's, round robin (3 games)
7:00 Basketball . . . . The Forum
men's, final (1 game, 3-4 places)
7:30 Water Polo . . . .
Pepperdine University . . . .
. . . . final round (2 games)
8:00 Fencing . L.B. Convention Center
. . . . . sabre, men's team, finals

Friday, August 10

AM   EVENT
8:00 Canoeing . . . . . . Lake Casitas
. . . . men's 500-m, finals
. . . . . . women's 500-m, finals
8:00 Field Hockey . . . .
Field East L.A. College . . . . . .
. . . . men's, final (1 game,
11-12 places) . . . .
women's, round robin (1 game)
8:30 Water Polo . . . .
Pepperdine University . . . .
. . . . final round (2 games)
9:00 Tennis . . . . UCLA
. . . . . . semifinals (4 matches)
9:00 Yachting . . . Long Beach Marina
Olympic boardsailing (exhibition)
9:30 Athletics . . . . . . L.A. Coliseum
. men's high jump, qualifications
. . . women's 4 x 400-m relay,
first round . . . .
men's 4 x 400-m relay, first round
. . . . . . women's discus throw,
qualifications . . . .
. . . . . women's 4 x 100-m relay
first round . . . .

. . . . . . men's 4 x 100-m relay,
first round . . . .
10:00 Archery . . . . . El Dorado Park
. . . . women's 70-m
. . . . men's 90-m
10:00 Basketball . . . . The Forum
. . . . men's, final round
(2 games, 5-8 places) . . . .
10:00 Fencing . L.B. Convention Center
épée, men's team, preliminaries
11:00 Team Handball . . . .
CSU, Fullerton . . . .
. . . . men's, final round
(2 games, 9-12 places) . . . . . .

PM   EVENT
12:00 Wrestling . . . .
Anaheim Convention Center . . .
. . . . freestyle (57, 68,
82, 100 kg), preliminaries . . . .
. freestyle (52, 74, over 100 kg),
finals . . . .
1:15 Field Hockey . . . .
Field East L.A. College . . . . . .
. . . . men's, finals
(2 games, 7-10 places) . . . . . .
women's, round robin (1 game)
1:30 Water Polo . . . .
Pepperdine University . . . .
. . . . final round (2 games)
2:00 Equestrian . . . . Santa Anita Park
. . . . ind. dressage
2:30 Archery . . . . . . El Dorado Park
. . . . women's 60-m
. . . . men's 70-m
4:00 Athletics . . . . . . L.A. Coliseum
. . . . women's high jump, final
. . . . women's 100-m hurdles,
semifinal
men's 4 x 400-m relay, semifinal
. . . women's 4 x 400-m relay,
semifinal . . . .
. . . . men's discus throw, final
. . . men's 1,500-m, semifinal
. . women's 100-m hurdles, final
. . . . . women's 3,000-m, final
men's 3,000-m steeplechase, final
4:00 Judo . . . . CSU, L.A.
. . . . heavyweight
4:30 Diving . . . . USC
. . . . women's platform, finals
6:00 Gymnastics . . . .
Pauley Pavilion, UCLA . . . . . .
. . . . rhythmic, preliminaries
6:00 Wrestling . . . .
Anaheim Convention Center . . .
. . freestyle (52, 57, 68, 74, 82,
100, over 100 kg), preliminaries
. freestyle (48, 62, 90 kg), finals
6:30 Team Handball . . . .
CSU, Fullerton . . . .
. . . . men's, final round
(2 games, 5-8 places) . . . .
6:30 Volleyball . . . Long Beach Arena
. . . . men's, final round
(2 matches, 5-8 places) . . . . . .
7:00 Basketball . . . . The Forum
men's, final (1 game, 1-2 places)
7:00 Soccer . . . . Rose Bowl
final round (1 game, 3-4 places)
7:30 Water Polo . . . .
Pepperdine University . . . .
. . . . final round (2 games)

Saturday, August 11

AM   EVENT
8:00 Canoeing . . . . . . Lake Casitas
. . . . men's 1,000-m, finals
8:00 Athletics . . . . . . L.A. Coliseum
. . . . . . men's 50-km walk, final
. . men's shot put, qualifications

. . . . women's 4 x 100-m relay,
semifinal . . . .
men's 4 x 100-m relay, semifinal
women's 800-m wheelchair, final
men's 1,500-m wheelchair, final
9:00 Yachting . . . Long Beach Marina
Olympic boardsailing, exhibition
9:15 Field Hockey . . . .
Field East L.A. College . . . .
men's, finals (3 games, 1-6 places)
10:00 Archery . . . . . El Dorado Park
. . . . women's 50-m
. . . . men's 50-m
10:00 Diving . . . . USC
. . men's platform, preliminaries
10:00 Fencing . L.B. Convention Center
épée, men's team, preliminaries
10:00 Tennis . . . . UCLA
. . . . finals (2 matches)
11:00 Boxing . . . .
L.A. Memorial Sports Arena . . .
. . . . final bouts

PM   EVENT
12:00 Volleyball . . . Long Beach Arena
. . . . men's, final round
(1 match, 3-4 places) . . . .
12:00 Wrestling . . . .
Anaheim Convention Center . . .
. . freestyle (57, 68, 82, 100 kg),
preliminaries . . . .
2:00 Team Handball . . . .
CSU, Fullerton . . . .
. . . finals (2 games, 1-4 places)
2:30 Archery . . . . . . El Dorado Park
. . . . women's 30-m
. . . . men's 30-m
3:00 Diving . . . . USC
. . . men's platform, preliminaries
4:00 Athletics . . . . . . L.A. Coliseum
. . . women's discus throw, final
. women's 4 x 100-m relay, final
. . . . . . men's high jump, final
. women's 4 x 100-m relay, final
. women's 4 x 400-m relay, final
. . . . men's shot put, final
. . . . . . women's 1,500-m, final
. . . . men's 1,500-m, final
. . . . men's 5,000-m, final
4:00 Judo . . . . CSU, L.A.
. . . . open category
6:00 Boxing . . . .
L.A. Memorial Sports Arena . . .
. . . . final bouts
6:00 Wrestling . . . .
Anaheim Convention Center . . .
. . freestyle (57, 68, 82, 100 kg),
finals
6:30 Volleyball . . . Long Beach Arena
men, finals (1 match, 1-2 places)
7:00 Soccer . . . . Rose Bowl
. . . . . final match (1-2 places)
7:00 Gymnastics . . . . UCLA
. . . . rhythmic, finals
8:00 Fencing . . . .
Long Beach Convention Center.
. . . . . épée, men's team, finals

Sunday, August 12

AM   EVENT
7:00 Equestrian . . . . Santa Anita Park
. . . . ind. jumping
11:00 Diving . . . . USC
. . . . men's platform, finals
5:15 Track and Field . . . .
L.A. Memorial Coliseum . . . . . .
. . . . . . men's, marathon (finish)
6:30 Closing Ceremony . . . .

LOS ANGELES 1984
20TH OLYMPIC GAMES

ATHLETICS (TRACK & FIELD)

Event	Gold		Silver		Bronze		Place	Country	Name	Time/Mark
100 METERS	USA	9.99 CARL LEWIS	USA	10.19 SAM GRADDY	CAN	10.22 BEN JOHNSON	4. 5. 8.	USA GBR JAM	Brown McFarlane Stewart	10.26 10.27 10.29
200 METERS	USA	19.80 CARL LEWIS	USA	19.96 KIRK BAPTISTE	USA	20.26 THOMAS JEFFERSON	4. 5. 6.	BRA FRG FRA	Batista da Silva Lübke Boussemart	20.30 20.51 20.55
400 METERS	USA	44.27 ALONZO BABERS	CIV	44.54 GABRIEL TIACOH	USA	44.71 ANTONIO McKAY	4. 5. 6.	AUS USA NGR	Clark Nix Uti	44.75 44.75 44.93
800 METERS	BRA	1:43.00 JOAQUIM CRUZ	GBR	1:43.64 SEBASTIAN COE	USA	1:43.83 EARL JONES	4. 5. 6.	KEN ITA KEN	Konchellah Sabia Koech	1:44.03 1:44.53 1:44.86
1,500 METERS	GBR	3:32.53 SEBASTIAN COE	GBR	3:33.40 STEVE CRAM	ESP	3:34.30 JOSÉ ABASCAL	4. 5. 6.	KEN USA SUI	Cheshire Spivey Wirz	3:34.52 3:36.07 3:36.97
5,000 METERS	MAR	13:05.59 SAÏD AOUITA	SUI	13:07.54 MARKUS RYFFEL	POR	13:09.20 ANTONIO LEITÃO	4. 5. 6.	GBR KEN KEN	Hutchings Kipkoech Cheruiyot	13:11.50 13:14.40 13:18.41
10,000 METERS	ITA	27:47.54 ALBERTO COVA	GBR	28:06.22 MICHAEL McLEOD	KEN	28:06.46 MICHAEL MUSYOKI	4. 5. 6.	ITA FRG KEN	Antibo Herle Bitok	28:06.50 28:08.21 28:09.01
3,000 METER STEEPLECHASE	KEN	8:11.80 JULIUS KORIR	FRA	8:13.31 JOSEPH MAHMOUD	USA	8:14.06 BRIAN DIEMER	4. 5. 6.	USA GBR SPA	Marsh Reitz Ramón	8:14.25 8:15.48 8:17.27
110-METER HURDLES	USA	13.20 ROGER KINGDOM	USA	13.23 GREGORY FOSTER	FIN	13.40 ARTO BRYGGARE	4. 5. 6.	CAN USA FRA	McKoy Campbell Caristan	13.45 13.55 13.71
400-METER HURDLES	USA	47.75 EDWIN MOSES	USA	48.13 DANNY HARRIS	FRG	48.19 HARALD SCHMID	4. 5. 6.	SWE SEN USA	Nylander Ba Hawkins	48.97 49.28 49.42
4 x 100-METER RELAY	USA	37.83	JAM	38.62	CAN	38.70	4. 5. 6.	ITA GER FRA		38.87 38.99 39.10
4 x 400-METER RELAY	USA	2:57.91	GBR	2:59.13	NIG	2:59.32	4. 5. 6.	AUS ITA BAR		2:59.70 3:01.44 3:01.60
20,000-METER WALK	MEX	1:23:13 ERNESTO CANTO	MEX	1:23:20 RAUL GONZÁLEZ	ITA	1:23:26 MAURIZIO DAMILANO	4. 5. 6.	CAN ITA ESP	Leblanc Mattioli Marin	1:24:29 1:25:07 1:25:32
50,000-METER WALK	MEX	3:47:26 RAÚL GONZÁLEZ	SWE	3:53:19 BO GUSTAFSSON	ITA	3:53:45 ALESSANDRO BELLUCCI	4. 5. 6.	FIN ITA USA	Salonen Ducceschi Schueler	3:58:30 3:59:26 3:59:46
LONG JUMP	USA	8.54 CARL LEWIS	AUS	8.24 GARY HONEY	ITA	8.24 GIOVANNI EVANGELISTI	4. 5. 6.	USA CHN BAH	Myricks Yuhuang Wells	8.16 7.99 7.97
TRIPLE JUMP	USA	17.26 ALFRED JOYNER	USA	17.28 MICHAEL CONLEY	GBR	16.87 KEITH CONNOR	4. 5. 6.	CHN FRG USA	Zhenxian Bouschen Banks	16.83 16.77 16.75
HIGH JUMP	FRG	2.35 DIETMAR MÖGENBURG	SWE	2.33 PATRIK SJÖBERG	CHN	2.31 ZHU JIANHUA	4. 5. 6.	USA USA CAN	Stones Norquist Ottey	2.31 2.29 2.29
POLE VAULT	FRA	5.75 PIERRE QUINON	USA	5.65 MIKE TULLY	USA	5.60 EARL BELL	4. 5. 6.	FRA FIN USA	Vigneron Pallonen Lytle	5.60 5.60 5.40
SHOT PUT	ITA	21.26 ALESSANDRO ANDREI	USA	21.09 MICHAEL CARTER	USA	20.97 DAVID LAUT	4. 5. 6.	USA SUI ITA	Wolf Günthör Montelatici	20.93 20.28 19.98

Event	Gold		Silver		Bronze		4th–6th		
DISCUS THROW	FRG 66.60 ROLF DANNEBERG		USA 66.30 MAC WILKINS		USA 65.46 JOHN POWELL		4. NOR Hjeltnes 5. USA Burns 6. FRG Wagner	65.28 64.98 64.72	
HAMMER THROW	FIN 78.08 JUHA TIAINEN		FRG 77.98 KARL-HANS RIEHM		FRG 76.68 KLAUS PLOGHAUS		4. ITA Bianchini 5. USA Green 6. FIN Huhtala	75.94 75.60 75.28	
JAVELIN THROW	FIN 86.76 ARTO HÄRKÖNEN		GBR 85.74 DAVID OTTLEY		SWE 83.72 KENTH ELDEBRINK		4. FRG Gambke 5. JPN Yoshida 6. ISL Vilhjálmsson	82.46 81.98 81.58	
DECATHLON	GBR 8,798 DALEY THOMPSON		FRG 8,673 JÜRGEN HINGSEN		FRG 8,412 SIEGFRIED WENTZ		4. FRG Kratschmer 5. FRA Motti 6. USA Crist	8,326 8,266 8,130	
100 METERS	USA 10.97 EVELYN ASHFORD		USA 11.13 ALICE BROWN		JAM 11.16 MERLENE OTTEY-PAGE		4. USA Bolden 5. JAM Jackson 6. CAN Bailey	11.25 11.39 11.40	
200 METERS	USA 21.81 VALERIE BRISCO-HOOKS		USA 22.04 FLORENCE GRIFFITH		JAM 22.09 MERLENE OTTEY-PAGE		4. GBR Smallwood-Cook 5. JAM Jackson 6. USA Givens	22.10 22.20 22.36	
400 METERS	USA 48.83 VALERIE BRISCO-HOOKS		USA 49.05 C. CHEESEBOROUGH		GBR 49.42 K. SMALLWOOD-COOK		4. CAN Payne 5. USA Leatherwood 6. FRG Thimm	49.91 50.25 50.37	
800 METERS	ROM 1:57.60 DOINA MELINTE		USA 1:58.63 KIM GALLAGHER		ROM 1:58.83 FITA LOVIN		4. ITA Dorio 5. GBR Baker 6. USA Wysocki	1:59.05 2:00.03 2:00.34	
1,500 METERS	ITA 4:03.25 GABRIELLA DORIO		ROM 4:03.76 DOINA MELINTE		ROM 4:04.15 MARICICA PUICA		4. FRG Gerdes 5. GBR Benning 6. GBR Boxer	4:04.41 4:04.70 4:05.53	
3,000 METERS	ROM 8:35.96 MARICICA PUICA		GBR 8:39.47 WENDY SLY		CAN 8:42.14 LYNN WILLIAMS		4. USA Bremser 5. SUI Bürki 6. POR Cunha	8:42.78 8:45.20 8:46.37	
MARATHON	USA 2:24:52 JOAN BENOIT		NOR 2:26:18 GRETE WAITZ		POR 2:26:57 ROSA MOTA		4. NOR Kristiansen 5. NZL Moller 6. GBR Welch	2:27:34 2:28:34 2:28:54	
100-METER HURDLES	USA 12.84 B. FITZGERALD-BROWN		GBR 12.88 SHIRLEY STRONG		USA 13.06 KIM TURNER FRA 13.06 MICHÈLE CHARDONNET		5. AUS Nunn 6. FRA Savigny	13.20 13.28	
400-METER HURDLE	MAR 54.61 NAWAL EL MOUTAWAKEL		USA 55.20 JUDI BROWN		ROM 55.41 CHRISTIANA COJOCARU		4. IND Usha 5. SWE Skoglund 6. AUS Flintoff	55.42 55.43 56.21	
4 x 100-METER RELAY	USA 41.65 ALICE BROWN JEANETTE BOLDEN CHANDRA CHEESEBOROUGH EVELYN ASHFORD		CAN 42.77 ANGELA BAILEY MARITA PAYNE ANGELLA TAYLOR FRANCE GAREAU		GBR 43.11 SIMMONE JACOBS KATHY SMALLWOOD-COOK B. GODDARD-CALLENDER HEATHER HUNTE-OAKES		4. FRA Bacoul/Gaschet Loval/Naigre 5. GER Oker/Schabinger Gaugel/Thimm 6. BAH Clarke/Davis Greene/Fowler	43.15 43.57 44.18	
4 x 400-METER RELAY	USA 3:18.29 LILLIE LEATHERWOOD SHERRI HOWARD VALERIE BRISCO-HOOKS CHANDRA CHEESEBOROUGH		CAN 3:21.21 CHARMAINE CROOKS JILLIAN RICHARDSON MOLLY KILLINGBECK MARITA PAYNE		FRG 3:22.98 HEIKE SCHULTE-MATTLER UTE THIMM HEIDE GAUGEL GABY BUSSMANN		4. GBR 5. JAM 6. ITA	3:25.51 3:27.51 3:30.82	
HIGH JUMP	FRG 2.02 ULRIKE MEYFARTH		ITA 2.00 SARA SIMEONI		USA 1.97 JONI HUNTLEY		4. FRA Ewanje-Épée 5. CAN Brill 6. AUS Browne	1.94 1.94 1.94	
LONG JUMP	ROM 6.96 A. CUŞIMIR-STANCIU		ROM 6.81 VALY IONESCU		GBR 6.80w SUE HEARNSHAW		4. USA Thacker 5. USA Joyner 6. AUS Lorraway	6.78 6.77 6.67	
SHOT PUT	FRG 20.48 CLAUDIA LOSCH		ROM 20.47 MIHAELA LOGHIN		AUS 19.19 GAEL MARTIN		4. GBR Oakes 5. CHN Meisu 6. GBR Head	18.14 17.96 17.90	
DISCUS THROW	HOL 65.36 RIA STALMAN		USA 64.86 LESLIE DENIZ		ROM 63.64 FLORENŢA CRACIUNESCU		4. FIN Lindholm 5. GBR Ritchie 6. FRG Manecke	62.84 62.58 58.56	
JAVELIN THROW	GBR 69.56 TESSA SANDERSON		FIN 69.00 TIINA LILLAK		GBR 67.14 FATIMA WHITBREAD		4. FIN Laaksalo 5. NOR Solberg 6. FRG Thyssen	66.40 64.52 63.26	

HEPTATHLON	AUS 6,390 GLYNIS NUNN	USA 6,385 JACKIE JOYNER	FRG 6,363 SABINE EVERTS	4. USA Greiner 6,281 5. GBR Simpson 6,280 6. FRG Braun 6,236

ARCHERY

FINAL STANDINGS	USA 2,616 DARRELL PACE	USA 2,564 RICHARD MCKINNEY	JPN 2,563 HIROSHI YAMAMOTO
FINAL STANDINGS	KOR 2,568 SEO HYANG-SOON	CHN 2,559 LI LINGJUAN	KOR 2,555 KIM JIN-HO

BASKETBALL

FINAL STANDINGS	USA	SPA	YUG
FINAL STANDINGS	USA	KOR	CHN

BOXING

LIGHT FLYWEIGHT 106 lbs. (48 kg)	USA PAUL GONZALEZ	ITA SALVATORE TODISCO	VEN JOSÉ MARCELINO BOLIVAR ZAM KEITH MWILA
FLYWEIGHT 112.5 lbs. (51 kg)	USA STEVE MCCRORY	YUG REDZEP REDZEPOVSKI	KEN IBRAHIM BILALI TUR EYUP CAN
BANTAMWEIGHT 119.5 lbs. (54 kg)	ITA MAURIZIO STECCA	MEX HECTOR LOPEZ	CAN DALE WALTERS DOM PEDRO NOLASCO
FEATHERWEIGHT 126 lbs. (57 kg)	USA MELDRICK TAYLOR	NGR PETER KONYEGWACHIE	TUR TURGUT AYKAC VEN OMAR CATARI PERAZA
LIGHTWEIGHT 132 lbs. (60 kg)	USA PERNELL WHITAKER	PUR LUIS ORTIZ	CMR MARTIN NDONGO EBANGA KOR CHUN CHIL-SUNG
LIGHT WELTERWEIGHT 140 lbs. (63.5 kg)	USA JERRY PAGE	THA DHAWEE UMPONMAHA	YUG MIRKO PUZOVIĆ ROM MIRCEA FULGER
WELTERWEIGHT 148 lbs. (67 kg)	USA MARK BRELAND	KOR AN YOUNG-SU	FIN JONI NYMAN ITA LUCIANO BRUNO
LIGHT MIDDLEWEIGHT 156 lbs. (71 kg)	USA FRANK TATE	CAN SHAWN O'SULLIVAN	FRA CHRISTOPHE TIOZZO FRG MANFRED ZIELONKA
MIDDLEWEIGHT 165.5 lbs. (75 kg)	KOR SHIN JOON-SUP	USA VIRGIL HILL	ALG MOHAMED ZAOUI PUR ARISTIDES GONZALES

LIGHT HEAVYWEIGHT 179 lbs. (81 kg)	○ YUG ANTON JOSIPOVIĆ	○ NZL KEVIN BARRY	● USA EVANDER HOLYFIELD ALG MUSTAPHA MOUSSA
HEAVYWEIGHT 200.5 lbs. (91 kg)	○ USA HENRY TILLMAN	○ CAN WILLIAM deWIT	● ITA ANGELO MUSONE NED ARNOLD VANDERLIJDE
SUPER HEAVYWEIGHT >200.5 lbs. (>91 kg)	○ USA TYRELL BIGGS	○ ITA FRANCESCO DAMIANI	● GBR ROBERT WELLS YUG SALIHU AZIZ

CANOEING

KAYAK SINGLES 500 METRES	○ NZL 1:47.84 IAN FERGUSON	○ SWE 1:48.18 LARS-ERIK MOBERG	● FRA 1:48.41 BERNARD BREGEON
KAYAK SINGLES 1000 METERS	○ NZL 3:45.73 ALAN THOMPSON	○ YUG 3:46.88 MILAN JANIĆ	○ USA 3:47.38 GREGORY BARTON
KAYAK PAIRS 500 METERS	○ NZL 1:34.21 IAN FERGUSON PAUL MacDONALD	○ SWE 1:35.26 PER-INGE BENGTSSON LARS-ERIK MOBERG	● CAN 1:35.41 HUGH FISHER ALWYN MORRIS
KAYAK PAIRS 1000 METERS	○ CAN 3:24.22 HUGH FISHER ALWYN MORRIS	○ FRA 3:25.97 BERNARD BREGEON PATRICK LEFOULON	● AUS 3:26.80 BARRY KELLY GRANT KENNY
KAYAK FOURS 1000 METERS	○ NZL 3:02.28 GRANT BRAMWELL IAN FERGUSON PAUL MacDONALD ALAN THOMPSON	○ SWE 3:02.81 PER-INGE BENGTSSON TOMMY KARLS LARS-ERIK MOBERG THOMAS OHLSSON	● FRA 3:03.94 FRANÇOIS BAROUH PHILIPPE BOCCARA PASCAL BOUCHERIT DIDIER VAVASSEUR
CANADIAN SINGLES 500 METERS	○ CAN 1:57.01 LARRY CAIN	○ DEN 1:58.45 HENNING JAKOBSEN	● ROM 1:59.86 COSTICA OLARU
CANADIAN SINGLES 1000 METERS	○ FRG 4:06.32 ULRICH EICKE	○ CAN 4:08.67 LARRY CAIN	● DEN 4:09.51 HENNING JAKOBSEN
CANADIAN PAIRS 500 METERS	○ YUG 1:43.67 MATIJA LJUBEK MIRKO NIŠOVIĆ	○ ROM 1:45.68 IVAN PATZAICHIN TOMA SIMIONOV	● SPA 1:47.71 ENRIQUE MIGUEZ NARCISCO SUÁREZ
CANADIAN PAIRS 1000 METERS	○ ROM 3:40.60 IVAN PATZAICHIN TOMA SIMIONOV	○ YUG 3:41.56 MATIJA LJUBEK MIRKO NISOVIĆ	● FRA 3:48.01 DIDIER HOYER ERIC RENAUD
KAYAK SINGLES 500 METERS	○ SWE 1:58.72 AGNETA ANDERSSON	○ FRG 1:59.93 BARBARA SCHÜTTPELZ	● NED 2:00.11 ANNEMIEK DERCKX
CANADIAN PAIRS 500 METERS	○ SWE 1:45.25 AGNETA ANDERSSON ANNA OLSSON	○ CAN 1:47.13 ALEXANDRA BARRÉ SUE HOLLOWAY	● GER 1:47.32 JOSEFA IDEM BARBARA SCHÜTTPELZ
KAYAK FOURS 500 METERS	○ ROM 1:38.34 AGAFIA CONSTANTIN NASTASIA IONESCU TECLA MARINESCU MARIA ŇTEFAN	○ SWE 1:38.87 AGNETA ANDERSSON ANNA OLSSON EVA KARLSSON SUSANNE WIBERG	● CAN 1:39.40 ALEXANDRA BARRÉ LUCIE GUAY SUE HOLLOWAY BARBARA OLMSTED

CYCLING

POINTS RACE 50 kilometers	BEL 37 ROGER ILEGEMS	FRG 15 UWE MESSERSCHMIDT	MEX 29 JOSÉ MANUEL YOUSHIMATZ SOTOMAYOR
1,000-METER SPRINT	USA MARK GORSKI	USA NELSON VAILS	JPN TSUTOMU SAKAMOTO
1,000-METER TIME TRIAL	FRG 1:06.10 FREDY SCHMIDTKE	CAN 1:06.44 CURTIS HARNETT	FRA 1:06.65 FABRICE COLAS
TEAM TIME TRIAL	ITA 1:58:28.0 MARCELLO BARTALINI MARCO GIOVANNETTI EROS POLI CLAUDIO VANDELLI	SUI 2:02:38.0 ALFRED ACHERMANN RICHARD TRINKLER LAURENT VIAL BENNO WISS	USA 2:02:46.0 RONALD KIEFEL ROY KNICKMAN DAVIS PHINNEY ANDREW WEAVER
4,000-METER INDIVIDUAL PURSUIT	USA 4:39.35 STEVE HEGG	FRG 4:43.82 ROLF GÖLZ	USA 4:44.03 LEONARD HARVEY NITZ
4,000-METER TEAM PURSUIT	AUS 4:25.99 MICHAEL GRENDA KEVIN NICHOLS MICHAEL TURTUR DEAN WOODS	USA 4:29.85 DAVID GRYLLS STEVE HEGG PATRICK MCDONOUGH LEONARD HARVEY NITZ	GER 4:25.60 REINHARD ALBER ROLF GÖLZ ROLAND GÜNTHER MICHAEL MARX
ROAD RACE 190.2 kilometers	USA 4:59:57 ALEXI GREWAL	CAN 4:59:57 STEVE BAUER	NOR 5:00:18 DAG OTTO LAURITZEN
ROAD RACE 79.2 kilometers	USA 2:11:14.0 CONNIE CARPENTER-PHINNEY	USA 2:11:14.0 REBECCA TWIGG	FRG 2:11:14.0 SANDRA SCHUMACHER

DIVING

PLATFORM	USA 710.91 GREGORY LOUGANIS	USA 643.50 BRUCE KIMBALL	CHN 638.28 LI KONGZHENG
SPRINGBOARD	USA 754.41 GREGORY LOUGANIS	CHN 662.31 TAN LIANGDE	USA 661.32 RONALD MERRIOTT
PLATFORM	CHN 435.51 ZHOU JIHONG	USA 431.19 MICHELLE MITCHELL	USA 422.07 WENDY WYLAND
SPRINGBOARD	CAN 530.70 SYLVIE BERNIER	USA 527.46 KELLY MCCORMICK	USA 517.62 CHRISTINE SEUFERT

EQUESTRIAN

THREE-DAY EVENT, INDIVIDUAL	NZL -51.60 MARK TODD	USA -54.20 KAREN STIVES	GBR -56.80 VIRGINIA HOLGATE
THREE-DAY EVENT, TEAM	USA -186.00 KAREN STIVES TORRANCE FLEISCHMANN J. MICHAEL PLUMB BRUCE DAVIDSON	GBR -189.20 VIRGINIA HOLGATE LUCINDA GREEN IAN STARK DIANA CLAPHAM	FRG -234.00 DIETMAR HOGREFE BETTINA OVERESCH CLAUS ERHORN BURKHARD TESDORPF
DRESSAGE, INDIVIDUAL	FRG 1,504 REINER KLIMKE	DEN 1,442 ANNE GRETHE JENSEN	SUI 1,364 OTTO HOFER
DRESSAGE, TEAM	FRG 4,955 REINER KLIMKE UWE SAUER HERBERT KRUG	SUI 4,673 OTTO HOFER CHRISTINE STÜCKELBERGER AMY-CATHÉRINE DE BARY	SWE 4,630 ULLA HÅKANSON INGAMAY BYLUND LOUISE NATHHORST

JUMPING, INDIVIDUAL	USA -4.00 0 **JOSEPH FARGIS**	USA -4.00 -8 **CONRAD HOMFELD**	SUI -8.00 0 **HEIDI ROBBIANI**
JUMPING THREE-DAY EVENT, TEAM	USA -12.00 **JOSEPH FARGIS** **CONRAD HOMFELD** **LESLIE BURR** **MELANIE AINSWORTH SMITH**	GBR -36.75 **MICHAEL WHITAKER** **JOHN WHITAKER** **STEVEN SMITH** **TIMOTHY GRUBB**	FGR -39.25 **PAUL SCHOCKEMÖHLE** **PETER LUTHER** **FRANKE SLOOTHAAK** **FRITZ LIGGES**

FENCING

ÉPEÉ, INDIVIDUAL	FRA **PHILIPPE BOISSE**	SWE **BJÖRNE VÄGGÖ**	FRA **PHILIPPE RIBOUD**
ÉPEÉ, TEAM	GER	FRA	ITA
FOIL, INDIVIDUAL	ITA **MAURO NUMA**	FRG **MATTHIAS BEHR**	ITA **STEFANO CERIONI**
FOIL, TEAM	ITA	FRG	FRA
SABER, INDIVIDUAL	FRA **JEAN-FRANÇOIS LAMOUR**	ITA **MARCO MARIN**	USA **PETER WESTBROOK**
SABER, TEAM	ITA	FRA	ROM
FOIL, INDIVIDUAL	CHN **LUAN JUJIE**	FRG **CORNELIA HANISCH**	ITA **DORINA VACCARONI**
FOIL, TEAM	FRG	ROM	FRA

FOOTBALL (SOCCER)

FINAL STANDINGS	FRA	BRA	YUG

FIELD HOCKEY

FINAL STANDINGS	PAK	FRG	GBR
FINAL STANDINGS	NED	FRG	USA

GYMNASTICS

ALL-AROUND, INDIVIDUAL	FRA 118.700 **KOJI GUSHIKEN**	USA 118.675 **PETER VIDMAR**	CHN 118.575 **LI NING**
ALL-AROUND, TEAM	USA	CHN	JPN
FLOOR EXERCISES	CHN 19.925 **LI NING**	CHN 19.775 **LOU YUN**	JPN 19.700 **KOJI SOTOMURA** FRA 19.700 **PHILIPPE VATUONE**
HORIZONTAL BAR	JPN 20.000 **SHINJI MORISUE**	CHN 19.975 **TONG FEI**	JPN 19.950 **KOJI GUSHIKEN**

HORSE VAULT	CHN 19.950 Lou Yun	CHN 19.825 Li Ning	
		JPN 19.825 Koji Gushiken	
		JPN 19.825 Shinji Morisue	
		USA 19.825 Mitchell Gaylord	

| PARALLEL BARS | USA 19.950
Bart Conner | JPN 19.925
Nobuyuki Kajitani | USA 19.850
Mitchell Gaylord |

| POMMELED HORSE | CHN 19.950
Li Ning | | USA 19.825
Timothy Daggett |
| | USA 19.950
Peter Vidmar | | |

| RINGS | JPN 19.850
Koji Gushiken | | USA 19.825
Mitchell Gaylord |
| | CHN 19.850
Li Ning | | |

| ALL-AROUND, INDIVIDUAL | USA 79.175
Mary Lou Retton | ROM 79.125
Ecaterina Szabó | ROM 78.675
Simona Pauca |

| ALL-AROUND, TEAM | ROM 392.20 | USA 391.20 | CHI 388.60 |

| BALANCE BEAM | ROM 19.800
Simona Pauca | | USA 19.650
Kathy Johnson |
| | ROM 19.800
Ecaterina Szabó | | |

| FLOOR EXERCISES | ROM 19.975
Ecaterina Szabó | USA 19.950
Julianne McNamara | USA 19.775
Mary Lou Retton |

| HORSE VAULT | ROM 19.875
Ecaterina Szabó | USA 19.850
Mary Lou Retton | ROM 19.750
Lavinia Agache |

| UNEVEN BARS | CHN 19.95
Ma Yanhong | | USA 19.80
Mary Lou Retton |
| | USA 19.95
Julianne McNamara | | |

| RHYTHMIC ALL-AROUND | CAN 57.950
Lori Fung | ROM 57.900
Doina Staiculescu | FRG 57.700
Regina Weber |

TEAM HANDBALL

| FINAL STANDINGS | YUG | FRG | ROM |

| FINAL STANDINGS | YUG | KOR | CHI |

JUDO

| EXTRA LIGHTWEIGHT
132.25 lbs. (60 kg) | JPN
Shinji Hosokawa | KOR
Kim Jae-Yup | GBR
Neil Eckersley |
| | | | GBR
Edward Liddie |

| HALF-LIGHTWEIGHT
143 lbs. (65 kg) | JPN
Yoshiyuki Matsuoka | KOR
Hwang Jung-Oh | FRA
Marc Alexandre |
| | | | AUT
Josef Reiter |

LIGHTWEIGHT 156.5 lbs. (71 kg)	○ **KOR** AHN BYEONG-KEUN	○ **ITA** EZIO GAMBA	○ **BRA** LUIS ONMURA	**GBR** KERRITH BROWN
HALF MIDDLEWEIGHT 172 lbs. (78 kg)	○ **FRG** FRANK WIENEKE	○ **GBR** NEIL ADAMS	○ **FRA** MICHEL NOWAK	**ROM** MIRCEA FRATIÇA
MIDDLEWEIGHT 189.5 lbs. (86 kg)	○ **AUT** PETER SEISENBACHER	○ **USA** ROBERT BERLAND	○ **JPN** SEIKI NOSE	**BRA** WALTER CARMONA
HALF HEAVYWEIGHT 209 lbs. (95 kg)	○ **KOR** HA HYOUNG-ZOO	○ **BRA** DOUGLAS VIEIRA	○ **ISL** BJARNI FRIDRIKSSON	**FRG** GÜNTER NEUREUTHER
HEAVYWEIGHT >209 lbs. (>95 kg)	○ **JPN** HITOSHI SAITO	○ **FRA** ANGELO PARISI	○ **KOR** CHO YONG-CHUL	**CAN** MARK BERGER
OPEN	○ **JPN** YASUHIRO YAMASHITA	○ **EGY** MOHAMED ALI RASHWAN	○ **ROM** MIHAI CIOC	**FRG** ARTHUR SCHNABEL

MODERN PENTATHLON

INDIVIDUAL	○ **ITA** 5,469 DANIELE MASALA	○ **SWE** 5,456 SVANTE RASMUSON	○ **ITA** 5,406 CARLO MASSULLO
TEAM	○ **ITA** 16,060 DANIELE MASALA CARLO MASSULLO PIERPAOLO CRISTOFORI	○ **USA** 15,568 MICHAEL STORM ROBERT LOSEY DEAN GLENESK	○ **FRA** 15,565 PAUL FOUR DIDIER BOUBE JOËL BOUZOU

ROWING

SINGLE SCULLS	○ **FIN** 7:00.24 PERTTI KARPPINEN	○ **FRG** 7:02.19 PETER-MICHAEL KOLBE	○ **CAN** 7:10.38 ROBERT MILLS
DOUBLE SCULLS	○ **USA** 6:36.87 BRADLEY LEWIS PAUL ENQUIST	○ **BEL** 6:38.19 PIERRE-MARIE DELOOF DIRK CROIS	○ **YUG** 6:39.59 ZORAN PANČIČ MILORAD STANULOV
QUADRUPLE SCULLS	○ **GER** 5:57.55 ALBERT HEDDERICH RAIMUND HÖRMANN DIETER WIEDENMANN MICHAEL DÜRSCH	○ **AUS** 5:57.98 PAUL REEDY GARY GULLOCK TIMOTHY MCLAREN ANTHONY LOVRICH	○ **CAN** 5:59.07 DOUG HAMILTON MIKE HUGHES PHIL MONCKTON BRUCE FORD
PAIR-OARED SHELL WITHOUT COXSWAIN	○ **ROM** 6:45.39 PETRU IOSUB VALER TOMA	○ **ESP** 6:48.87 FERNANDO CLIMENT LUIS LASÚRTEGUI	○ **NOR** 6:51.81 HANS MAGNUS GREPPERUD SVERRE LOKEN
PAIR-OARED SHELL WITH COXSWAIN	○ **ITA** 7:05.99 CARMINE ABBAGNALE GIUSEPPE ABBAGNALE GIUSEPPE DI CAPUA [COX]	○ **ROM** 7:11.21 DIMITRIE POPESCU VASILE TOMOIAGA DUMITRU RADACANU[COX]	○ **USA** 7:12.81 KEVIN STILL ROBERT ESPESETH DOUGLAS HERLAND [COX]

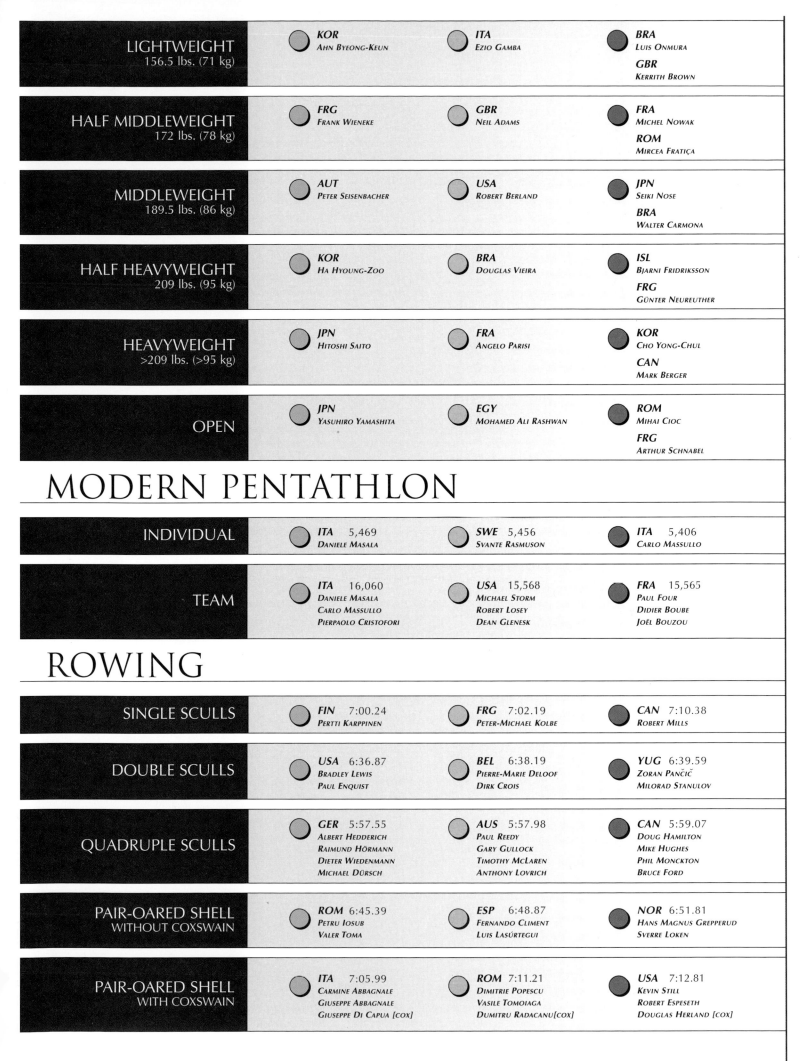

FOUR-OARED SHELL WITHOUT COXSWAIN	NZL 6:03.48 LESLIE O'CONNELL SHANE O'BRIEN CONRAD ROBERTSON KEITH TRASK	USA 6:06.10 DAVID CLARK JONATHAN SMITH PHILIP STEKL ALAN FORNEY	DEN 6:07.72 MICHAEL JESSEN LARS NIELSEN PER RASMUSSEN ERIK CHRISTIANSEN
FOUR-OARED SHELL WITH COXSWAIN	GBR 6:18.64	USA 6:20.28	NZL 6:23.68
EIGHT-OARED SHELL WITHOUT COXSWAIN	CAN 5:41.32	USA 5:41.74	AUS 5:43.40
SINGLE SCULLS	ROM 3:40.68 VALERIA RAČILĂ	USA 3:43.89 CHARLOTTE GEER	BEL 3:45.72 ANN HAESEBROUCK
DOUBLE SCULLS	ROM 3:26.75 MARIOARA POPESCU ELISABETA OLENIUC	NED 3:29.13 GREET HELLEMANS NICOLETTE HELLEMANS	CAN 3:29.82 DANIÈLE LAUMANN SILKEN LAUMANN
QUADRUPLE SCULLS	ROM 3:14.11	USA 3:15.57	DEN 3:16.02
PAIR-OARED SHELL WITHOUT COXSWAIN	ROM 3:32.60 RODICA ARBA-PUSCATU ELENA HORVAT	CAN 3:36.06 BETTY CRAIG TRICIA SMITH	GER 3:40.50 ELLEN BECKER IRIS VÖLKNER
FOUR-OARED SHELL WITH COXSWAIN	ROM 3:19.30	CAN 3:21.55	AUS 3:23.29
EIGHT-OARED SHELL WITH COXSWAIN	USA 2:59.80	ROM 3:00.87	NED 3:02.92

SHOOTING

RAPID-FIRE, PISTOL	JPN 595 TAKEO KAMACHI	ROM 593 CORNELIU ION	FIN 591 RAUNO BIES
FREE PISTOL	CHN 566 XU HAIFENG	SWE 565 RAGNAR SKANÅKER	CHN 564 WANG YIFU
SMALL-BORE RIFLE PRONE	USA 599 EDWARD ETZEL	FRA 596 MICHEL BURY	GBR 596 MICHAEL SULLIVAN
SMALL-BORE RIFLE THREE POSITIONS	GBR 1,173 MALCOLM COOPER	SUI 1,163 DANIEL NIPKOW	GBR 1,162 ALISTER ALLAN
RUNNING GAME TARGET	CHN 587 LI YUWEI	COL 584 HELMUT BELLINGRODT	CHN 581 HUANG SHIPING
AIR RIFLE	FRA 589 PHILIPPE HÉBERLÉ	AUT 587 ANDREAS KRONTHALER	GBR 587 BARRY DAGGER
SMALL BORE RIFLE THREE POSITIONS	CHN 581 WU XIAOXUAN	FRG 578 ULRIKE HOLMER	USA 578 WANDA JEWELL
SPORT PISTOL	CAN 585 LINDA THOM	USA 585 RUBY FOX	AUS 583 PATRICIA DENCH
AIR RIFLE	USA 393 PAT SPURGIN	ITA 391 EDITH GUFLER	CHN 389 WU XIAOXUAN
TRAP SHOOTING	ITA 192 LUCIANO GIOVANNETTI	PER 192 FRANCISCO BOZA	USA 192 DANIEL CARLISLE
SKEET SHOOTING	USA 198 MATTHEW DRYKE	DEN 196 OLE RASMUSSEN	ITA 196 LUCA SCRIBANI ROSSI

SWIMMING

100-METER FREESTYLE	USA 49.80 Ambrose Gaines	AUS 50.24 Mark Stockwell	SWE 50.31 Per Johansson
200-METER FREESYTLE	FRG 1:47.44 Michael Groß	USA 1:49.10 Michael Heath	FRG 1:49.69 Thomas Fahrner
400-METER FREESTYLE	USA 3:51.23 George DiCarlo	USA 3:51.49 John Mykkanen	AUS 3:51.79 Justin Lemberg
1500-METER FREESTYLE	USA 15:05.20 Michael O'Brien	USA 15:10.59 George DiCarlo	FRG 15:12.11 Stefan Pfeiffer
100-METER BACKSTROKE	USA 55.79 Rick Carey	USA 56.35 David Wilson	CAN 56.49 Michael West
200-METER BACKSTROKE	USA 2:00.23 Rick Carey	FRA 2:01.75 Frédéric Delcourt	CAN 2:02.37 Cameron Henning
100-METER BREASTSTROKE	USA 1:01.65 Steven Lundquist	CAN 1:01.99 Victor Davis	AUS 1:02.97 Peter Evans
200-METER BREASTSTROKE	CAN 2:13.34 Victor Davis	AUS 2:15.79 Glenn Beringen	SUI 2:17.41 Etienne Dagon
100-METER BUTTERFLY	FRG 53.08 Michael Groß	USA 53.23 Pablo Morales	AUS 53.85 Glenn Buchanan
200-METER BUTTERFLY	AUS 1:57.04 Jon Sieben	FRG 1:57.40 Michael Groß	VEN 1:57.51 Rafael Vidal Castro
200-METER INDIVIDUAL MEDLEY	CAN 2:01.42 Alex Baumann	USA 2:03.05 Pablo Morales	GBR 2:04.38 Neil Cochran
400-METER INDIVIDUAL MEDLEY	CAN 4:17.41 Alex Baumann	BRA 4:18.45 Ricardo Prado	AUS 4:20.50 Robert Woodhouse
4 X 100-METER FREESTYLE RELAY	USA 3:19.03	AUS 3:19.68	SWE 3:22.69
4 X 200-METER FREESTYLE RELAY	USA 7:15.69	GER 7:15.73	GBR 7:24.78
4 X 100-METER MEDLEY RELAY	USA 3:39.30	CAN 3:43.23	AUS 3:43.25
100-METER FREESTYLE	USA 55.92 Carrie Steinseifer / USA 55.92 Nancy Hogshead		NED 56.08 Annemarie Verstappen
200-METER FREESTYLE	USA 1:59.23 Mary Wayte	USA 1:59.50 Cynthia Woodhead	NED 1:59.69 Annemarie Verstappen
400-METER FREESTYLE	USA 4:07.10 Tiffany Cohen	GBR 4:10.27 Sarah Hardcastle	GBR 4:11.49 June Croft
800-METER FREESTYLE	USA 8:24.95 Tiffany Cohen	USA 8:30.73 Michelle Richardson	GBR 8:32.60 Sarah Hardcastle
100-METER BACKSTROKE	USA 1:02.55 Theresa Andrews	USA 1:02.63 Betsy Mitchell	NED 1:02.91 Jolanda de Rover
200-METER BACKSTROKE	NED 2:12.38 Jolanda de Rover	USA 2:13.04 Amy White	ROM 2:13.29 Anca Patrascoiu

Event	Gold	Silver	Bronze
100-METER BREASTSTROKE	NED 1:09.88 PETRA VAN STAVEREN	CAN 1:10.69 ANNE OTTENBRITE	FRA 1:10.70 CATHERINE POIROT
200-METER BREASTSTROKE	CAN 2:30.38 ANNE OTTENBRITE	USA 2:31.15 SUSAN RAPP	BEL 2:31.40 INGRID LEMPEREUR
100-METER BUTTERFLY	USA 59.26 MARY T. MEAGHER	USA 1:00.19 JENNA JOHNSON	FRG 1:01.36 KARIN SEICK
200-METER BUTTERFLY	USA 2:06.90 MARY T. MEAGHER	AUS 2:10.56 KAREN PHILLIPS	FRG 2:11.91 INA BEYERMANN
200-METER INDIVIDUAL MEDLEY	USA 2:12.64 TRACY CAULKINS	USA 2:15.17 NANCY HOGSHEAD	AUS 2:15.92 MICHELE PEARSON
400-METER INDIVIDUAL MEDLEY	USA 4:39.24 TRACY CAULKINS	AUS 4:48.30 SUZANNE LANDELLS	FRG 4:48.57 PETRA ZINDLER
400 x 100-METER FREESTYLE RELAY	USA 3:43.43	NED 3:44.40	GER 3:45.56
400 x 100-METER MEDLEY RELAY	USA 4:08.34	GER 4:11.97	CAN 4:12.98
SYNCHRONIZED SOLO	USA 198.467 TRACIE RUIZ	CAN 195.300 CAROLYN WALDO	JPN 187.050 MIWAKO MOTOYOSHI
SYNCHRONIZED DUET	USA 195.584 TRACIE RUIZ CANDY COSTIE	CAN 194.234 SHARON HAMBROOK KELLY KRYCZKA	JPN 187.992 SAEKO KIMURA MIWAKO MOTOYOSHI

VOLLEYBALL

	Gold	Silver	Bronze
FINAL STANDINGS	USA	BRA	ITA
FINAL STANDINGS	CHN	USA	JPN

WATER POLO

	Gold	Silver	Bronze
FINAL STANDINGS	YUG	USA	GER

WEIGHT LIFTING

Class	Gold	Silver	Bronze
FLYWEIGHT 114.61 lbs. (52 kg)	CHN 235.0 ZENG GUOQIANG	CHN 235.0 ZHOU PEISHUN	JPN 232.5 KAZUSHITO MANABE
BANTAMWEIGHT 123 lbs. (56 kg)	CHN 267.5 WU SHUDE	CHN 265.0 LAI RUNMING	JPN 252.5 MASAHIRO KOTAKA
FEATHERWEIGHT 132 lbs. (60 kg)	CHN 282.5 CHEN WEIQIANG	ROM 280.0 GELU RADU	TPE 272.5 TSAI WEN-YEE
LIGHTWEIGHT 148.75 lbs. (67.5 kg)	CHN 320.0 YAO JINGYUAN	ROM 312.5 ANDREI SOCACI — FIN 312.5 JOUNI GRÖNMAN	
MIDDLEWEIGHT 165 lbs. (75 kg)	FRG 340.0 KARL-HEINZ RADSCHINSKY	CAN 335.0 JACQUES DEMERS	ROM 332.5 DRAGOMIR CIOROSLAN
LIGHT HEAVYWEIGHT 181.5 lbs. (82.5 kg)	ROM 355.0 PETRE BECHERU	AUS 342.5 ROBERT KABBAS	JPN 340.0 RYOJI ISAOKA

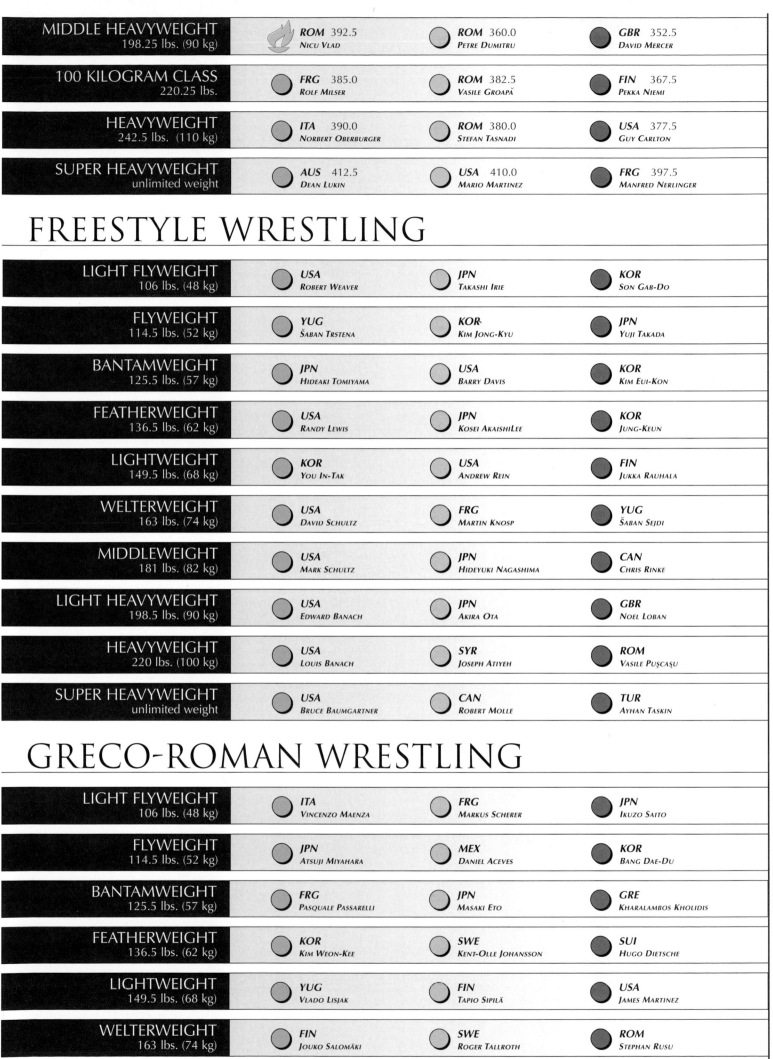

MIDDLE HEAVYWEIGHT 198.25 lbs. (90 kg)	ROM 392.5 Nicu Vlad	ROM 360.0 Petre Dumitru	GBR 352.5 David Mercer
100 KILOGRAM CLASS 220.25 lbs.	FRG 385.0 Rolf Milser	ROM 382.5 Vasile Groapǎ	FIN 367.5 Pekka Niemi
HEAVYWEIGHT 242.5 lbs. (110 kg)	ITA 390.0 Norbert Oberburger	ROM 380.0 Stefan Tasnadi	USA 377.5 Guy Carlton
SUPER HEAVYWEIGHT unlimited weight	AUS 412.5 Dean Lukin	USA 410.0 Mario Martinez	FRG 397.5 Manfred Nerlinger

FREESTYLE WRESTLING

LIGHT FLYWEIGHT 106 lbs. (48 kg)	USA Robert Weaver	JPN Takashi Irie	KOR Son Gab-Do
FLYWEIGHT 114.5 lbs. (52 kg)	YUG Šaban Trstena	KOR Kim Jong-Kyu	JPN Yuji Takada
BANTAMWEIGHT 125.5 lbs. (57 kg)	JPN Hideaki Tomiyama	USA Barry Davis	KOR Kim Eui-Kon
FEATHERWEIGHT 136.5 lbs. (62 kg)	USA Randy Lewis	JPN Kosei AkaishiLee	KOR Jung-Keun
LIGHTWEIGHT 149.5 lbs. (68 kg)	KOR You In-Tak	USA Andrew Rein	FIN Jukka Rauhala
WELTERWEIGHT 163 lbs. (74 kg)	USA David Schultz	FRG Martin Knosp	YUG Šaban Sejdi
MIDDLEWEIGHT 181 lbs. (82 kg)	USA Mark Schultz	JPN Hideyuki Nagashima	CAN Chris Rinke
LIGHT HEAVYWEIGHT 198.5 lbs. (90 kg)	USA Edward Banach	JPN Akira Ota	GBR Noel Loban
HEAVYWEIGHT 220 lbs. (100 kg)	USA Louis Banach	SYR Joseph Atiyeh	ROM Vasile Puşcaşu
SUPER HEAVYWEIGHT unlimited weight	USA Bruce Baumgartner	CAN Robert Molle	TUR Ayhan Taskin

GRECO-ROMAN WRESTLING

LIGHT FLYWEIGHT 106 lbs. (48 kg)	ITA Vincenzo Maenza	FRG Markus Scherer	JPN Ikuzo Saito
FLYWEIGHT 114.5 lbs. (52 kg)	JPN Atsuji Miyahara	MEX Daniel Aceves	KOR Bang Dae-Du
BANTAMWEIGHT 125.5 lbs. (57 kg)	FRG Pasquale Passarelli	JPN Masaki Eto	GRE Kharalambos Kholidis
FEATHERWEIGHT 136.5 lbs. (62 kg)	KOR Kim Weon-Kee	SWE Kent-Olle Johansson	SUI Hugo Dietsche
LIGHTWEIGHT 149.5 lbs. (68 kg)	YUG Vlado Lisjak	FIN Tapio Sipilä	USA James Martinez
WELTERWEIGHT 163 lbs. (74 kg)	FIN Jouko Salomäki	SWE Roger Tallroth	ROM Stephan Rusu

MIDDLEWEIGHT 181 lbs. (82 kg)	ROM Ion Draica	GRE Dimitrios Thanopoulos	SWE Sören Claeson
LIGHT HEAVYWEIGHT 198.5 lbs. (90 kg)	USA Steven Fraser	ROM Ilie Matei	SWE Frank Andersson
HEAVYWEIGHT 220 lbs. (100 kg)	ROM Vasile Andrei	USA Greg Gibson	YUG Jozef Tertei
SUPER HEAVYWEIGHT unlimited weight	USA Jeffrey Blatnick	YUG Refik Memišević	ROM Victor Dolipschi

YACHTING

FINN MONOTYPE	NZL 34.70 Russell Coutts	USA 37.00 John Bertrand	CAN 37.70 Terry Neilson
470 CLASS	ESP 33.70 Luis Doreste Roberto Molina	USA 43.00 Stephen Benjamin Christopher Steinfeld	FRA 49.40 Thierry Peponnet Luc Pillot
BOARDSAILING	NED 27.70 Stephan van den Berg	USA 46.00 Randall Steele	NZL 46.60 Bruce Kendall
STAR CLASS	USA 29.70 William Earl Buchan Stephen Erickson	GER 41.40 Joachim Griese Michael Marcour	ITA 43.50 Giorgio Gorla Alfio Peraboni
FLYING DUTCHMAN	USA 19.70 William Carl Buchan Jonathan McKee	CAN 22.70 Terry McLaughlin Evert Bastet	GBR 48.70 Jonathan Richards Peter Allam
TORNADO CLASS	NZL 14.70 Christopher Timms Rex Sellers	USA 37.00 Randy Smyth Jay Glaser	AUS 50.40 Christopher Cairns John Anderson
SOLING CLASS	USA 33.70 Robert Haines Edward Trevelyan Roderick Davis	BRA 43.40 Torben Grael Daniel Adler Ronaldo Senfft	CAN 49.70 Hans Fogh John Kerr Steve Calder

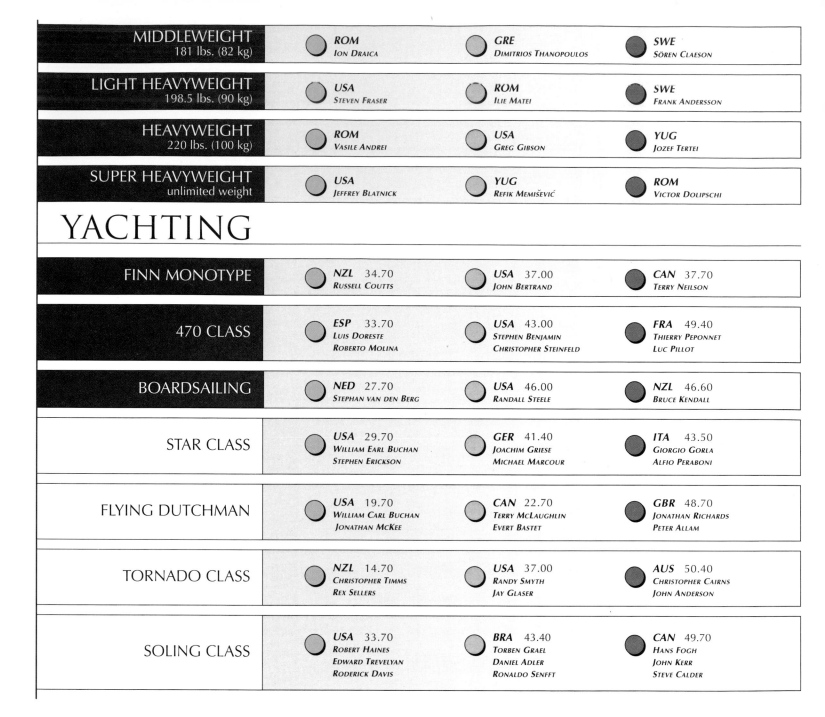

NATIONAL MEDAL COUNT

COMPETITORS   COUNTRIES: 140   ATHLETES: 6,797   MEN: 5,230   WOMEN: 1,567

	GOLD	SILVER	BRONZE	TOTAL		GOLD	SILVER	BRONZE	TOTAL		GOLD	SILVER	BRONZE	TOTAL		GOLD	SILVER	BRONZE	TOTAL
USA	83	61	30	174	YUG	7	4	7	18	POR	1		2	3	IRL		1		1
GER	17	19	23	59	NED	5	2	6	13	JAM		1	2	3	EGY		1		1
ROM	20	16	17	53	FIN	4	2	6	12	NOR		1	2	3	COL		1		1
CAN	10	18	16	44	NZL	8	1	2	11	TUR			3	3	SYR		1		1
GBR	5	11	21	37	BRA	1	5	2	8	VEN			3	3	THA		1		1
CHN	15	8	9	32	SUI		4	4	8	MAR	2			2	CIV		1		1
ITA	14	6	12	32	MEX	2	3	1	6	NGR		1	1	2	TPE			1	1
JPN	10	8	14	32	DEN		3	3	6	GRE		1	1	2	DOM			1	1
FRA	5	7	16	28	ESP	1	2	2	5	PUR		1	1	2	CMR			1	1
AUS	4	8	12	24	BEL	1	1	2	4	ALG			2	2	ISL			1	1
KOR	6	6	7	19	AUT	1	1	1	3	PAK	1			1	ZAM			1	1
SWE	2	11	6	19	KEN	1		2	3	PER		1		1					

Saturday, February 13

PM	EVENT
1:00	Opening Ceremony . . . . McMahon Stadium . . . .
2:30	Hockey. Olympic Sadddledome . . . . round robin (1 game)
4:30	Hockey . . . . Sadddledome . . . . round robin (1 game)
6:30	Hockey . . . . Saddledome . . . . round robin (1 game)

Sunday, February 14

AM	EVENT
10:00	Luge . . . . Canada Olympic Park . . . . . . men's, 1st & 2nd runs
10:00	Cross-Country Skiing. . Canmore . . . . women's 10-km

PM	EVENT
1:30	Ski Jumping . . . . Canada Olympic Park . . . 70-m
2:30	Hockey . . . . Saddledome . . . . round robin
3:00	Curling . . . . . Max Bell Arena . . . . round robin
5:00	Speed Skating . . . Olympic Oval . . . . men's 500-m
6:30	Hockey . . . . Saddledome . . . . round robin
6:45	Figure Skating . . . . Saddledome . . . . pairs short program

Monday, February 15

AM	EVENT
8:30	Curling . . . . . . Max Bell Arena . . . . round robin
10:00	Luge . . . . Canada Olympic Park . . . . . . men's, 3rd & 4th runs
10:00	Cross-Country Skiing. . Canmore . . . . men's 30-km
11:30	Alpine Skiing . . . . Nakiska . . . . men's downhill

PM	EVENT
2:15	Hockey . . . . Saddledome . . . . round robin
6:00	Hockey . . . . Saddledome . . . . round robin
6:15	Hockey . . . . Saddledome . . . . round robin

Tuesday, February 16

AM	EVENT
8:30	Curling . . . . . . Max Bell Arena . . . . round robin
10:00	Hockey . . . . Saddledome . . . . round robin
10:00	Luge . . . . Canada Olympic Park . . . . women's, 1st & 2nd runs
10:30	Alpine Skiing . . . . Nakiska . . . . men's combined downhill

PM	EVENT
2:00	Hockey . . . . Saddledome . . . . round robin
6:00	Figure Skating . . . . Saddledome . . . . pairs free skate
6:15	Hockey . . . . Saddledome . . . . round robin

Wednesday, February 17

AM	EVENT
8:00	Figure Skating . . . . F.D.B. Olympic Arena . . . . men's compulsories
8:30	Curling . . . . . . Max Bell Arena . . . . round robin
10:00	Cross-Country Skiing. . Canmore . . . . women's 5-km
10:30	Alpine Skiing . . . . Nakiska . . . . . . men's combined slalom
11:00	Speed Skating . . . Olympic Oval . . . . men's 5,000-m
11:30	Disabled Skiing . . . . . Canmore . . . . cross-country 5-km

PM	EVENT
2:00	Hockey . . . . Saddledome . . . . round robin
2:15	Hockey . . . . Saddledome . . . . round robin
6:15	Hockey . . . . Saddledome . . . . round robin

Thursday, February 18

AM	EVENT
10:00	Luge . . . Canada Olympic Park . . . . women's, 3rd & 4th runs

PM	EVENT
2:00	Hockey . . . . Saddledome . . . . round robin
2:15	Hockey . . . . Saddledome . . . . round robin
6:00	Speed Skating . . . Olympic Oval . . . . men's 1,000-m
6:15	Hockey . . . . Saddledome . . . . round robin
6:30	Figure Skating . . . . Saddledome . . . . men's short program

Friday, February 19

AM	EVENT
10:00	Luge . . . . Canada Olympic Park . . . . . . double, 1st & 2nd runs
10:00	Cross-Country Skiing. . Canmore . . . . men's 15-km

PM	EVENT
12:00	Alpine Skiing . . . . Nakiska . . . . women's downhill
2:00	Hockey . . . . Saddledome . . . . round robin
2:15	Hockey . . . . Saddledome . . . . round robin
6:00	Curling . . . . . . Max Bell Arena . . . . semifinals
6:15	Hockey . . . . Saddledome . . . . round robin

Saturday, February 20

AM	EVENT
10:00	Bobsled. . Canada Olympic Park . . . . . . 2-man, 1st & 2nd runs
10:30	Alpine Skiing . . . . Nakiska . . women's combined downhill
11:00	Biathlon . . . . Canmore . . . . men's 20-km

PM	EVENT
1:00	Curling . . . . . . Max Bell Arena . . . . finals
1:00	Hockey . . . . Saddledome . . . . round robin
2:15	Hockey . . . . Saddledome . . . . round robin
5:00	Speed Skating . . . Olympic Oval . . . . men's 1,500-m
5:15	Figure Skating . . . . Saddledome . . . . men's free skate
6:15	Hockey . . . . Saddledome . . . . round robin

Sunday, February 21

AM	EVENT
9:00	Figure Skating . . . . Saddledome . . . . dance compulsories
10:00	Cross-Country Skiing. . Canmore . . . . . . women's 4 x 5-km relay
11:30	Alpine Skiing . . . . Nakiska
	. . . . women's combined slalom

PM	EVENT
12:00	Speed Skating . . . Olympic Oval . . . . men's 10-km
12:30	Alpine Skiing . . . . Nakiska . . . . men's super G
12:30	Disabled Skiing . . . . Canada Olympic Park . . . . giant slalom
1:30	Hockey . . . . Saddledome . . . . round robin
1:30	Freestyle Skiing . . . . Canada Olympic Park . . . aerials
5:00	Hockey . . . . Saddledome . . . . round robin
6:15	Hockey . . . . Saddledome . . . . round robin

Monday, February 22

AM	EVENTS
10:00	Cross-Country Skiing . Carnmore . . . . . . men's 4 x 10-km relay
10:00	Hockey . . . . Saddledome . . . . round robin
10:00	Bobsled. . Canada Olympic Park . . . . . . 2-man, 3rd & 4th runs
11:30	Alpine Skiing . . . . Nakiska . . . . women's super G

PM	EVENT
1:30	Freestyle Skiing . . . . . . Nakiska . . . . moguls
2:00	Hockey . . . . Saddledome . . . . round robin
6:00	Short-Track Speed Skating . Max Bell Arena . men's 1,500-m . . . . women's 500-m
6:00	Figure Skating . . . . Saddledome . . . . dance original set pattern
6:00	Speed Skating . . . Olympic Oval . . . . women's 500-m
6:30	Hockey . . F.D.B. Olympic Arena . . . . round robin

Tuesday, February 23

AM	EVENT
10:00	Short-Track Speed Skating . . . . Max Bell Arena . . . men's 500-m
10:00	Ski Jumping . . . . Canada Olympic Park . . . . 90-m individual
11:00	Biathlon . . . . Canmore . . . . men's 10-km

PM	EVENT
1:30	Nordic Combined . . . . Canada Olympic Park . . . . jumping, team
2:15	Hockey . . F.D.B. Olympic Arena . . . . medal round
5:15	Figure Skating. . . . Saddledome . . . . dance free skate
6:00	Speed Skating . . . Olympic Oval . . . . women's 3,000-m
6:15	Hockey . . F.D.B. Olympic Arena . . . . medal round

Wednesday, February 24

AM	EVENT
8:00	Figure Skating . . . . F.D.B. Olympic Arena . . . . women's compulsories
10:00	Nordic Combined. . . . Canmore . . . . team 3 x 10-km relay
10:30	Hockey . . . . Saddledome . . . . medal round
10:30	Alpine Skiing . . . . Nakiska . . . . women's giant slalom

PM	EVENT
1:30	Ski Jumping . . . . Canada Olympic Park . . . . team
2:30	Hockey . . . . Saddledome . . . . medal round
6:00	Short-Track Speed Skating . . . . Max Bell Arena . men's 1,000-m . . women's 3,000-m relay, heats
6:30	Hockey . . . . Saddledome . . . . medal round

Thursday, February 25

AM	EVENT
10:00	Cross-Country Skiing. . Canmore . . . . women's 20-km
10:30	Alpine Skiing . . . . Nakiska . . . . men's giant slalom

PM	EVENT
1:30	Hockey . . . . Saddledome . . . . medal round
2:00	Freestyle Skiing . . . . Canada Olympic Park . . . ballet
6:00	Short-Track Speed Skating . . . . Max Bell Arena . men's 3,000-m . . women's 1,000-m relay finals
6:30	Figure Skating . . . . Saddledome . . . . . . women's short program

Friday, February 26

AM	EVENT
10:30	Hockey . . . . Saddledome . . . . medal round
10:30	Alpine Skiing . . . . Nakiska . . . . women's slalom
11:00	Biathlon . . . . Canmore . . . . 4 x 7.5-km relay

PM	EVENT
2:30	Hockey . . . . Saddledome . . . . medal round
6:00	Speed Skating . . . Olympic Oval . . . . women's 1,000-m
6:30	Hockey . . . . Saddledome . . . . medal round

Saturday, February 27

AM	EVENT
8:30	Cross-Country Skiing. . Canmore . . . . men's 50-km
10:00	Bobsled. . Canada Olympic Park . . . . . . 4-man, 1st & 2nd runs
10:30	Alpine Skiing . . . . Nakiska . . . . men's slalom

PM	EVENT
1:00	Hockey . . . . Saddledome . . . . medal round
5:00	Speed Skating . . . Olympic Oval . . . . women's 1,500-m
5:30	Figure Skating. . . . Saddledome . . . . women's free skate

Sunday, February 28

AM	EVENT
10:00	Bobsled. . Canada Olympic Park . . . . . . 4-man, 3rd & 4th runs
10:00	Nordic Combined. . . . Canmore 15-km
10:00	Hockey . . . . Saddledome . . . . medal round

PM	EVENT
1:30	Nordic Combined . . . . Canada Olympic Park . . . . jumping, individual
2:00	Hockey . . . . Saddledome . . . . medal round
3:00	Speed Skating . . . Olympic Oval . . . . women's 5,000-m
6:00	Figure Skating . . . . Saddledome . . . . exhibition
7:30	Closing Ceremony . . . . McMahon Stadium . . . .

CALGARY 1988
15TH OLYMPIC WINTER GAMES

BIATHLON

10 KILOMETERS	**GDR** 25:08.1 FRANK-PETER ROETSCH	**URS** 25:23.7 VALERY MEDVEDTSEV	**URS** 25:29.4 SERGEY CHEPIKOV
20 KILOMETERS	**GDR** 56:33.3 FRANK-PETER ROETSCH	**URS** 56:54.6 VALERY MEDVEDTSEV	**ITA** 57:10.1 JOHANN PASSLER
4 x 7.5-KILOMETER RELAY	**URS** 1:22:30.0 DMITRY VASILYEV SERGEY CHEPIKOV ALEKSANDR POPOV VALERY MEDVEDTSEV	**FRG** 1:23:37.4 ERNST REITER STEFAN HÖCK PETER ANGERER FRITZ FISCHER	**ITA** 1:23:51.5 WERNER KIEM GOTTLIEB TASCHLER JOHANN PASSLER ANDREAS ZINGERLE

BOBSLED

TWO-MAN	**URS** 3:53.48 JĀNIS KIPURS VLADIMIR KOZLOV	**GDR** 3:54.19 WOLFGANG HOPPE BOGDAN MUSIOL	**GDR** 3:54.64 BERNHARD LEHMANN MARIO HOYER
FOUR-MAN	**SUI** 3:47.51 EKKEHARD FASSER KURT MEIER MARCEL FÄSSLER WERNER STOCKER	**GDR** 3:47.58 WOLFGANG HOPPE DIETMAR SCHAUERHAMMER BOGDAN MUSIOL INGO VOGE	**URS** 3:48.26 JĀNIS KIPURS GUNTIS OSIS JURIS TONE VLADIMIR KOZLOV

FIGURE SKATING

SINGLES	**USA** 3.0 BRIAN BOITANO	**CAN** 4.2 BRIAN ORSER	**URS** 7.8 VIKTOR PETRENKO
SINGLES	**GDR** 4.2 KATARINA WITT	**CAN** 4.6 ELIZABETH MANLEY	**USA** 6.0 DEBRA THOMAS
PAIRS	**URS** 1.4 YEKATERINA GORDEYEVA SERGEY GRINKOV	**URS** 2.8 YELENA VALOVA OLEG VASILYEV	**USA** 4.2 JILL WATSON PETER OPPEGARD
DANCE	**URS** 2.0 NATALYA BESTEMYANOVA ANDREY BUKIN	**URS** 4.0 MARINA KLIMOVA SERGEY PONOMARENKO	**CAN** 6.0 TRACY WILSON ROBERT MCCALL

ICE HOCKEY

FINAL STANDINGS	**URS**	**FIN**	**SWE**

LUGE

SINGLE	**GDR** 3:05.548 JENS MÜLLER	**FRG** 3:05.916 GEORG HACKL	**URS** 3:06.274 YURY KHARCHENKO

TWO-SEATER	**GDR** 1:31.940 JÖRG HOFFMANN JOCHEN PIETZSCH	**GDR** 1:32.039 STEFAN KRAUßE JAN BEHRENDT	**FRG** 1:32.274 THOMAS SCHWAB WOLFGANG STAUDINGER
SINGLE	**GDR** 3:03.973 STEFFI WALTER-MARTIN	**GDR** 3:04.105 UTE OBERHOFFNER-WEIß	**GDR** 3:04.181 CERSTIN SCHMIDT

ALPINE SKIING

DOWNHILL	**SWI** 1:59.63 PIRMIN ZURBIGGEN	**SWI** 2:00.14 PETER MUELLER	**FRA** 2:01.24 FRANCK PICCARD
SLALOM	**ITA** 1:39.47 ALBERTO TOMBA	**FRG** 1:39.53 FRANK WOERNDL	**LIE** 1:39.84 PAUL FROMMELT
GIANT SLALOM	**ITA** 2:06.37 ALBERTO TOMBA	**AUS** 2:07.41 HUBERT STROLZ	**SWI** 2:08.39 PIRMIN ZURBIGGEN
SUPER GIANT SLALOM	**FRA** 1:39.66 FRANK PICCARD	**AUS** 1:40.96 HELMUT MAYER	**SWE** 1:41.08 LARS-BOERJE ERIKSSON
COMBINED	**AUS** 36.55 HUBERT STROLZ	**AUS** 43.45 BERNHARD GSTREIN	**SWI** 48.24 PAUL ACCOLA
DOWNHILL	**FRG** 1:52.64 MARINA KIEHL	**SWI** 1:25.86 BRIGITTE OERTLI	**CAN** 1:26.61 KAREN PERCY
SLALOM	**SWI** 1:36.69 VRENI SCHNEIDER	**YUG** 1:38.37 MATEJA SVET	**FRG** 1:38.40 CHRISTA KINSHOFER-GUETLEIN
GIANT SLALOM	**SWI** 2:06.49 VRENI SCHNEIDER	**FRG** 2:07.42 CHRISTA KINSHOFER-GÜETHLEIN	**SWI** 2:07.72 MARIA WALLISER
SUPER GIANT SLALOM	**AUS** 1:19.03 SIGRID WOLF	**SWI** 1:20.03 MICHELA FIGINI	**CAN** 1:20.29 KAREN PERCY
COMBINED	**AUS** 29.25 ANITA WACHTER	**SWI** 29.48 BRIGITTE OERTLI	**SWI** 51.28 MARIA WALLISER

NORDIC SKIING

	Gold	Silver	Bronze
15 KILOMETERS, CLASSICAL	URS 41:18.9 MIKHAIL DEVYATYAROV	NOR 41:33.4 PÅL GUNNAR MIKKELSPLASS	URS 41:48.5 VLADIMIR SMIRNOV
30 KILOMETERS, FREESTYLE	URS 1:24:26.3 ALEKSEY PROKUROROV	URS 1:24:35.1 VLADIMIR SMIRNOV	NOR 1:25:11.6 VEGARD ULVANG
50 KILOMETERS, CLASSICAL	SWE 2:04:30.9 GUNDE ANDERS SVAN	ITA 2:05:36.4 MAURILIO DE ZOLT	SUI 2:06:01.9 ANDI GRÜNENFELDER
4 x 10-KILOMETER RELAY	SWE 1:43:58.6 JAN BO OTTOSSON THOMAS WASSBERG GUNDE ANDERS SVAN TORGNY MOGREN	URS 1:44:11.3 VLADIMIR SMIRNOV VLADIMIR SAKHNOV MIKHAIL DEVYATYAROV ALEKSEY PROKUROROV	TCH 1:45:22.7 RADIM NYC VÁCLAV KORUNKA PAVEL BENC LADISLAV ŠVANDA
5 KILOMETERS, CLASSICAL	URS 55:53.6 TAMARA TIKHONOVA	URS 56:12.8 ANFISA REZTSOVA	URS 57:22.1 RAISA SMETANINA
10 KILOMETER, CLASSICAL	URS 30:08.3 VIDA VENCIENÉ	URS 30:17.0 RAISA SMETANINA	FIN 30:20.5 MARJO MATIKAINEN
20 KILOMETER, FREESTYLE	URS 55:53.6 TAMARA TIKHONOVA	URS 56:12.8 ANFISA REZTSOVA	URS 57:22.1 RAISA SMETANINA
4 x 5-KILOMETER RELAY FREESTYLE	URS 59:51.1 SVETLANA NAGEYKINA NINA GAVRYLYUK TAMARA TIKHONOVA ANFISA REZTSOVA	NOR 1-01:33.0 TRUDE DYBENDAHL MARIT WOLD ANNE JAHREN MARIANNE DAHLMO	FIN 1-01:53.8 PIRKKO MÄÄTTÄ MARJA-LIISA KIRVESNIEMI-HÄMÄLÄINEN MARJO MATIKAINEN JAANA SAVOLAINEN

SKI JUMPING

	Gold	Silver	Bronze
LARGE HILL	FIN 224.0 MATTI NYKÄNEN	NOR 207.9 ERIK JOHNSEN	YUG 207.7 MATJAŽ DEBELAK
LARGE HILL, TEAM	FIN 634.4 MATTI NYKÄNEN ARI-PEKKA NIKKOLA TUOMO YLIPULLI JARI PUIKKONEN	YUG 625.5 PRIMOŽ ULAGA MATJAŽ ZUPAN MATJAŽ DEBELAK MIRAN TEPEŠ	NOR 596.1 OLE EIDHAMMER JON KJORUM OLE FIDJESTOL ERIK JOHNSEN
SMALL HILL	FIN 229.1 MATTI NYKÄNEN	TCH 212.1 PAVEL PLOC	TCH 211.8 JIŘI MALEC

NORDIC COMBINED

	Gold	Silver	Bronze
INDIVIDUAL	SUI 432.230 HIPPOLYTE KEMPF	AUT 429.375 KLAUS SULZENBACHER	URS 422.590 ALLAR LEVANDI
TEAM	FRG 792.08 THOMAS MÜLLER HANS-PETER POHL HUBERT SCHWARZ	SUI 791.40 FREDY GLANZMANN HIPPOLYTE KEMPF ANDRÉAS SCHAAD	AUS 785.90 HANSJÖRG ASCHENWALD GÜNTHER CSAR KLAUS SULZENBACHER

SPEED SKATING

	Gold	Silver	Bronze
500 METERS	GDR 36.45 UWE-JENS MEY	NED 36.76 JAN YKEMA	JPN 36.77 AKIRA KUROIWA

1000 METERS		URS 1:13.03 Nikolay Gulyaev		GDR 1:13.11 Uwe-Jens Mey		URS 1:13.19 Igor Zhelezovsky
1,500 METERS		GDR 1:52.06 André Hoffmann		USA 1:52.13 Eric Flaim		AUT 1:52.31 Michael Hadschieff
5,000 METERS		SWE 6:44.63 Tomas Gustafson		NED 6:44.98 Leendert Visser		NED 6:45.92 Gerard Kemkers
10,000 METERS		SWE 13:48.20 Tomas Gustafson		AUT 13:56.11 Michael Hadschieff		NED 14:00.55 Leendert Visser
500 METERS		USA 39.10 Bonnie Blair		GDR 39.12 Christa Rothenburger		GDR 39.24 Karin Kania-Busch-Enke
1,000 METERS		GDR 1:17.65 Christa Rothenburger		GDR 1:17.70 Karin Kania-Busch-Enke		USA 1:18.31 Bonnie Blair
1,500 METERS		NED 2:00.68 Yvonne van Gennip		GDR 2:00.82 Karin Kania-Busch-Enke		GDR 2:01.49 A. Ehrig-Schöne-Mitscherlich
3,000 METERS		NED 4:11.94 Yvonne van Gennip		GDR 4:12.09 A. Ehrig-Schöne-Mitscherlich		GDR 4:16.92 Gabi Zange-Schönbrunn
5,000 METERS		NED 7:14.13 Yvonne van Gennip		GDR 7:17.12 A. Ehrig-Schöne-Mitscherlich		GDR 7:21.61 Gabi Zange-Schönbrunn

NATIONAL MEDAL COUNT

COMPETITORS   COUNTRIES: 57   ATHLETES: 1,423   MEN: 1,110   WOMEN: 313

	GOLD	SILVER	BRONZE	TOTAL		GOLD	SILVER	BRONZE	TOTAL		GOLD	SILVER	BRONZE	TOTAL		GOLD	SILVER	BRONZE	TOTAL
URS	10	9	7	26	FIN	4	1	2	7	NOR		3	2	5	FRA	1		1	2
GDR	9	10	6	25	NED	3	2	2	7	CAN		2	3	5	LIT			1	1
SWI	5	5	5	15	SWE	4		2	6	YUG		2	1	3	JPN			1	1
AUT	3	5	2	10	USA	2	1	3	6	TCH		1	2	3	LIE			1	1
GER	2	4	2	8	ITA	2	1	2	5	LIT	1		1	2					

RECORD OF THE XXIII OLYMPIAD

OFFICERS OF THE INTERNATIONAL OLYMPIC COMMITTEE

H. E. Juan Antonio Samaranch — President
H. E. Louis Guirandou-N' Diaye — First Vice President
Alexandru Siperco — Second Vice President
Ashwini Kumar — Third Vice- President

Other Executive Members:
Virgilio de Leon
Prince Alexandre Mérode
Julian K. Roosevelt
Richard W. Pound
Major Sylvio de Magalhaes Padilhal

INTERNATIONAL OLYMPIC COMMITTEE MEMBERSHIP DURING THE XXIII OLYMPIAD

ARRIVALS: 22

—— 1984 ——

July 25	Turgut Atakol	Turkey
	Princess Nora	Liechtenstein
	Chong Kyu Park	South Korea
	David Siebandze	Swaziland

—— 1985 ——

June 6	Henry O. Adefope	Nigeria
	Francisco Elizalde	Philippines
	Carlos Ferrer	Spain
	Robert Helmick	USA
	Albert Prince	Monaco

—— 1986 ——

October 16	Un Yong Kim	South Korea
	Lambis Nikolaou	Greece
	Anita DeFrantz	USA
	Jean-Claude Ganga	Congo

—— 1987 ——

May 11	Ivan Slavkov	Bulgaria
	Anthonius Geesink	Netherlands
	Slobodan Filipovic	Yugoslavia
	Seuili Wallwork	Samoa

—— 1988 ——

May 11	H. R. H. Princess Anne	Great Britain
	Fidel Carasquilla Mendoza	Colombia
	Edward Wilson	Netherlands
	Wu Ching-kuo	Chinese Taipei
	Rampaul Ruhe	Mauritius

DEPARTURES: 17

—— 1984 ——

None

—— 1985 ——

March 8	Alejandro Rivera Bascur*	Chile
June 6	Pedro de Gue II	Spain
	Douglas Roby	USA
	Adetokunbo Ademola	Nigeria
December 3	Chong Kyu Park*	South Korea

—— 1986 ——

March 27	Julian Kean Roosevelt*	USA
August 18	Nikolaos Nissiotis*	Greece
October 18	Julio Gerlein Comelin*	Colombia
November 8	Cornelis Kerdel*	Netherlands

—— 1987 ——

May 12	Vladimir Stoytchev	Bulgaria
	Boris Bakrac	Yugoslavia
August 19	Ydnekatchew Tessema*	Ethiopia
December 31	Henry Hsu	Chinese Taipei
	Cecil Lancelot Cross	New Zealand

—— 1988 ——

January 18	Konstantin Andrianov*	USSR
February 11	Luke of Pavenham	Great Britain
April 9	Turgut Atakol*	Turkey

* Died in office; all others resigned

Net increase in the IOC membership: 5

Total IOC membership by the end of the XXIII Olympiad: 92

OFFICERS OF THE UNITED STATES OLYMPIC COMMITTEE

16th Quadrennial, January 31, 1981-February 9, 1985

William E. Simon
Simon was elected USOC president January 31, 1981. His term spanned the XXII and the XXIII Olympiads.

Other elected officers were:
John B. Kelly Jr., First Vice President
Dr. Evie Dennis, Second Vice President
Robert H. Helmick, Third Vice President
Stephen B. Sobel, Secretary
Lawrence Houghton, Treasurer
Richard G. Kline, Counselor
Lt. Col. F. Don Miller, Executive Director
Retired, February 11, 1985

17th Quadrennial, February 9, 1985-March 2, 1989

John B. Kelly Jr.
Kelly was elected USOC president on February 9, 1985. His term was to span the XXIII and XXIV Olympiads, but he died on March 2, 1985.

Other elected officers were:
Robert H. Helmick, First Vice President
Dr. Evie Dennis, Second Vice President
Stephen B. Sobel, Third Vice President
Andras Toro, Secretary
Howard Miller Jr., Treasurerr
Richard Kline, Counselor
Gen. George D. Miller, Executive Director

Robert H. Helmick, who had been serving as first vice president, ascended to the USOC presidency on March 21, 1985, completing his first term on February 18, 1989.

General Miller, who had been President Kelly's choice for the new USOC executive director, was elected by the board in October 1984, and began his tenure on February 12, 1985, less than month before Kelly's death. The relationship between Helmick and Miller was troubled from the beginning, although Miller is creditied with the hiring of the first full-time USOC Development Director and arranging for the USOC to derive 10 per cent of the revenues paid to the IOC by U.S. television networks. President Helmick fired General Miller on August 22, 1987. The Assistant Executive Director, Baaron B. Pittenger assumed Miller's duties on August 23rd.

HONORARY PRESIDENTS OF THE UNITED STATES OLYMPIC COMMITTEE

Starting with President Grover Cleveland, who accepted the then honorary presidency of what was the American Olympic Association in December, 1895, every United States president has agreed to serve in this capacity. During the XXIII Olympiad, President Ronald Reagan was the honorary president of the USOC.

OLYMPIC AWARDS

THE OLYMPIC ORDER

The Olympic Order, created in 1974, is awarded to a person who has expressed the Olympic ideal through his or her action, who has attained remarkable accomplishment in sport, or who has rendered outstanding service to the Olympic cause, either through personal achievement or contribution to the development of sport. The award consists of a medal and has three degrees: gold, silver, and bronze. The recipient also gets a gold, silver, or bronze necklace that takes the form of two laurel wreaths with the Olympic rings in the center. The medal and the necklace are accompanied by a diploma detailing the recipient's achievement.

RECIPIENTS

THE GOLD OLYMPIC ORDER

1984 François Mitterrand, France
Peter V. Ueberroth, United States
Branko Mikulicl, Yugoslavia

1985 His Majesty King Juan Carlons de Borbon, Spain
Erich Honecker, East Germany
Nicholas Ceauscu, Romania

1986 Wan Li, China

1987 His Excellency Todor Jivkov, Bulgaria
His Majesty King Bhumibol Adulyade, Thailand
His Excellency Kenan Evren, Turkey

THE SILVER OLYMPIC ORDER

1984 Hélène Ahrweiler, France
Abdelhamid Rachdi Alami, Morocco
Abdul Hamid Al-Hajji, Kuwait
Dr. Kinichi Asano, Japan
Si Mohamed Baghadi, Algeria
Motohiko Ban, Japan
Herma Bauma, Austria
Bo Bengtson, Sweden
Aldo Bergamashi, Italy
Abebe Bikila, Ethiopia
Fred Blay, Liberia
Emeric Blum, Yugoslavia
Jean Borotra, France
Tom Bradley, United States
Gian-Carlo Brusati, Italy
José Maria Cagigal, Spain
Paolo Cappabianca, Italy
Juan José Castillo, Spain
Harry H. Cavan, Great Britain
Miroslav Cerar, Yugoslavia
Nadia Comaneci, Romania
George Craig, New Zealand
Beppe Croce, Italy
Abilio Ferreira D'almeida, Brazil
Horst Dassler, West Germany

Alain Danet, France
Sandy Duncan, Great Britain
Abdelaziz Elshafei, Egypt
Milan Ercegan, Yugoslavia
Suat Erler, Turkey
René Frank, Belgium
Shunji Fujii, Japan
Akira Fujita, Japan
Knolly Henderson, Trinidad & Tobago
Antonin Himl, Czechoslovakia
Pierre Hirschy, Switzerland
Paul Högberg, Sweden
Bert Isatitsch, Austria
Ahmed Karabegovic, Yugoslavia
Pal Kovacs, Hungary
Paul Libaud, France
Hero Lupescu, Romania
Samuel Mbogo Kamau, Kenya
The Honorable Ibrahim Mbomba Njoya, Cameroon
Colonel F. Don Miller, United States
Kenjiro Mizuno, Japan
Julio Enrique Monagas, Puerto Rico
Primo Nebiolo, Italy
Renzo Nostini, Italy
Fred B. Oberlander, Canada
Nelson Paillou, France
Luis Azemar Puig de la Bellacasa, Spain
Marian Renke, Poland
Walter J.M.A. von Rosberg, Netherlands Antilles
Günther Sabetski, West Germany
Keith Shervington, Jamaica
Zhong Shitong, China
Anto Sucic, Yugoslavia
Artur Takac, Yugoslavia
Stanko Tomic, Yugoslavia
Harry Usher, United States
Uglijesa Uzelac, Yugoslavia
Olegario Vazquez Razquez Raña, Mexico
Paul Zifferen, United States

1985 Sir Adetokunbo Ademola, Nigeria
Haralambie Alexa, Romania
Sheik Esa Bin Rashed Al Khalifa, Bahrain
Hanji Aoki, Japan
Abdel Azim Ashry, Egypt
Tsegaw Ayele, Egypt
Edmund William Barker, Singapore
Domenico Bruschi, San Marino
Cristine Caron, France
Bud Greenspan, United States
Josef Grudzien, Poland
Hermann Jannsen, Nigeria
John B. Kelly, United States
Ferdinand Siregar Mangombar, Indonesia
Kenkichi Oshima, Japan
Lord Porritt, New Zealand
Bedrich Poula, Czechoslovakia
Ludwig Prokop, Austria
André Gustavo Richer, Brazil
Raimundo Saporta, Spain
William Simon, United States
Borislav Stankovic, Yugoslavia
Joseph Lluis Vilaseca, Spain
Walter Wasservogel, Austria
Jean Weymann, Switzerland

1986 Carlos Orsio de Almeida, Brazil
Lachezar Avramov, Bulgaria
John Akii Bua, Uganda
Mahmoud Ba, Mauritania
Bernhard Baier, West Germany
Istvan Buda, Hungary
Liselott Diem, West Germany
Juston Durand, Benin
Isaac Froimovich, China
Boris Georgiev Nikolov, Bulgaria
Carlos de Godo, Spain
Roberto C. Goizueta, United States
Antoine Khoury, Lebanon
Cheick Kouyate, Mali
Jean-Arnould Leew, Belgium

Air Vice Marshal C.L. Metha, India
Nikolaos Nissiotis, Greece
Chong-Kyu Park, South Korea
Clèanthis Paleologos, Greece
Pedro Perez Duenas Cuba
Ahmed Mohammed Qaatabi, South Yemen
Max Rinkenburger, West Germany
Douglas F. Roby, United States
*Julian K. Roosevelt, United States
*Roger Rousseau, Canada
Ricardo José Russomando, Argentina
Andrej Starovoitov, Soviet Union
Otto Szymiczek, Greece
William Thayer Tutt, United States
Tàdeusz Ulatowski, Poland
Georges Vichos, Greece
George Wieczisk, East Germany
Lev Yashin, Soviet Union
Huang Zhong, China

1987 Francisco Ferreira Alves, Portugal
Boris Bakrac, Yugoslavia
Gavrila Barani, Romania
John Joseph Brown, Australia
Abdel Moniem El Bah, Libya
Julio Gerlein Comelin, Colombia
Ramiro Tavares Goncalves, Brazil
Rudolf Hellmann, East Germany
Chen Jinkai, China
Alberto Juantorena, Cuba
Erich Kamper, Austria
Cornelius Kerdel, the Netherlands
L.N. Khurana, India
Jean-Claude Killy, France
Philip Othmar Krumm, United States
Colonel Zdzislaw Ludwik Krzyszkowiak, Poland
Li Menghua, China
Geoffroy de Navacelle, France
Sergio Orsi, Italy
Lassina Palenfo, Ivory Coast
Marcel Parche, Switzerland
Janusz Przedpelski, Poland
Haluk San, Turkey
Teofilo Stevenson Lorenzo, Cuba
Vladimir Stoytchev, Bulgaria
Leon Stukelj, Yugoslavia
Brian Wightman, Fiji

THE BRONZE OLYMPIC ORDER

1984 Francisco Alguersauri Duran, Spain
Duarte Manuel de Almeida Bello, Portugal
Siegfried Brietzke, West Germany
Muhammad Naqi Butt, Pakistan
Alain Danet, France
Bogomil Nonev, Bulgaria
Jal Pardovala, Italy
Alberto Passadore, Uruguay
Josef Szalay, Hungary
Ashenafi Youria, Ethiopia

1985 No bronze awards made.
1986 No bronze awards made.
1987 No bronze awards made.

OFFICIAL PUBLICATIONS OF THE INTERNATIONAL OLYMPIC COMMITTEE

THE OLYMPIC CHARTER

The Olympic Charter provides the official rules, procedures, and protocols of the IOC, which are periodically updated by vote of the membership at an IOC Session. Three editions were issued during the XXIII Olympiad: Edition 27 in July, 1984 (in French and English), Edition 28 in June, 1985 (in French, English, and Spanish), and Edition 29 in May, 1987 (in French, English, and Spanish).

THE OLYMPIC REVIEW

Starting in January 1970, the IOC's *Lettre d' informations* became the *Olympic Review*, the eleventh version of the IOC's monthly publication. It is printed in English and French. There were 41 issues of the *Olympic Review* during the XXIII Olympiad:

#201-#202	July-August 1984
#203	September 1984
#204	October 1984
#205	November 1984
#206	December 1984
#207	January 1985
#208	February 1985
#209	March 1985
#210	April 1985
#211-#212	May-June 1985
#213	July 1985
#214	August 1985
#215	September 1985
#216	October 1985
#217-#218	November-December 1985
#219	January 1986
#220	February 1986
#221	March 1986
#222-#223	April-May 1986
#224	June 1986
#225	July 1986
#226	August 1986
#227	September 1986
#228	October 1986
#229-#230	November-December 1986
#231-#232	January-February 1987
#233	March 1987
#234	April 1987
#235-#236	May-June 1987
#237	July 1987
#238	August 1987
#239	September 1987
#240	October 1987
#241	November 1987
#242	December 1987
#243-#244	January-February 1988
#245	March 1988
#246	April 1988
#247	June 1988
#248	July 1988
#249	August 1988

THE OLYMPIC MESSAGE

For some years the editorial staff of the *Olympic Review* felt the need for an official IOC publication for educational purposes, which could articulate the harmony between sport and culture. Based on a decision made at the XI Olympic Congress at Baden-Baden in 1981, the *Olympic Message*, a quarterly with its own unique format, was issued. The *Quarterly* had its own sequential numbering system and a new subscriber base, which included not only the Olympic family, but international media sources, libraries, clubs, and interested individuals. There were 14 issues during the XXIII Olympiad.

#8	December 1984	#15	September 1986
#9	March 1985	#16	December 1986
#10	June 1985	#17	March 1987
#11	September 1985	#18	August 1987
#12	December 1985	#19	December 1987
#13	March 1986	#20	April 1988
#14	June 1986	#21	July 1988

THE IOC HANDBOOK

This publication lists the names and addresses of members of the IOC, the NOCs, and the IFs, as well as further information on Olympic-related associations. The IOC decided in 1967 that the *IOC Handbook* would be published after each IOC Session. Issues during the XXIII Olympiad included:

1984	*IOC Handbook*	1986	*IOC Handbook*
1985	*IOC Handbook*	1987	*IOC Handbook*

ACKNOWLEDGMENTS

The publisher would like to thank the following for their invaluable assistance to 1st Century Project and World Sport Research & Publications: Gov. Francisco G. Almeda (Philippine Olympic Committee, Manila); Sheik Fahad Al-Ahmad Al-Sabah (Olympic Committee of Kuwait); Don Anthony; Maj. Gen. Charouck Arirachakaran (Olympic Committee of Thailand, Bangkok); Bibliothèque National de France (Paris); Marie-Charlotte Bolot (University of the Sorbonne Cultural Library and Archives, Paris); Boston Public Library; British Museum and Library (London); Gail Britton; Richard L. Coe; Anita DeFrantz (IOC Member in the United States); Margi Denton; Carl and Lieselott Diem - Archives/Olympic Research Institute of the German Sport University Cologne; Edward L. Doheny, Jr. Library (University of Southern California, Los Angeles); Robert G. Engel; Miguel Fuentes (Olympic Committee of Chile, Santiago); National Library of Greece (Athens); Hollee Hazwell (Columbiana Collection, Columbia University, New York); Rebecca S. Jabbour and Bill Roberts (Bancroft Library, University of California at Berkeley); Diane Kaplan (Manuscripts and Archives, Sterling Library, Yale University, New Haven); David Kelly (Sport Specialist, Library of Congress, Washington, D.C.); Fékrou Kidane (International Olympic Committee, Lausanne); Peter Knight; Dr. John A. Lucas; Los Angeles Public Library; Blaine Marshall; Joachaim Mester, President of the German Sport University Cologne; Ed Mosk; Geoffroy de Navacelle; New York Public Library; Olympic Committee of India (New Delhi); Richard Palmer (British Olympic Association, London); C. Robert Paul; University of Rome Library and Archives; Margaret M. Sherry (Rare Books and Special Collections, Firestone Library, Princeton University); Dr. Ruth Sparhawk; Gisela Terrell (Special Collections, Irwin Library, Butler University, Indianapolis); The Officers, Directors and Staff (United States Olympic Committee, Colorado Springs); University Research Library, (University of California at Los Angeles); John Vernon (National Archives, Washington, DC); Emily C. Walhout (Houghton Library; Harvard University); David Wallechinsky; Herb Weinberg; Dr. Wayne Wilson, Michael Salmon, Shirley Ito (Paul Ziffren Sports Resource Center Library, Amateur Athletic Foundation of Los Angeles); Patricia Henry Yeomans; Nanci A. Young (Seeley G. Mudd Manuscript Library, Princeton University Archives); Dr. Karel Wendl, Michéle Veillard, Patricia Eckert, Simon Mandl, Ruth Perrenoud, Nikolay Guerguiev, Fani Kakridi-Enz , Laura Leslie Pearman, and Christine Sklentzas (International Olympic Committee Olympic Studies and Research Center, Lausanne); and Pat White (Special Collections, Stanford University Library, Palo Alto).

The publishers recognize with gratitude the special contributions made for Volume 21 by Madame Monique Berlioux; Tanis Biedler (The Calgary Herald); Ian Blackwell, Andrew Wrighting (Popperfoto, Northampton); Val Ching (Allsport, Pacific Palisades); Beth Davis (Figure Skating Hall of Fame, Colorado Springs); Preston Levi (International Swimming Hall of Fame, Ft. Lauderdale); Deborah Goodsite, Danny Baudanza (The Bettmann Archive, New York); Ken Kishimoto, Shigeaki Matsubara (Photo Kishimoto, Tokyo); Andy Kiss (Duomo, New York); Glennda Leslie, Brenda McCafferty (City of Calgary Archives); Alexandra Leclef Mandl, Catherine Fasel Chapuis (International Olympic Committee Photo Archives, Lausanne); John Nixon (Long Photography, Los Angeles); Patricia Olkiewicz, Cindy Slater (United States Olympic Committee Library and Photo Archives, Colorado Springs); Amy Poffenbarger (Raleigh USA, Kent); Philip Pritchard (Hockey Hall of Fame Archive, Toronto); Tom West and Gladys Serafino (Canadian Olympic Hall of Fame, Calgary); David Wood (Desrosiers Dance Theatre, Toronto); Jahn A. van Zuijlen, Dr. Marjet Derks (Netherlands Sports Museum, Lelystad).

The Publishers would also like to thank the following individuals, institutions and foundations for providing initial funding for the project: The Amelior Foundation (Morristown, New Jersey); Roy and Mary Cullen (Houston); The English, Bonter, Mitchell Foundation (Ft. Wayne, Indiana); Adrian French (Los Angeles); The Knight Foundation (Miami); The Levy Foundation (Philadelphia); and, Jonah Shacknai (New York). And for completion funding: Michael McKie, Optimax Securities, Inc. (Toronto); Graham Turner, Fraser & Beatty (Toronto); and Century of Sport Partnership (Toronto).

And a special thanks to Barron Pittenger (Assistant Executive Director, United States Olympic Committee, September 1981 to August 1987 and Executive Director, August 1987 to December 1989).

BIBLIOGRAPHY

Albertson, Lisa H. (ed.). *Athens to Atlanta: 100 Years of Glory*. Salt Lake City, Utah: Mikko Laitinen Commemorative Publications, 1993.

Albertson, Lisa H. (ed.). *Chamonix to Lillehammer: The Glory of the Olympic Winter Games*. Salt Lake City, Utah: Mikko Laitinen Commemorative Publications, 1994.

Benoit, Joan, with Sally Baker. *Running Tide*. New York: Knopf, 1987.

Davis, Michael D. *Black American Women in Olympic Track and Field*. Jefferson, NC: McFarland & Co., 1992.

Duncanson, Neil. *The Fastest Men on Earth: The 100m Olympic Champions*. London: Willow Books, 1988.

Gordon, Harry. *Australia at the Olympic Games*. St. Lucia, Queensland: University of Queensland Press, 1994.

Halberstam, David. *The Amateurs*. New York: Penguin Books, 1986.

Hill, Christopher R. *Olympic Politics*. Manchester: Manchester University Press, 1992.

Howell, Reet & Max. *Aussie Gold : A Celebration of Every Australian Olympic Gold Medal Winner Since 1896*. Albion, Queensland: Brooks Waterloo, 1988.

King, Frank W. *It's How You Play the Game: The Inside Story of the Calgary Olympics*. Calgary: Script: the writers' group, inc., 1988.

Lewis, Carl with Jeffrey Marx. *Inside Track: My Professional Life in Amateur Track and Field*. New York: Simon and Schuster, 1990.

Miller, David. *Olympic Revolution: The Olympic Biography of Juan Antonio Samaranch*. London: Pavilion, 1992.

Miller, David. *Sebastian Coe: Coming Back*. London: Sidgwick & Jackson, 1984.

Perelman, Richard B. *Olympic Retrospective: The Games of Los Angeles*. Los Angeles : The Los Angeles Olympic Organizing Committee, 1985.

Pound, Richard W. *Five Rings Over Korea: The Secret Negotiations Behind the 1988 Olympic Games in Seoul*. Boston: Little, Brown and Company, 1994.

Retton, Mary Lou & Bela Karolyi with John Powers. *Mary Lou: Creating and Olympic Champion*. New York: McGraw-Hill Book Co., 1986.

Segrave, Jeffrey O. and Donald Chu (eds.). *The Olympic Games in Transition*. Champaign, IL: Human Kinetic Books, 1988.

Simson, Vyv & Andrew Jennings. *The Lords of the Rings: Power, Money and Drugs in the Modern Olympics*. London: Simon & Schuster, 1992.

Thompson, Daley with Neil Wilson. *Daley: The Last Ten Years*. London: Willow Books, 1986.

Ueberroth, Peter with Richard Levin & Amy Quinn. *Made in America: His Own Story*. New York: Morrow, 1985.

Wallechinsky, David. *The Complete Book of the Olympics*. Boston: Little, Brown and Company, 1992.

Brownlee, Shannon. "Yanks on the Move." *Sports Illustrated*, January 27, 1988.

Cooper, Christin. "Women's Alpine." *Skiing*, January 1988.

Cramer, Ben. "Olympic Cheating: The inside story of illicit doping and the U.S. cycling team." *Rolling Stone*, February 14, 1985.

Demak, Richard. "The Coolest Under Fire." *Sports Illustrated*, February 29, 1988.

Gammon, Clive. "The Eagle Has Landed." *Sports Illustrated*, March 14, 1988.

Govier, Katherine. "The Land of Beginning Again." *Maclean's*, February 15, 1988.

Greenberg, Al. "Peerless Pirmin." *Skiing*, January 1988.

Howe, Nicholas. "The Swiss Prove Mortal." *Skiing*, September 1988.

Howse, John. "Grief on the Oval." *Maclean's*, February 29, 1988.

Howse, John. "The End of an Era." *Maclean's*, March 7, 1988.

Howse, John. "Trying to Prevent a Free Ride." *Maclean's*, June 22, 1987.

Johnson, William O. "Losers of Renown." *Sports Illustrated*, January 27, 1988.

Johnson, William O. "The Swiss Golden Boy." *Sports Illustrated*, January 27, 1988.

Johnson, William O. "One of Three for Z." *Sports Illustrated*, February 29, 1988.

Johnson, William O. "Gone with the Wind." *Sports Illustrated*, February 29, 1988.

Keefler, Danielle. "A Blood Feud on the Trails." *Maclean's*, February 29, 1988.

Kirkpatrick, Curry. "The Man Who Never Loses." *Sports Illustrated*, July 30, 1984.

Kirkpatrick, Curry. "La Bomba." *Sports Illustrated*, January 3, 1992.

Leerhsen, Charles. "Everyone Into the Pool." *Newsweek*, July 9, 1984.

Leo, John. "Alert: Nukes Away!" *Time*, February 29, 1988.

Levin, Bob. "Flight of the Finn." *Maclean's*, February 29, 1988.

Manning, Richard. "Swimming Away With It." *Newsweek*, August 13, 1984.

Moore, Kenny. "Spinning Straw Into Gold." *Sports Illustrated*, December 24, 1984.

Moore, Kenny. "Two Aces On A Collision Course." *Sports Illustrated*, June 23, 1984.

Newman, Bruce. "La Bomba's A Real Blast." *Sports Illustrated*, January 25, 1988.

O'Hara, Jane. "Looking Golden But Missing the Ring." *Maclean's*, February 29, 1988.

Read, Ken. "Tomba Triumphant." *Skiing*, September 1988.

Reilly, Rick. "Felled by a Heavy Heart." *Sports Illustrated*, February 22, 1988.

Reilly, Rick. "This Flaim was Bright." *Sports Illustrated*, February 29, 1988.

Skow, John. "A Tidal Wave of Winners." *Time*, August 13, 1984.

Skow, John. "A Soaring, Majestic Slowness." *Time*, August 20, 1984.

Skow, John. "Super-Z Zips and Zaps Them All." *Time*, February 15, 1988.

Skow, John. "Three, Two, One...Airborne!" *Time*, February 29, 1988.

Smith, Gary. "The Great Leap Upward." *Sports Illustrated*, July 18, 1984.

Smith, Gary. "There's Gold on His Menu." *Sports Illustrated*, July 18, 1984.

Smolowe, Jill. "The Soaring, Spinning Battle of the Brians." *Time*, February 15, 1988.

Smolowe, Jill. "This Soldier's No Toy." *Time*, February 29, 1988.

Stathoplos, Demme. "No One Does It Better." *Sports Illustrated*, July 18, 1984.

Sullivan, Robert. "Inflexible Fliers." *Sports Illustrated*, February 29, 1988.

Sullivan, Robert. "Slippin' and Slidin'." *Sports Illustrated*, March 7, 1988.

Swift, E.M. "Double the Pleasure." *Sports Illustrated*, January 29, 1988.

Swift, E.M. "A Magical Twosome." *Sports Illustrated*, January 29, 1988.

Underwood, John. "No Goody Two-Shoes." *Sports Illustrated*, March 10, 1969.

Wallace, Bruce. "A Shakeup in Olympic Hockey." *Maclean's*, February 29, 1988.

Witteman, Paul A. "The Jests of the Rest." *Time*, February 29, 1988.

Wolff, Alexander. "Flight of the Finns." *Sports Illustrated*, January 10, 1994.

Wood, Chris. "Upsets on the Slopes." *Maclean's*, February 29, 1988.

Wood, Chris. "Medals on the Mountain." *Maclean's*, March 7, 1988.

Excerpts from:

The *New York Times*
The *Los Angeles Times*

PHOTO CREDITS

INDEX

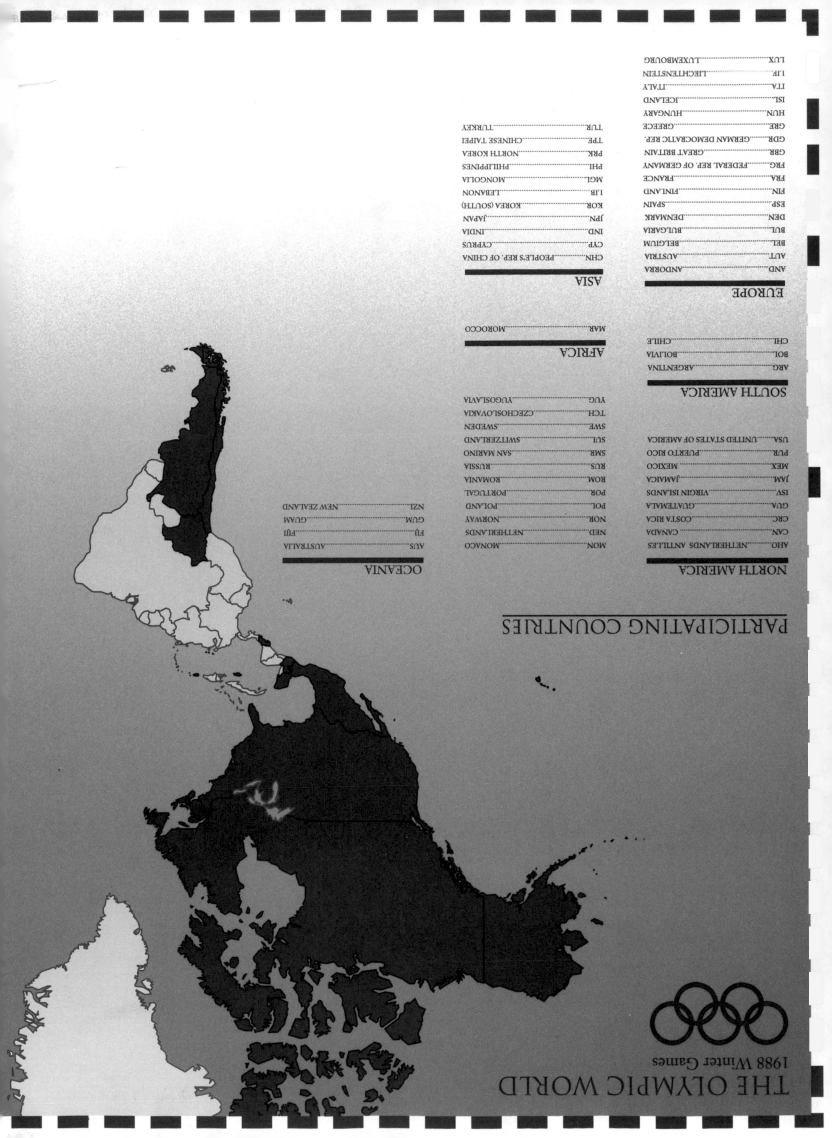